THE PLOT OF SHAME

US MILITARY EXECUTIONS IN EUROPE DURING WWII

Paul Johnson

FRONTLINE BOOKS

THE PLOT OF SHAME
US Military Executions in Europe During WWII

First published in Great Britain in 2023 by

Frontline Books
An imprint of
Pen & Sword Books Ltd
Yorkshire – Philadelphia

Copyright © Paul Johnson, 2023

ISBN 978 1 39901 177 8

The right of Paul Johnson to be identified as
Author of this work has been asserted by him in accordance
with the Copyright, Designs and Patents Act 1988.

A CIP catalogue record for this book is
available from the British Library

All rights reserved. No part of this book may be reproduced or
transmitted in any form or by any means, electronic or mechanical
including photocopying, recording or by any information storage and retrieval system,
without permission from the Publisher in writing.

Typeset in 10.5/13 pt Palatino by SJmagic DESIGN SERVICES, India.

Printed and bound in the UK by CPI Group (UK) Ltd.

Pen & Sword Books Ltd incorporates the imprints of Pen & Sword Archaeology, Atlas,
Aviation, Battleground, Discovery, Family History, History, Maritime, Military, Naval,
Politics, Social History, Transport, True Crime, Claymore Press, Frontline Books, Praetorian
Press, Seaforth Publishing and White Owl

For a complete list of Pen & Sword titles please contact

PEN & SWORD BOOKS LTD
47 Church Street, Barnsley, South Yorkshire, S70 2AS, England
E-mail: enquiries@pen-and-sword.co.uk
Website: www.pen-and-sword.co.uk

Or

PEN AND SWORD BOOKS
1950 Lawrence Rd, Havertown, PA 19083, USA
E-mail: Uspen-and-sword@casematepublishers.com
Website: www.penandswordbooks.com

Contents

Acknowledgements		vi
List of Abbreviations		vii
Introduction		1
Chapter 1	US Military Court Martials and Executions	5
Chapter 2	The Executioners	13
Chapter 3	No Resting Place in the Plot of Shame	18
Chapter 4	1943: Murder, Rape and Ten Hanged	28
Chapter 5	1944: The Heat of Battle	52
Chapter 6	1944: August – Summer Madness	93
Chapter 7	1944: The Year Ends	134
Chapter 8	1945: The Spoils of War	187
Chapter 9	The Execution of Private Edward Donald Slovik	220
Chapter 10	A Case of Double Murder	224
Chapter 11	A Grave Mystery	229
Chapter 12	In Circumstances Unknown	234
Sources and Bibliography		235
Index		237

Acknowledgements

My grateful thanks go to all those listed below, without whose assistance this publication may not have been possible. In particular, I would like to thank Colonel French L. MacLean (US Army retd), author of the book *The Fifth Field* (Schiffer Publishing), whose cooperation, guidance and generosity is greatly appreciated.

Doug Banks – Colourise History
Michelle Bates
Jill Boatwright
Sandford Chandler
Miranda Chumbley
Joseph LoPinto
Martin Mace
Eve Martin
Rebecca Mileham
Winston Ramsay – *After the Battle* magazine
Carol Tyler – American Battle Monuments Commission (ABMC)
David Venditta
Simon Webb

List of Abbreviations

ABMC	American Battle Monuments Commission
CP	Command Post
DTC	Disciplinary Training Centre
ETO	European Theatre of Operations
GCM	General Courts Martial
HMS	His Majesty's Ship
JAG	Judge Advocate General
MBS	Mediterranean Base Section
MP	Military Policeman
MTO	Mediterranean Theatre of Operations
NATO	North-African Theatre of Operations
OD	Olive Drab
PBS	Peninsular Base Section
PFC	Private First Class
PX	Post Exchange
RAF	Royal Air Force
T/5	Technician Fifth Grade
USAAF	United States Army Air Force

Introduction

There were over 12,000 General Court Martials (GCM) conducted by the US Army in the European, Mediterranean and North African theatres of operations during the Second World War. The charges were varied but there were many soldiers who were indicted for the crimes of murder, rape or a combination of both. Many of them would receive terms of imprisonment but a small proportion were executed for their actions. This is their story.

Firstly, this is not an in-depth study of the US military justice system during the Second World War. That would require far more print space than is available here. Neither does it seek to retry the assailants, nor judge their victims, accusers or executioners, yet it may raise an eyebrow regarding the behaviours and attitudes of the period. The purpose here is to provide the reader with a brief introduction to and overview of the soldiers of the US Army who were executed for civil crimes in the European, Mediterranean and North African theatres of operations in the period between 1942 and 1945, and whose bodies were secretly buried in a little-known location in Northern France. More importantly, the aim is to look a little closer, wherever possible, at the victims who, all too often, remain in the shadows.

During a time of global conflict, a substantial proportion of US military personnel behaved in an honest and exemplary fashion throughout the entire period of their service. However, with approximately 12 million men and women serving their country across the globe there were bound to be a few bad apples. Those who committed serious civil crimes, such as rape and murder, would find themselves appearing before a General Court Martial, a panel of officers who, where an assailant was found guilty, were duty bound to sentence the criminal to a period of incarceration or execution.

Ultimately, 142 soldiers would perish at the hands of a hangman or a firing squad across all the theatres of operations, inclusive of the South-West Pacific and China/Burma theatres. Of these men, the majority committed their crimes in the European, Mediterranean and North African theatres. For ease of reference, I have simply classed these theatres as 'Europe' on the basis that most of these men are buried in one location, which, to this day, is not open to visitors.

The Oise-Aisne American Cemetery sits on the outskirts of the community of Fère-en-Tardenois, France. Its four immaculately tended plots, maintained by the American Battle Monuments Commission (ABMC), contain the remains of 6,012 US soldiers who died whilst fighting in the vicinity during the First World War. But the cemetery also holds a dark secret. Located behind the superintendent's office, on the opposite side of the entrance to the main cemetery, and hidden from view, is another resting place, Plot 'E'. Here can be found the remains of those US Army servicemen who, following a GCM, were sentenced to death and executed. Originally, their bodies were buried near the site of their execution and later concentrated into temporary military cemeteries. Then, in 1949, at the height of the US Return of the Dead Program, their remains were stealthily removed from these locations and re-interred in what has become known as the 'Plot of Shame' and often referred to by the staff who maintain the site at the cemetery as 'The Fifth Field'. Every man had been dishonourably discharged from the US Army just prior to their execution and are regarded as the 'the dishonourable dead'. No US flag is permitted to fly over the plot, which is marked with a small single granite cross. The graves are arranged in four neat rows and marked by nothing other than a flat stone indicator the size of a credit card, etched with a sequential number engraved in black. The remains lay with their backs turned to the main cemetery. Access is difficult, and visitors are not encouraged.

The only person originally interred in the plot who was not a rapist or murderer was Private Eddie Slovik, who was executed for desertion on 31 January 1945. In 1987, President Ronald Reagan gave permission for his remains to be exhumed and returned to the United States for reburial, but this was not to take place until 1990. Additionally, in the same year, the Pentagon granted permission for the body of Private Alex F. Miranda to be disinterred from Plot 'E' and reburied in the Santa Ana Cemetery, California, following a campaign by his nephew, Louis Martinez, to have his body returned home.

The stories of all those US servicemen who were executed across Europe during the Second World War are featured here, but it should be

Chapter 1

US Military Court Martials and Executions

All but one of those executed by the military between November 1942 and August 1945 committed murder, rape or a combination of these two crimes. These two offences are described in the following brief terms.

Murder is regarded as the killing of a human being with malice aforethought and without legal justification or excuse. The malice may exist at the time the act is committed and may consist of knowledge that the act which causes death will probably cause death or grievous bodily harm. The law presumes malice where a deadly weapon is used in a manner likely to and does in fact cause death and an intent to kill may be inferred from an act of the perpetrator which manifests a reckless disregard of human life.

Rape was deemed, at the time, to be unlawful carnal knowledge of a woman by force and without her consent. Any penetration of her genitals is sufficient carnal knowledge, whether emission occurs or not. The force involved in the act of penetration is alone sufficient where there is in fact no consent.

The Articles of War

At the commencement of the Second Word War the US military operated under the terms of 121 Articles of War, which had been revised and enacted by Congress in June 1920. The military justice system continued to operate under these rulings until 31 May 1951, when the Uniform Code of Military Justice came into effect. The Articles of War relevant to the crimes discussed in this book are outlined below and are, in the main, those which each perpetrator breached, and under which executions were conducted. A soldier facing a GCM would be charged with breaching the article(s) of war in relation to their crime. Failure to advise an individual of their rights would, on occasion, be used as part of their defence and thus the sentencing might be reduced or amended. The Articles that were most commonly used are quoted below.

The 24th Article of War

> This demands that every accused, before being interviewed (or interrogated) be informed of his rights against self-incrimination. Every person in the military service, when asked, is required to make a statement, even if that statement is an election to remain silent. If he chooses to speak, he must be warned that anything he says can be used against him in future legal proceedings. The interviewer may not issue any threats nor make any promises. If there is anything in his statement, the accused believes could be incriminating it is the accused's privilege to leave it out of the statement. The interviewer must use all means to ensure that the accused understands these rights.

The 58th Article of War

> Any person subject to military law who deserts or attempts to desert the service of the United States shall, if the offense be committed in time of war, suffer death or such other punishment as a court-martial may direct, and, if the offense be committed at any other time, any punishment, excepting death, that a court-martial may direct. (On February 3, 1942, desertion was made eligible to be a capital offense by Executive Order 9048.)

The 92nd Article of War

> Any person subject to military law who commits murder or rape shall suffer death or imprisonment for life, as a court-martial may direct; but no person shall be tried by court-martial for murder or rape committed within the geographical limits of the States of the Union in time of peace.

The 93rd Article of War

> Any person subject to military law who commits manslaughter, mayhem, arson, burglary, housebreaking, robbery, larceny, embezzlement, perjury, forgery, sodomy, assault with intent to commit any felony, assault with intent to do bodily harm with a dangerous weapon, instrument, or other thing, or assault with intent to do bodily harm, shall be punished as a court-martial may direct.

The Visting Forces Act – A Note

On 6 August 1942, the United Kingdom saw the introduction of the Visiting Forces Act. Essentially, this was a judicial restraint that prevented members of the US military and naval forces from being tried before British civil or military courts. Instead, they would be tried solely by US military courts. The Act, introduced following correspondence between the US ambassador, John Gilbert Winant, and the British Secretary of State for War, Anthony Eden, was brought into being on the basis that the United States would be sending significant numbers of their armed forces to the United Kingdom and, as time went by, those numbers would increase. The US authorities pressed that point with the British government with what was described as 'great vigour and earnestness'. It is suggested that US military courts took a harder line than British civil courts when it came to capital crimes. However, there is some evidence to indicate that this was, in fact, not the case and some US servicemen appear to have benefited from this closed environment.

Court Martials

During the Second World War, the US Army used three types of court martial, as described below.

Summary Court Martial
This could only impose a sentence of no more than one month's confinement, restriction to a certain area for no more than three months and could fine a soldier a maximum of two-thirds of his monthly pay.

Special Court Martial
This could sentence a soldier to a maximum of six months' confinement and fine a soldier a maximum of two-thirds of his monthly pay for a maximum period of six months.

General Court Martial (GCM)
A GCM could impose the death sentence and other punishments. It consisted of a minimum of five members, with the most senior officer becoming the court's president. One of the panel officers had the task of a law officer, which was usually a member of the Judge Advocate General's department, who would advise the panel on matters of law and make rulings on matters of law and was also a voting member of the panel. The prosecution case was presented by a Trial Judge Advocate. The defence case was presented by a Defence Counsel.

In the case of a GCM, all the voting in the conviction and sentencing phases of the trial were by secret written ballot. A verdict of not guilty was final and the trial would end. When a guilty verdict was returned, the court would then hear any mitigating evidence as well as the accused's previous disciplinary record. For any offence that had a mandatory death sentence, the court was required to return a unanimous guilty verdict. In a case where there was a choice of death or life imprisonment, a unanimous decision was required in the sentencing phase. For a sentence of ten years to life imprisonment, three-quarters of the court panel was needed. All other convictions required a two-thirds majority decision. Fractions were in favour of the defendant. So, with a court panel of seven officers, a conviction required five officers to vote in favour. So, it was possible for a seven-member court who were hearing a case of murder to have a five-two split in favour of conviction and then a unanimous seven votes for a death sentence. After sentencing, the case would be reviewed by the approving authority, usually the Divisional commander, assisted by his Judge Advocate. They could not amend the sentence but could state an opinion. The next stage in the process was the confirming authority. In peacetime, this was the US president, but in wartime, the Commanding General of the Army in the Field was the one person who could confirm or reduce the sentence but could not increase the severity of the sentence.

In addition to the approving and confirming authorities, a special Board of Review, consisting of at least three Judge Advocates, would review the case. The confirming authority could not direct the execution of a death sentence until this body had informed them that the record of the trial was 'legally sufficient' to support a death sentence. The Article of War which covers those reviews is quoted below.

Article 50½, Review/Rehearing

> The Judge Advocate General shall constitute, in his office, a board of review consisting of not less than three officers of the Judge Advocate General's Department. Before any record of trial in which there has been adjudged a sentence requiring approval or confirmation by the President under the provisions of article 46, article 48, or article 51 is submitted to the President, such record shall be examined by the board of review. The board shall submit its opinion, in writing, to the Judge Advocate General, who shall, except as herein otherwise provided, transmit the record and the board's opinion, with his recommendations, directly to the Secretary of War for the action of the President.

Execution

The procedures for conducting an execution were carefully documented in the 'Procedure for Military Executions', War Department Pamphlet 27-4.

Hanging

For a hanging sturdy gallows would be constructed according to the diagrams in the pamphlet in a location where there was some privacy afforded. The length of the drop would be calculated based upon the condemned man's weight and height to ensure a broken neck. On the day of execution, the condemned man would be read the order of execution in his cell and then brought to the gallows. At the foot of the thirteen stairs, his wrists would be bound behind, and then he would be helped up the stairs onto the platform where he would take his place on the trapdoor. Whilst his ankles were being bound, the officer in charge would ask if he had anything to say and allow him to make any statement he wished. The chaplain would then ask the same question. Once the condemned finished his statements, or declined, the hood would be pulled over his head and the noose adjusted in a precise manner to ensure he would break his neck in the fall. In a moment, the trap would be sprung. After a brief time, the officer in charge would send the medical officer(s) beneath the gallows, and they would monitor the vital signs of the condemned until they pronounced him dead. His remains would then be removed and taken to the place of burial.

Death By Musketry
All those who were executed by musketry (firing squad) were shot within the confines of a Disciplinary Training Centre (DTC), with the exception of Private Eddie Slovik. In these cases, an area would be prepared so that the bullets would be captured after passing through the condemned and not ricochet. A sturdy post would be securely placed in the ground in a position to allow the firing squad to take at least twenty-five paces to their places. The order of execution would be read to the condemned in his cell, and then he would be brought to the range where his wrists would be bound. His chest and ankles would be bound to the post to prevent him slumping before or after being shot. The condemned would then be given time to make his final statement to the witnesses and to the chaplain. A highly visible target would be pinned on his shirt over his heart, sometimes by a doctor using his stethoscope, and he would be blindfolded. The officer in charge would order the firing squad of eight to twelve men, 'Squad? Ready …, Aim …, Fire!' After the condemned was pronounced dead by medical officers, he would be removed from the post and taken to the place of burial.

Burial
Once a prisoner had been pronounced dead, their body would be removed from the point of execution and wrapped in a covering. The body would be handed over to a Graves Registration Officer, who would have arrangements in place to bury the body in the nearest US Military Cemetery. When the Return of the Dead Program was in operation, between May 1946 and December 1951, many of the executed men were reinterred in one of the nearest ABMC cemeteries, such as Cambridge, England. However, it seems a decision was made in 1949 not to allow these men to rest amongst the honoured dead, and they were removed from the ground and reburied in Plot 'E' at the Oise-Aisne American Cemetery at Fère-en-Tardenois, France. One wonders what General John Joseph Pershing would have felt about these men being buried in a cemetery where so many of the soldiers he commanded in Europe still rest. Pershing died on 15 July 1948, and it was shortly after this that the site was chosen for the burial of the dishonoured.

In the period between November 1942 and September 1945, the US military carried out at least ninety-nine executions in the European and North African zones. All the men executed were of junior rank. Six of the condemned soldiers met their end by firing squad, the remainder being hanged. A high proportion, more than 80 per cent, were of black, Hispanic or Native American heritage. Ninety-six men were moved from their original burial location to the Oise-Aisne American Cemetery, two of which were never convicted of a crime, although their deaths occurred whilst they were in custody. Two of these were later repatriated to the United States. There were a further four men who were executed but whose bodies were returned to the US and were never buried in the Oise-Aisne American Cemetery.

The Return of the Dead – A Brief Overview

For families and friends, bringing home the body of a loved one is a significant part of the grieving process and the United States was the only country to repatriate its deceased soldiers after both the First and Second World Wars. Following the conclusion of the Second World War, the return of US war dead would become the greatest reburial effort in the history of the United States, and one of the most overlooked chapters of the post-war period. In June 1943, the Quartermaster General of the US Army had already begun drawing up plans regarding the disposition of US war dead and in May 1946, Congress unanimously approved the Return of the Dead Program. But public opinion was split, as well as that of many families. Some argued it would be sacrilegious and disrespectful to move the dead. Others pleaded for the return of their fallen husbands, sons and brothers. A survey of 249,000 next of kin was undertaken during summer 1946, after which it was decided the next of kin could choose to have their relative buried in a US national cemetery, a private cemetery or an American cemetery nearest the deceased's site of temporary burial.

The Office of the Quartermaster General oversees Mortuary Affairs, the branch tasked with retrieving, identifying and burying US and Allied military personnel. This was a job that would fall to the American Graves Registration Service, the Transportation Corps and thousands of civilian employees. Moving from country to country, the gruesome, sober work involved locating graves, disinterring and formally identifying remains, preparing bodies for permanent burials and sending them home by ship and train. The overseas transportation for the duration of the repatriation period was provided by an Army Mortuary Fleet composed primarily of converted Liberty ships that could each carry around 6,500 caskets. When the federally funded repatriation programme ended on Monday, 31 December 1951, more than 171,000 bodies had been returned home to their loved ones for a final burial, whilst another 110,000 were laid to rest in 14 new military cemeteries, most of them in Europe. But amongst this momentous procession of honoured dead were those whose bodies would rarely be returned to their families, instead, they would be removed from their grave, some on more than one occasion, and reburied in secret. These were not the bodies of men who had been lost on the battlefield, but those of the executed, soldiers who had committed capital crimes, paid the ultimate penalty and were reburied in a location known only to the US government.

Chapter 2

The Executioners

Whilst a hangman, or the members of a firing squad, may apply the mechanics of a death sentence, it is the point of confirmation that really determines if a soldier should live or die. This heavy burden lays with the President of the United States, but in a theatre of war the decision falls upon the Commanding General of the Army in the Field.

The confirming officers for the men who were executed in the North-African Theatre of Operations (NATO), Mediterranean Theatre of Operations (MTO) and European Theatre of Operations (ETO) during the Secord World War were:

Lieutenant General Omar Nelson Bradley	5
General Jacob Loucks Devers	8
Lieutenant General Joseph Taggart McNarney	16
General of the Army Dwight David Eisenhower	71

The Commanding Generals who confirmed the death sentences of convicted servicemen. Left to right: Lieutenant Omar Nelson Bradley, General Jacob Loucks Devers, Lieutenant General Joseph Taggart McNarney and General of the Army Dwight David Eisenhower.

Although the court papers were reviewed at several points before the Commanding Officer made a final decision, the process, perhaps, provides a small insight into how the US military viewed the black solider during the Second World War. This is encapsulated in the words of Lieutenant General Joseph Taggart McNarney, who, whilst serving as the military governor of the American zone from 1945 to 1947, refused to appoint any African American service members as part of his staff and said that, 'It would take 100 years before the Negro will develop to the point where he will be on a parity with white Americans.' This ideological stance may possibly have influenced his decision-making process when confirming death sentences. McNarney authorised the execution of sixteen soldiers, only one of whom was white.

Master Sergeant John Clarence Woods – The Clumsy Hangman

When it first came to carrying out an execution in the ETO, the US Army, surprisingly, found that it had no qualified hangman. The sixteen hangings that took place in Shepton Mallet, England, were all carried out by British hangmen. By August 1944, with the Allied campaign in Normandy in full flow, Eisenhower became acutely aware that he had a significant problem. Thomas Pierrepoint had to be flown out to the combat zone to carry out the execution of Private Clarence Whitfield, but a recently released pamphlet from the War Department made it clear that where judicial hangings were to be carried out, 'the trap will be actuated personally by the officer charged with the execution of the sentence'. This is something that commanders in the field did not want to impose upon their commissioned officers, and so a hangman was desperately sought. Eventually a private was found who

Master Sergeant John Clarence Woods.

was an experienced hangman, or so he claimed. In a single day he was promoted to the rank of master sergeant and quickly began a career that was filled with controversy and ended in the fog of mystery.

    John Clarence Woods was born on 5 June 1911 in Wichita, Kansas. After completing his first year of high school he dropped out and, in 1929, he enlisted in the US Navy, which he later deserted. After being apprehended, he was convicted by a GCM and was dismissed for being mentally unstable and unsuitable for military service. Despite this, he was inducted into the army on 30 August 1943, and following his basic training at Fort Leavenworth, Kansas, he was assigned to Company 'B' of the 37th Engineer Combat Battalion, 5th Engineer Special Brigade on 30 March 1944. Woods may have taken part in the landings on Omaha Beach on 6 June 1944 with his unit, but he never discussed his past, and there is some inference that he did not see any combat service. Woods made every effort to keep to himself, although he gained a reputation as a hard drinker. He was assigned to the Loire DTC and is known to have hanged at least thirty-four soldiers and assisted with five others in the ETO. In October 1946, he gained international notoriety as the official hangman for the International Military Tribunal at Nürnberg. There, he executed ten senior German military and civilian officials who had been convicted of crimes against humanity. There was a significant question mark over his capabilities during his time as a hangman, given that several of his executions went horribly wrong, with the prisoner suffering considerably before they finally died. Woods was electrocuted on 21 July 1950 on Eniwetok Atoll, at a time when the US government was using the location for the testing of nuclear weapons. There are those who believe his death was shrouded in mystery, but it appears to have been nothing more than an unfortunate accident. He is buried in the city cemetery in Toronto, Kansas, a small town 60 miles east of Wichita, where he had lived with his wife.

Thomas Pierrepoint and Albert Pierrepoint

Thomas William Pierrepoint and his nephew, Albert Pierrepoint, were amongst the most prolific hangmen in British history. Between them and their assistants, Alexander Riley and Herbert Morris, they were to be involved in the execution of seventeen US servicemen during the Second World War.

    Thomas, born in Sutton Bonington, Nottinghamshire, on 6 October 1870, began working as a hangman in 1906 under the influence of his brother, Henry, who had been on the list of official executioners since

Above left: Thomas Pierrepoint, the only British executioner to hang a US serviceman in a combat zone.

Above right: Albert Pierrepoint, the renowned British executioner.

1901. Sadly, Henry was a heavy drinker, and it would be this that eventually led Thomas to make a formal complaint in July 1910, when his brother arrived drunk at a prison the day before an execution and excessively berated him. As a result, Henry was removed from the list of executioners. During the Second World War, Thomas was appointed by the US military as their official executioner and was responsible for the hangings that took place inside Shepton Mallet Prison, Somerset, which was then titled the US 2912th DTC. In this role Thomas carried out executions not only for murder but also rape which, at the time, was a capital crime under US military law, although not in British law. In seven of these cases he was assisted by his nephew, Albert, who was principal hangman for the remaining executions. His career spanned 39 years and ended in 1946, by which time he is thought to have carried out 294 hangings. Thomas died on 11 February 1954, aged 83.

Albert Pierrepoint would become Britain's most renowned executioner. Born in Clayton, Yorkshire, on 30 March 1905, he was one of five children. He first became an assistant executioner in September 1932 and would become a lead executioner by October 1941, when he hanged the gangland killer Antonio 'Babe' Mancini. During the Second World War he hanged fifteen German spies, as well as US servicemen. After the war he, like Master Sergeant John Clarence Woods, carried out the execution of numerous German war criminals, Nazi sympathisers and British traitors. Albert disliked any publicity connected to his role and was unhappy that his name had been announced to the press by General Sir Bernard Montgomery. When he was followed across an airfield by the press, he described it as being 'as unwelcome as a lynch mob'. As the tide of British opinion began to change, Pierrepoint undertook several executions that gained notoriety, including the last woman to be hanged in the UK, Ruth Ellis. Following a dispute with the Home Office he resigned from his post in 1956 and requested that his name be removed from the list of executioners. He and his wife, Anne, ran a pub until they retired to the seaside town of Southport in the 1960s. Albert Pierrepoint died on 10 July 1992, aged 87, having carried out an estimated 435 hangings.

Chapter 3

No Resting Place in the Plot of Shame

There have been claims that the four soldiers featured in this chapter, who were executed for their crimes, were later buried in the Plot 'E', but this is not the case. These four men, listed in chronological order, were buried in temporary locations and then reinterred in the United States through the Return of the Dead Program.

Sunday, 27 December 1942, England
Victim   Second Lieutenant Robert James Cobner (white)
                Age: 25
                Service No.: O-1100488
                Unit: Company 'C', 827th Engineer Battalion (Aviation)
                Murdered
Assailant   Private David Cobb (black)
                Age: 21
                Service No.: 34165248
                Unit: Company 'C', 827th Engineer Battalion (Aviation)

The case of Private David Cobb is intriguing, not only because of the controversial circumstances surrounding his actions, but also by the fact that his body was never buried in the Plot of Shame at Oise-Aisne American Cemetery, a point that often appears to have been overlooked. His victim was Second Lieutenant Robert James Cobner. Born at Edgewood, Allegheny County, Pennsylvania, on 1 August 1917, Cobner was the first child of English-born steel-mill worker Charles E. Cobner and his Scottish wife, Ann. He enlisted in the US Army on 11 July 1941 at Fort George G. Meade, Maryland, and his education and capabilities saw

Private David Cobb.

him posted to Officer Candidate School. Upon graduation, he was commissioned as a second lieutenant, being assigned to the 827th Engineer Aviation Battalion, the role of which was to construct airfields for the 8th US Army Air Force (USAAF) in the United Kingdom. The unit was deployed to the ETO on 16 December 1942 and were first stationed at Desborough Camp, Northamptonshire.

One of the men for whom Cobner was responsible was Private David Cobb. Born on 14 November 1921, he was the second son of the Revd Howard Chester and Addie Mae Cobb (née Chambers) of Dothan, Houston County, Alabama. Cobb voluntarily enlisted into the US Army in Fort McClellan, Alabama, on 8 January 1942, and underwent basic training at Fort Dix, New Jersey. Not regarded as the perfect soldier, he was posted to the UK. On the night of 26 December 1942, Cobb, having only been overseas for eleven days, was assigned to guard duty. This tedious task lasted for some 8 hours, between midnight and 8.00 a.m. Although he was initially relieved, he was sent back to continue guard duty after having only 2 hours off because prisoners were being held in the guardhouse. At 11.45 a.m., Second Lieutenant Robert James Cobner, the Officer of the Day, arrived to have some beds moved and to inspect the guardhouse. When Cobner directed Cobb to assist in the moving of the beds, the soldier refused. Cobb, who was very agitated at only having a short period of relief, was carrying his rifle draped across his shoulders in a casual manner and was ordered to stand to attention whilst addressing an officer, and to put his uniform into proper order, otherwise he would find himself being restricted. Cobb disdainfully replied that he didn't care if he was restricted for six months, he wasn't going to do it. The young officer then directed the Sergeant of the Guard, Corporal William Mason Jr, to arrest the soldier, and ordered Cobb to surrender his rifle. When Cobb refused, Lieutenant Cobner ordered Mason to take the weapon. Cobb then pointed the rifle at Mason, who immediately backed off, and when Lieutenant Cobner approached him, Cobb turned the rifle on the young officer and fired a single shot which killed him instantly when the bullet penetrated his heart.

Cobb appeared before a GCM, held in the Guildhall, Cambridge, on 6 January 1943. Here it was determined he had killed the lieutenant whilst the officer was performing his duty. The jury swiftly recommended the death sentence and a Board of Review, held on 1 March 1942, determined the court was legally constituted and the verdict appropriate. Cobb was moved to the US Army's DTC in Shepton Mallet, Somerset, where he was executed at 1.00 a.m. on 12 March 1943 by Thomas and Albert Pierrepoint. Lieutenant Colonel Gillard and eighteen witnesses were present at the execution. There is some indication that Thomas Pierrepoint's handling of the execution was both brusque and lacked patience. This is perhaps not surprising, given that British executions usually took place at 8.00 a.m., rather than 1.00 a.m., the preferred choice of the Americans. Cobb's body was originally buried in Brookwood American Military Cemetery, Surrey, but at the request of his family was returned to his widow and is buried in an unmarked grave next to his sister, Ruby Lee Cobb, in the North Highland Street Cemetery in Dothan, Houston County, Alabama.

The body of Second Lieutenant Robert James Cobner rests in Plot D, Row 3, Grave 50 in the American Military Cemetery, Cambridge. His military awards include the American Defense Service Medal, the American Campaign Medal, the European African Middle East Campaign Medal and the World War II Victory Medal. Remember him.

Sunday, 10 January 1943, England
Victim   PFC Harry Mosby Jenkins (white)
                Age: 25
                Service No.: 3304258
                Unit: 116th Infantry Regiment
                Murdered
Assailant   Private Harold Adolphus Smith (white)
                Age: 21
                Service No.: 14045090
                Unit: Headquarters Company, 1st Tank Destroyer
                    Group

PFC Harry Mosby Jenkins.

Harry Mosby Jenkins was born in Madison, Virginia, on 7 June 1917, the son of Ashby and Martha Jenkins. A farm worker, he joined the US Army on 1 May 1941 at Richmond, Virginia, and following his basic training became a member of the 116th Infantry Regiment, part of the 29th Infantry Division. With the entry of the United States into the Second World War, Harry was posted to the ETO, where he was based at Chiseldon Camp, Wiltshire. It would be here that his life would end, not because of battle but because of a brief altercation with another soldier.

Harold Adolphus Smith was born on 4 January 1923 in La Grange, Troup City, Georgia. His father, Loyd, was 21 years old and his mother, Zellah, was just 13. With the permission of his parents, he enlisted in the US Army on 4 February 1941. Like Jenkins, he found himself stationed at Chiseldon Camp, serving with the Headquarters Company of the 1st Tank Destroyer Group. On 31 December 1942, Smith was being held in the guardhouse, awaiting trial for stealing a jeep. After receiving his pay, he and another general prisoner, Private Harry English, escaped from confinement and made their way to London by train where they rented a room at the Royal Hotel in Russell Square. Smith was soon out of money and returned to Chiseldon Camp on 9 January 1943. Here, he was given a sandwich by two members of a guard detail, Corporal Amos R. Buchanan and PFC Richard B. Payne, both from Company 'E', 116th Infantry Regiment. The guards took him to their barracks, where he spent the night and remained until approximately 3.30 p.m. the following day. Men coming into the barracks from guard duty dropped their pistols 'in the nearest convenient spot'. During the day Smith took, without authority, a US Army .45 calibre pistol, holster, web belt and three clips of ammunition. He strapped this equipment to his waist, under his overcoat, and walked out of the barracks at about 4.00 p.m., checking the clip in the pistol as he went.

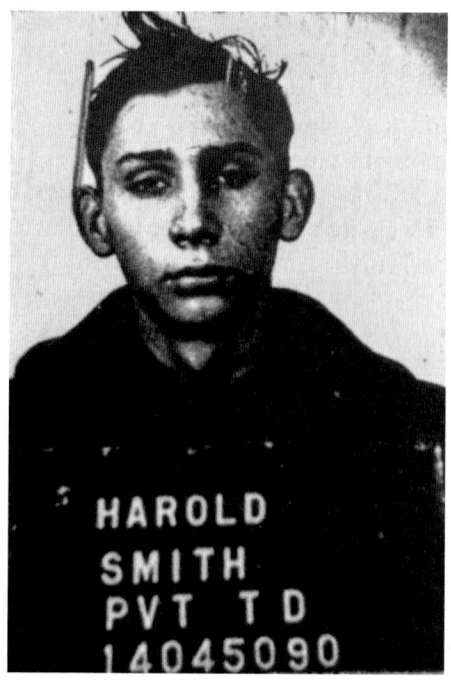

Private Harold Adolphus Smith. (*JAG File*)

At this moment, Private Harry Jenkins was mounting a guard outside the barracks. According to Smith's statement, he thought the guard was the one who had given him the sandwich. Smith walked towards Jenkins and said, 'Hiya bud.' Jenkins said, 'What the hell did you say?' Smith replied, 'I just said hiya bud.' Jenkins then said, 'What do you mean by that?' Smith retorted, 'Just hiya bud.' Smith then said that at this moment he and Jenkins were about 4ft apart. Smith saw that Jenkins then moved his right hand towards his holstered gun. Smith withdrew the pistol from under his overcoat and fired two shots at Jenkins, who fell to the ground. Smith then holstered the gun and ran away from the scene and made his way back to London.

At about 2.30 a.m. on Monday, whilst sleeping in a chair at the YMCA, Smith was woken up by a London policeman and arrested. He was then handed over to the US Military Police. Jenkins was taken to Swindon Hospital at about 4.30 p.m. on 9 January 1943, suffering from shock and gunshot wounds. Jenkins has a wound in the left side of his back, one in his left arm, one in his left thigh and one in his right thigh, with one of the bullets passing right through his body. He died the next evening.

Smith appeared before a GCM at Bristol on 12 March 1943, where he pleaded not guilty to the crime. A witness told Smith's trial that, upon hearing the two shots, he had rushed out of his hut and upon reaching the mortally wounded soldier, was told that it was Smith that had shot him. There was some argument from the defence counsel concerning the age of the defendant, but this was deemed to be inaccurate. Smith was found guilty and sentenced to death by hanging. Following a review of the court proceedings, the death sentence was confirmed by Lieutenant General Jacob Loucks Devers. Smith was executed on 25 June 1943 at Shepton Mallet Prison by Thomas and Albert Pierrepoint. He was initially buried in a temporary grave at Brookwood American Military Cemetery. Some modern records suggest his body was later removed to the Oise-Aisne American Cemetery, but this is not the case. It appears that after the war, under the terms of the Return of the Dead Program, his family arranged for his remains to be returned to his hometown of La Grange, Georgia.

Private Harry Mosby Jenkins was returned to the United States under the Return of the Dead Program, and is buried in Etlan Cemetery, Etlan, Madison County, Virginia. Remember him.

Saturday, 28 August 1943, Algeria

Victim	Private Alfred Edwin Raby (white)
	Age: 28
	Service No.: 36123309
	Unit: 18th Replacement Battalion
	Murdered
Assailants	Private Edwin P. Jones (white)
	Age: 23
	Service No.: 15045804
	Private Fred Thomas Bailey (white)
	Age: 25
	Service No.: 33090327
	Unit: 27th Armoured Field Artillery Battalion, 1st Armoured Division

The graves of Private Alfred Edwin Raby and Private Edwin P. Jones. The remains of each man were shipped to the United States under the Return of the Dead Program.

There was a need to reinforce control in militarised zones using the Military Police. The role was not a popular one, and Military Policemen (MPs) were often spat on, assaulted and, on occasions, killed by their comrades. One MP was Private Alfred Edwin Raby. Born in Detroit, Michigan, on 29 January 1915, he was the son of William Raby and Clara George. After completing his formal education, Edwin worked on the production line at the Ford Motor Company plant at River Rouge, west of Detroit. He enlisted in the US Army on 16 July 1941 and, after serving in the military for a year, married his sweetheart, Jane Kaczynski, in Detroit on 11 July 1942, just before being shipped overseas.

Edwin P. Jones was born on 16 February 1920, the eldest son of a rural Kentucky farmer. He was one of eight children, four boys and four girls, and his family had a difficult upbringing despite their hard-working parents. Sadly, his brother, Willie, was killed in August 1941 during a fight at a roadhouse when a local troublemaker, Earl 'Pedro' Kistner, fired two shots from a pistol, one of which killed Willie whilst the other struck Edwin in the chest, damaging a lung. Although Kistner was charged with murder, a subsequent hearing, held by Judge F.S. Vance, found there was insufficient evidence for an indictment and Kistner walked free.

At about 8.30 p.m. on 28 August 1943, a group of eight soldiers were sitting on a step drinking wine in the Algerian village of Assi Ben Okba. Amongst the group were Private Edwin P. Jones and Private Fred T. Bailey. Two MPs drove up and told the men they could not drink the wine and requested that they surrender of the bottle. After some conversation, the men were permitted to drink the wine, after which the MPs broke the bottle and drove away. Whilst the wine was being consumed, Bailey told the policemen they were poor sports and said, 'We will come back tomorrow night and show you a thing or two.' The soldiers then made their way to their bivouacs, but Jones and Bailey decided to return to the village. Jones loaded his .45 pistol with a clip and placed a cartridge in the chamber and they returned to Assi Ben Okba, walking down the street where they had previously encountered the MPs. The village was off limits to any military personnel after 10.00 p.m., so when an MP, Private Allen Lewis, heard a commotion going on, he took his motorcycle to investigate. He found Jones and Bailey, along with two other men, attempting to run other soldiers out of town. Bailey wanted to take the motorcycle and Lewis could see things were getting out of hand, so he went for help. He returned a brief time later with a truck and four MPs, including Private Norman E. Hippert and Private Alfred E. Raby.

At the same time, Second Lieutenant Charles M. Hunter, MP, arrived in his jeep. The MPs were now in a scuffle with the soldiers and, as Hunter approached them, Jones began running his hands up and down his pockets. The MPs attempted to search him but as they were struggling, he broke free and produced the pistol. Jones fired three shots, one of which struck Alfred Raby in the chest, killing him instantly. Another shot and seriously wounded Norman Hippert, who had to roll behind the truck to escape the gunfire. Jones waved the pistol at the rest of the MPs saying, 'If any of you other pricks move, I'll mow you all down.' He then disappeared around a corner but was soon captured.

Both Jones and Bailey were brought before a GCM at Oran, Algeria, on 21 September 1943, and pleaded not guilty to the charges. Bailey, who had three previous convictions by summary courts martial, was sentenced to dishonourable discharge, forfeiture of all pay and allowances due or to become due and confinement at hard labour for one year and nine months. Jones, however, was sentenced to death. He was hanged at the MBS Stockade, Oran, Algeria, on 5 January 1944 by Major Arthur S. Imell. His body was buried at the US Military Cemetery in Oran. Under the Return of the Dead Program, his remains were brought back to the United States and, on 21 August 1949, he was buried next to his younger brother, Willie, in the family plot at the Drennan Chapel Cemetery, Henry County, Kentucky.

Private Alfred Edwin Raby was brought home to his beloved wife under the same programme and is buried in the Mount Olivet Cemetery, Detroit, Michigan. Remember him.

Saturday, 5 August 1944, France
Victim   Yvonne Emilienne Eugenia Vaudevire, French civilian (white)
                    Age: 39
                    Raped
Assailant   Private Theron Watts McGann (white)
                    Age: 23
                    Service No.: 39332102
                    Unit: Company 'A', 32nd Signal Construction Battalion

On the evening of 5 August 1944, two women seeking refuge from the war were living together, along with two young children, in Quibou, a tiny village some 7 miles south-west of Saint-Lô. Paulette Martin was a refugee from Cherbourg and Yvonne Vaudevire was a 39-year-old refugee from Paris. Company 'A', 32nd Signal Construction Battalion was bivouacked close to the village. Amongst the men of the unit was 23-year-old Private Theron Watts McGann, from Portland, Oregon. The soldier was a troubled individual with a criminal past. That evening there was a hard knock on the door of the home the women shared. Yvonne Vaudevire, who spoke no English, opened it and saw a US soldier in the doorway who asked, 'How about pulling a piece?' Yvonne replied, 'No, impossible', whereupon the soldier forced his way into the house and went over to Paulette Martin, who could speak some English, placed his hand on his revolver, which was in a holster, seized her around the waist and asked, 'Will you pull a piece?' She answered, 'No, impossible; tomorrow.' He replied, 'No, tonight.' Frightened by the soldier's demeanour, Paulette told Yvonne, 'Get out of the door, so I can go out and call for help', but Yvonne refused. The soldier went over to the door, locked it and put the key in his pocket. Holding the revolver, he lined up the two women in front of him, one behind the other. Yvonne, being afraid, raised her arms and said, 'Yes, I consent', telling him, as best she could, not to shoot. The soldier led her into the kitchen where there was a sofa, he removed her clothing in a rough manner, leaving her entirely naked, and placed her garments on the sofa. He sat down and placed her on his lap, naked, facing him, where he then indulged in sexual intercourse with her. The act was over within about 20 to 30 minutes, during which time Paulette Martin remained in the kitchen, on the other side of the room, and covered her eyes with her hands. The soldier looked steadily at Paulette all the time, continually pointed his revolver at her and never put the weapon down for a moment. When he had finished, the soldier got up and left, locking the door behind him.

On 28 August 1944, Private Theron Watts McGann appeared before a GCM at Fougerolles du Plessis, a small town 60 miles south of Saint-Lô. He pleaded not guilty, despite confessing to the crime, and chose not to take to the witness stand, perhaps resigning himself to his fate. He had enlisted in the US Army on 13 May 1943, and evidence would demonstrate he had been sentenced on two occasions for car theft and also had a drinking problem. His character was described as poor, and a medical report described him as 'constitutional psychopathic'. This was a problem that arose for the US and British forces during the Second World War. The shortage of manpower as the war progressed often led to the recruitment of men who were, to some degree, psychologically unfit for service, but were still accepted into the ranks. It is suggested by author William Bradford Huie that those men considered as temperamentally unstable, maladjusted, sexually perverted or overly nervous totalled almost 1.5 million, from an army of about 10 million.

The trial was short, and in less than 2½ hours the brown-haired, blue-eyed American was found guilty and sentenced to death. The sentence was confirmed by General Dwight D. Eisenhower on 27 October. McGann was transported to Saint-Lô in preparation for execution. Temporary gallows were erected in the courtyard of a building in the northern section of the city, close to a building that had been so severely damaged that all that remained were four outer walls. On the morning of 20 November 1944, with the rain falling, a group of officials, witnesses and spectators gathered in the courtyard. After being asked if he had any last words, which he did not, a black hood was placed over McGann's head, a noose adjusted around his neck and then Major Mortimer H. Christian dropped him through the trapdoor. About 13 minutes later, at 10.16 a.m., Captain Albert M. Summerfield began to confirm the soldier as dead, and as he uttered the words 'I pronounce …', the wall of the adjacent building collapsed, scattering the group of onlookers. Once he had composed himself, the medical officer completed the task and McGann was pronounced dead. His body was removed from the site and taken to the US Military Cemetery at Marigny for burial. Like the others in this chapter, he was never moved to the Oise-Aisne American Cemetery but, instead, at the request of the family, was returned to Portland, Oregon, for burial.

There is no official record to confirm that Yvonne Vaudevire was amongst those who witnessed McGann's execution, but Sergeant Emmett N. Bailey Jr, who was present, claimed that she was there. Small recompense for the few moments of her life in which a memory was created, one that would never leave her. Remember her.

Chapter 4

1943: Murder, Rape and Ten Hanged

Friday, 7 May 1943, Algeria
Victim   Corporal William Lynn Tackett (white)
                Age: 21
                Service No.: 6982857
                Unit: 218th Military Police Company
                Murdered
Assailant   Private Charles H. Smith (white)
                Age: 33
                Service No.: 36337437
                Unit: 540th Engineer Regiment

William Lynn Tackett was born on 15 February 1922 in Henrico, Virginia, the son of Thomas Jefferson Tackett and Helen Marie Lynn. His mother, was an army nurse who had been stationed at a number of military hospitals, including Oteen, North Carolina, before marrying his father, who was serving as a sergeant in the Quartermaster Corps in Washington. The couple married in 1920 and produced two children, Thomas and William. Tragically, Helen passed away just a week after her second wedding anniversary on 13 July

Corporal William Lynn Tackett.

1922, having contracted tuberculosis. Thomas, who was now working at the Federal Shipyard in New Jersey, had help to raise the children from Rose Lynn, Helen's sister. The couple married on 19 July 1924 and would produce two children of their own, Margaret and John. In a bitter twist, Rose passed away on 6 August 1930, leaving Thomas with four children. A third sister, Margaret, stepped in to help and, it seems love blossomed again, and she and Thomas married in 1934. By 1942, William had enlisted in the army and, on completion of his basic training, was shipped overseas, serving with the 218th Military Police Company in the Algerian port of Oran, a key location for US forces in North Africa, who were making last-minute preparations for the invasion of Sicily. His older brother, Thomas, was also in North Africa, serving with the Army Air Corps.

On 7 May 1943, Corporal Tackett was on duty in the city along with another MP, Private Sephus Joe Stinnett. They were on watch outside a brothel named 'Villa de Roses' where servicemen were waiting to enter the premises. MPs were on hand to ensure that the troops, many of whom had been drinking, did not get too excited or out of hand. In the line was Private Charles Smith, a man with an extensive criminal record. Born on 6 October 1909, in Salem, Missouri, he was known to be quick-tempered and had been arrested on many occasions for minor offences. However, in 1930, he carried out a robbery in Granite City, Illinois, for which he received a twenty-year jail sentence. He was released after serving seven years at Menard Prison. Smith was drafted into the army on 11 May 1942 at Chicago, Illinois, and following the completion of his basic training was shipped to North Africa. That afternoon he had been drinking heavily and was making a nuisance of himself. He made several attempts to enter the brothel but, due to his drunken state, was refused access. It was not long before an enraged Smith began to cause more trouble and Stinnett was forced to eject the unruly soldier, telling him it was time he was going home. Now, further enraged, Smith threatened to cut the MP's throat. Stinnett, having decided he needed to arrest the soldier, came forward but Corporal William Lynn Tackett attempted to calm the situation. He told Stinnett to go back inside, then approached Smith with the objective of encouraging him to leave. Tackett tapped Smith on the shoulder and started to lead him away from the establishment. The MP did not get far. In less than eight steps, Smith whipped out a knife and slashed Tackett across the throat, inflicting a gushing wound. Tackett immediately fell to the ground. Pharmacist's Mate John F. Brookmeyer of the US Navy attempted to give first aid to the stricken soldier but major blood vessels had been severed. He helped place Corporal Tackett into a jeep, after which he was transported to hospital but died on the way. Smith tried to escape but was brought down by another soldier and swiftly arrested.

Smith was brought before a GCM on 21 May 1943, in Oran. His defence was that he was drunk and did not know what he was doing. Smith testified on his own behalf, stating he had consumed ten or twelve glasses of red wine that evening, adding that he did not know whether he had struck the victim, or even how he left the 'Villa de Roses'. The court found Smith guilty of murder, on the basis that the accuracy and depth of the wound was such that it was clear his intention was malicious and he was sentenced to death. Following approval and review, the sentence was confirmed by General Dwight D. Eisenhower. On 6 September 1943, Major Arthur S. Imell, the commander at the DTC in Oran, arranged for nine commissioned officers to be present as official witnesses at the hanging in Algiers. At 7.00 a.m., Major Imell is believed to have cut the rope that activated the trapdoor sending Smith to his death, which was officially pronounced at 7.20 a.m. His body was originally buried in the US Military Cemetery in Oran. Like so many others, in 1949 his body was secretly removed from its temporary grave and transported to the Oise-Aisne American Cemetery, where he lays in Plot 'E', Row 4, Grave 77.

Corporal William Lynn Tackett is buried with honour in the American Military Cemetery at Carthage, Tunisia. His remains are in Plot H, Row 19, Grave 19. Remember him.

Friday, 28 May 1943, Algeria
Victim	Carmen Nunez, Algerian civilian
	Age: 10
	Raped and murdered
Assailant	Private James E. Kendrick (white)
	Age: 21
	Service No.: 14026995
	Unit: Headquarters Battery, 14th Armoured Field Artillery Battalion

The files concerning the cases detailed here often contain limited information about the victims. Modern technology, and the growing availability of access to archives, provides the opportunity to look a little closer at everyone, but this is rarely the case when the victim is from a poor native background. On 2 June 1943, near the village of Debrousseville, Algeria, the body of Carmen Nunez, a French Algerian girl, who was not quite 10 years old and small for her age, was found face down in the dirt. A disabled child, she had club feet, one of which had been bandaged, and when a doctor turned her tiny body over, he saw that her facial muscles and tissues were entirely gone, eaten by maggots. A US doctor established that she had been raped, and that her death was caused by asphyxiation due to her nose and mouth being forced into the ground by pressure on the back of her neck. In her right hand was a clump of grass, the result of a grasping hand, clawed 'in the agony of death'.

On Christmas Eve 1942, Private James E. Kendrick, a 21-year-old white soldier from Picayune, Mississippi, had landed in Casablanca, French Morocco, assigned to the 14th Armoured Field Artillery Battalion, part of the US 2nd Armoured Division. On 28 May he had been seen driving a truck containing Carmen and her younger brother, François. Kendrick had befriended the little girl's family, who lived in Ferme Blanche, Algeria, outside of Mascara, whilst his unit was stationed close to their village, often visiting and giving the children chewing gum and candy. That fateful afternoon Kendrick had driven Mr Nunez, a barber, to the camp where he would cut the hair of the soldiers based there. Kendrick then returned to the Nunez home and, against the wishes of their mother, he took the children for a ride in the truck on the basis they were going to pick up their father. Despite her objections, Kendrick picked up the two children, placed them in the truck and drove off. A short time after he left, François returned home carrying $20 and told his mother that the American wanted to buy some wine but had driven off with Carmen in his vehicle. She was not seen alive again. Later that evening, Staff Sergeant Elden V. Kietzman interviewed Kendrick and asked him what had happened to the girl, but the soldier denied any knowledge of seeing her or knowing what had happened to her. The following morning, the child's mother confronted Kendrick in his camp area and, sheepishly, he told her, 'Me no kill. I haven't seen the child.' First Lieutenant Gerald P. Blakeman, Provost Marshal, then interrogated Kendrick, fully believing that the soldier was connected to the child's disappearance, but the young man continued to deny he knew anything about it and claimed that he had not returned to the village after dropping Mr Nunez at the bivouac area.

On 2 June, Kendrick was taken to the Judge Advocate Major Benjamin P. Brentz, who, along with two other officers, began an interrogation. Soon realising that he was in deep trouble, the soldier, who was later described as being 'a poor character with unsatisfactory performance', began to change his story. He claimed that he was drunk and that during the journey to the camp he had driven over a bump and the child had been thrown out of the vehicle, with one of the wheels running over her. Not knowing what to do with the injured child, he decided to drive out to a location near Debrousseville, where he left her. Brentz immediately organised a search party, led by Kendrick, who later that day found the girl's body in an open field, about 2 miles off the Fornaka–Perregaux road. Tyre tracks from a heavy military vehicle led to a point where bloodstained underwear was found, and about 160ft further on the body of the child was discovered. Before her body was turned over, a large brown stain could be seen on the ground close to her genital area, which was believed to be dried blood. Major Brentz ordered photographs of the scene be taken, and these would be used in court later. Captain Theodore W. Plume, US Medical Corps, provided a graphic description of the child's injuries and how she had met her death at the hands of her killer. Captain William C. Smith, who stood with Kendrick some 40ft or so from the body whilst it was examined, asked him if he wished to revise his statement. The soldier confirmed he did, and Smith advised him of his rights. But it seems that Kendrick maintained that it was all a terrible accident and he had dumped the child's body in a panic, after she fell from his truck.

Just ten days later, on 12 June 1943, Kendrick appeared before a GCM at 2nd Armoured Division Headquarters, where he testified in his own defence. Born on 22 March 1922, he had attended eight years of grade school and one year of high school before quitting to become a truck driver. He enlisted in the US Army in Montgomery, Alabama, on 29 October 1940 and after completing training as a motorcycle mechanic joined the 2nd Armoured Division at Fort Benning, Georgia. It was noted that he had ten previous court-martial convictions. He claimed that he had been so drunk on 28 May that he could not see the road, that the little girl had offered him sex, which he accepted, and following this act, she had suffered some form of epileptic fit when climbing back into his truck. Whilst some medical experts stated that death from suffocation was feasible for epileptics, it was almost certainly not the case in this instance. Numerous witnesses saw him driving the truck on the afternoon of the crime, non of whom stated he appeared drunk, and family members testified that he had driven away with the children without their permission. It was clear to the court that Kendrick had acted with 'design, and premeditation characterised his every movement'. He was found guilty of murder and carnal knowledge, both of which were violations of the 92nd Article of War and sentenced to death by hanging.

General Dwight D. Eisenhower, commanding NATO, confirmed the sentence on 29 June. With preparations for the invasion of Sicily paramount in the minds of operational leaders, the execution was delayed until 17 July. At 6.25 a.m. that morning, Kendrick stood before Major Matthew C. Stewart, Commanding Officer of the Oran DTC. After having the court decision read out to him before a small group of officers and witnesses, he was summarily hanged. His body was buried in the US Military Cemetery in Oran, but in 1949 it was removed and secretly transported to the Oise-Aisne American Cemetery, and reinterred in Plot 'E', Row 1, Grave 5.

The body of Carmen Nunez would have been dealt with in accordance with the customs and religion of her country. Remember her.

Wednesday, 14 July 1943, England

Victim	Doris May Staples, British civilian (white)
	Age: 35
	Murdered
Assailant	Private John H. Waters (white)
	Age: 38
	Service No.: 32337934
	Unit: Engineer Model Makers Detachment

Doris May Staples was a free-spirited woman. Born on 25 November 1906, she was the daughter of Arthur Staples and May Le Huray, whose home was in Saint-Pierre-Port, Guernsey, in the Channel Islands. With the onset of the Second World War, and the Nazi invasion of Europe, Doris and her father moved to England, where they settled in Hammersmith, West London. A dressmaker by trade, her skills were in demand at a time when clothing was rationed, outfits often needing to be adapted, and military personnel were seeking alterations and repairs to their uniforms. The air assault by the German Luftwaffe had made London a very unsafe place to live and Doris moved again and took up residence in Reading Road, Henley-on-Thames, Oxfordshire. She was a woman who wanted to savour life and had a number of male friends with whom she would socialise. One, a US soldier, was a favourite but

Doris May Staples, a woman determined to enjoy life.

it seems he was posted to North Africa, most likely as part of Operation Torch. Doris wasted no time and in January 1943, she met another US soldier, Private John Henry Waters serving with the Engineer Model Makers Detachment, attached to RAF Medmenham.

Born on 1 October 1905 in Perth Amboy, Middlesex County, New Jersey, Waters had married in 1925 and separated from his wife in 1928 because of family difficulties, but was not divorced. By April 1930, he was being held in the New York State Reformatory at Elmira, Chemung, New York, known as 'The Hill', where, under the 'Elmira System', inmates were given the opportunity to undertake vocational training in various trades and extra-curricular activities such as a prison band, newspaper and various athletic leagues. Here he was employed as a modeller in the plaster shop. Although he had never attended school, he was able to read and write and would eventually make a living as a model maker in terracotta and ornamental plaster, a skill that would later be required by the Allied forces when creating plans and models for operational purposes. On 16 May 1942, when Waters arrived at Fort Jay on Governors Island, New York, he was optimistic that he was embarking on a new phase of life as he entered service with the US Army. Little did he know that within just eighteen months his life would end, not with honour on the battlefield but dangling from a hangman's noose in a damp and dingy corner of a British prison. The path to this dreadful conclusion was a bittersweet one, filled with love, lust, jealousy, pain and, ultimately, murder.

In July 1942, the US Engineer Model Makers Detachment arrived in England, where they were stationed at Phyllis Court, Henley-on-Thames, Oxfordshire, a former private club described as a Regency country house with fine views of the River Thames through its large French windows. This was a pleasant place to work, being spacious and well lit, and was conducive to model making. John Waters arrived at Phyllis Court on 4 October 1942. He met Doris Staples in January 1943, and a short time after their relationship became a sexual one. However, Doris had an eye on other men, and it seems there was also still a place in her heart for the soldier in North Africa. It appears that she also often told Waters lies and their relationship turned sour when he became aware that she had been seeing other men. At the same time, he had received a notice concerning an allotment of his pay to his wife, from whom he had been separated for many years. This set him on a path to murder.

At about 12.30 p.m. on the afternoon of 14 July 1943, Waters made his way to 11a Greys Road, Henley-on-Thames, where Doris was working in a tailor's shop owned by Issy Aaronson, but he found she was not there, so he left. He returned 2 hours later, and after speaking for a moment to Doris and passing her a note, he left the premises to return to his detachment. The Royal Air Force maintained the guard at Phyllis Court, which operated entirely under RAF regulations, personnel being supplied by both the British and Americans proportionally based on the number of men from each unit stationed there. At 4.00 p.m. that day, Waters took his turn at guard duty, where he was handed a Webley .38 revolver and twelve rounds of ammunition. As soon as his comrade left the area, Waters walked out of Phyllis Court and made his way back to the shop, where Doris was working with two other women, Rebecca Woolf and Gertrude Hurst. At 4.30 p.m., there was a tap on the window of the shop, and one of the women remarked, 'He's here again', to which Doris replied, 'What does he want now? I had better go out and see what he wants.' She did so, and held a brief conversation with Waters, saying at one point, 'I can't come out with you now, Johnny, I'm working.' Aaronson, irritated by the ever present American, told her to stop gossiping and get back to work. Events now moved very swiftly to a catastrophic height. As Doris went back into the shop, she attempted to close the door behind her, but Waters put his foot in the way, to prevent her from doing so. He then entered the shop, pulled out the pistol, which he was wearing on a lanyard around his neck, and fired three shots into her back. Waters then approached Doris, who had collapsed on the floor, and fired another two rounds into her body. Having shot Doris five times, he turned the gun on himself and, saying to Rebecca Woolf, 'Not you, Betty', he shot himself under the chin. However, this was not the end of the drama and Waters was still a danger.

Rebbeca Wolf ran, screaming, from the shop to get help and Gertrude Hurst attempted to climb over a fence in the backyard to escape the bloodbath. A passer-by raced to the police station to sound the alarm and at about 4.45 p.m., Inspector Henry Morris arrived to find a group of people surrounding the shop, one of whom shouted, 'Look out, he has got a gun.' Two US soldiers, Captain Harrison P. Reed and Sergeant Henry E. Cloud, who were also serving with the model makers detachment, then arrived on the scene. Reed shouted, 'Are you all right, Johnny? Throw out your gun.' There was no reply, and the weapon was not thrown out. At this point, a tear-gas grenade was hurled through the door of the shop. Any hope that this would put an end to what seemed to be developing into a siege was dashed when somebody in the crowd called to the Americans, 'He's just moved!' A moment later, two shots rang out. One smashed a window on the other side of the road, and the other ricocheted off the surface of the road, sending the crowd diving for cover. Reed and Cloud, who had made there way to the rear of the premises, clambered over the fence and found John Waters slumped in an outside toilet, bleeding heavily from a wound to his jaw, but clinging to life. He was taken to hospital where it was determined the bullet had passed through his chin, the floor of his mouth, tongue and hard palate and lodged in the left frontal region of the brain. Later, it migrated through his brain and had to be surgically removed.

A board of officers convened on 27 October 1943 to determine Waters' sanity and found that he was sane and responsible for his actions on the day of the crime. However, due to his injuries, Waters did not appear before a GCM until 29 November 1943, which was held in Watford, Hertfordshire. He was suffering from partial blindness, convulsions and headaches, and was unable to remember significant events. A doctor stated that Waters had most likely suffered intellectual deterioration with the passage of time, including his ability to remember. He pleaded not guilty to all the charges against him and both his company commander and first sergeant testified that he was a good soldier and a particularly good model technician. He then took to the stand and claimed he could not remember going on guard duty, going to town, being in the tailor's shop, seeing the victim or committing the shooting. The court convicted Waters of three charges: murder, leaving his guard post and maiming himself. He was then sentenced to death by hanging. Brigadier General Ewart G. Plank approved the verdict and the sentence. But it seems that there was both a public outcry in the town with many residents signing a petition for clemency and an official plea for leniency amongst senior officers, who called for the sentence to be commuted. This was not because of any mitigating circumstances but simply due to the fact that, considering Waters' injuries, if his head was jerked backwards by a rope he might be prone to decapitation or if his injured jaw gave way under the strain of being hanged, the rope could actually slip over his head and he would drop to the ground. However, after 'full consideration and considerable discussion', General Dwight D. Eisenhower directed that the sentence should be carried out.

At 12.53 a.m. on 10 February 1944, Major James C. Cullens, Commanding Officer of the 2912th DTC, led a group of eighteen officials and witnesses to the execution chamber. Guards escorted the condemned man into the chamber 2 minutes later. Thomas Pierrepoint then placed the white hood over his head and adjusted the noose around his neck, whilst his assistant, Alexander Riley, strapped Waters' ankles together. Cullens gave a silent signal to the executioners and Waters dropped to his death. Major Thomas O. Otto pronounced him dead at 1.19 a.m. His body was then was taken to Brookwood American Military Cemetery in Surrey, where it was buried, marked with a temporary wooden cross, to which was attached one of his ID tags, the other being buried with him. In 1948, his body was removed and transferred to the American Military Cemetery, Cambridge. Then, in 1949, it was dug up for a second time and secretly transported to the Oise-Aisne American Cemetery, where it rests in Plot 'E', Row 2, Grave 46. It seems a little ironic that the US military would go to great lengths to help a man recover from self-inflicted injuries, only to then execute him.

Doris May Staples is buried in Henley-on-Thames Cemetery, Oxfordshire. Remember her.

Saturday, 17 July 1943, Italy
Victim   Giovianana Incatasciato Morana, Italian civilian
      Raped
Assailants Private Willie A. Pittman (black)
      Age: 25
      Service No.: 34400976
      Private Harvey Stroud (black)
      Age: 22
      Service No.: 33215131
      Private Armstead White (black)
      Age: 29
      Service No.: 34401104
      Private David White (black)
      Age: 24
      Service No.: 34400884
      Unit: Company 'C', 249th Quartermaster Battalion

By May 1943, German forces had been swept from Tunisia, and Allied commanders believed their forces were at a strength where they were ready to conduct operations on the enemy's soil. The invasion of Sicily, codenamed 'Operation Husky', began on 10 July 1943. Amongst the troops of the US II Corps were the 249th Quartermaster Battalion, an African American unit. A week after the landings, on 17 July 1943, four black American soldiers arrived at the home of Giovanni Morana in Marretta, a small village near Gela. In the house were Morana, his wife, Giovianana, their 3-year-old daughter and several other relatives who were visiting. Three of the soldiers entered the house and ordered the relatives to leave, after which Giovianana was grabbed by the arm, but she managed to break free and hide under a bed. One of the attackers dragged her out, handed his rifle to a companion, stripped her of all her clothing, threw her on the bed and raped her. Morana heard his wife struggling and calling for help, and he attempted to appease the attackers but was helpless as he had been forced against a wall, his daughter in his arms, with a rifle pointed at him. Each of the soldiers then took it in turn to rape Giovianana, forcing her husband and daughter to watch the vile assaults. No sooner had the soldiers left than one of the relatives rushed to a nearby Command Post at Barrafranca, operated by troops of the US 1st Infantry Division, known as the Big Red One. A detail was ordered to search the location where the attack had taken place and quickly arrested eight black soldiers in the vicinity. An attempt was then made to arrest a further four black soldiers, but they made good their escape. These were soon identified as Privates Harvey Stroud, Armstead White, Willie A. Pittman and David White.

The four men were swiftly arrested and, the following morning, Major Mitchell Abraham Mabardy, the Provost Marshall for US II Corps, commenced an investigation. He took statements from all four men, with each of them admitting they had sex with Giovianana and each implicating their three comrades. Mabardy arranged for all twelve men to be taken to the scene of the assault, where they were paraded before the victim and her husband. All the accused were identified separately by the couple. The four young men were tried at Caltanissetta, Sicily, on 21 July 1943, just four days after the assault. The trials, ordered by Lieutenant General Omar Bradley, were held separately at the insistence of the defence counsel and took place between 2.00 p.m. and midnight. The judge and jury, in every case, were the same, and each man was promptly found guilty and sentenced to death. Giovianana had bruises on her arm, which were shown in court, and she bravely testified that she had not consented to the acts, and that her husband, who was holding their daughter, was continually restrained by one of the other soldiers as each man took his turn with her.

Private David White, a married man, was the first to appear before the GCM. Born in Shamrock, Dixie County, Florida, on 12 July 1919, he had been in the army for less than a year. He pleaded not guilty to the crime, but his counsel offered no defence, and he was never called to the witness stand to testify his innocence. His trial lasted just 3 hours 30 minutes. Private Harvey Stroud would appear before the court next. Born on 26 March 1921 in Merwell, Georgia, he had joined the US Navy in early 1940 but was discharged from the service on 17 July 1941 on a charge of antagonism. He then entered service with the US Army on 31 October 1942. Stroud pleaded not guilty to the crime, but then admitted taking part in the assault and had stopped raping Giovianana when he realised what he was doing. He begged the court for mercy which was not forthcoming. Stroud, whose trial lasted 2 hours 45 minutes, was given the same sentence as White. The third trial was that of Private Armstead White. Born in Paul, Conecuh County, Alabama, on 28 April 1914, his was to be the shortest of all the four trials, lasting just 60 minutes. Although he had pleaded not guilty, he did not take to the witness stand and was quickly sentenced to death. Military justice was now moving swiftly and there was no gap between that of Armstead White and the last man to stand trial, Private Willie A. Pittman. Born in Campbellton, Jackson County, Florida, on 26 August 1918, he had joined the army on 5 September 1942 and was also married. He also pleaded not guilty and, although he took to the witness stand, could not demonstrate any form of justification for his actions. Just 10 minutes before midnight, he was sentenced to death.

The four men were held in confinement at Termini Imerese, Palermo, whilst a Board of Review went over their cases to ensure that the court was legally constituted. General Dwight D. Eisenhower confirmed the sentences on 4 August 1943 but withheld the order directing the execution as the US Army was now faced with a dilemma. There was still no official US Army hangman to carry out the executions. Ultimately, Eisenhower instructed Brigadier General Joseph Vincent DePaul Dillon to act as both presiding officer and executioner. On 30 August 1943, all four soldiers were transported to a location south of Campofelice di Rocella, on the northern coast of Sicily, where they were to be hanged. The location had been chosen by Lieutenant General to ensure that the Sicilian public could not witness the executions. These

Brigadier General Joseph Vincent DePaul Dillon.

took place in the early morning light, in the presence of nine senior US Army officers, five chaplains and Giovanni Morana, who had been forced to watch his wife's brutal rape ordeal. The body of each man was dropped through the trapdoor of the gallows by Brigadier General Joseph Vincent DePaul Dillon, then wrapped in a mattress cover and buried at the US Military Cemetery at Caronia. This, however, would be the beginning of a long road to a final resting place. The men's bodies were removed from Caronia in April 1947 and reinterred in the US Military Cemetery at Monte Soprano, but were scheduled to be moved again, this time to the US Military Cemetery at Nettuno, although this does not appear to have happened. In February 1949, with the US war-dead programme in full swing, their bodies were again removed from the ground and transported to Naples. From here they were shipped to Epinal, France, where they were held in storage. On 4 April 1949, in total secrecy, their bodies were finally laid to rest in Plot 'E' at the Oise-Aisne American Cemetery. Private David White is buried in Row 3, Grave 72, Private Armstead White lays in Row 2, Grave 47, Private Willie A. Pittman rests in Row 3, Grave 50. The body of Private Harvey Stroud was originally buried in Row 1, Grave 2 but was relocated in 1951 to Row 2, Grave 26, the fifth and final time his body was to be buried.

Doubtless, Giovianana Incatasciato Morana lived out her life on the isle of Sicily but would never forget the day that four members of a liberating army came to her home, held her husband and child hostage and defiled her young body. Remember her.

Tuesday, 28 September 1943, England
Victims	Cynthia June Lay, British civilian (white)
	Age: 19
	Murdered
	Muriel Joyce Rosalie Fawden, British civilian (white)
	Age: 22
	Raped
Assailant	Private Lee Andrew Davis (black)
	Age: 21
	Service No.: 18023362
	Unit: 'C' Company, 248th Quartermaster Battalion (Service)

On 28 September 1943, two friends who worked at Savernake Hospital, on the outskirts of Marlborough, Wiltshire, decided to go to an afternoon film showing together, seeing *Once Upon a Honeymoon*, starring Cary

Cynthia June Lay, who was shot dead by Private Lee Andrew Davis.

Grant and Ginger Rogers. Cynthia June Lay, a 19-year-old assistant cook, and her friend, 22-year-old Muriel Fawden, an assistant to the chief accountant, left the cinema at about 7.45 p.m. and walked back up London Hill to the hospital. June, as she preferred to be known, was born in Petersfield, Hampshire, and her life is a little bit of a mystery. What is known is that by the time she was 15 she was a resident at St Mary's Home in Salisbury, Wiltshire, a facility operated by Augustinian nuns. The purpose of the facility was to help marginalised women – mainly single mothers, the homeless and sex-trade workers – by providing them with shelter and teaching them a trade, and it was common practice at the time for pregnant women who were unmarried to disappear from their home area and start a new life through the facility. It is not known why June was a resident there but in 1939 she was training to be a domestic servant. After this she began working at Savernake Hospital.

Muriel Fawden's life also appears to have had a tragic element to it. Her father, Frederick Thomas Fawden, had worked for the Great Western Railway at Bristol before the First World War. On 25 November 1916 he married Rosalie Rebecca Tucker, the daughter of a railway engine driver. He was conscripted into service with the British Army, serving with the Railways Operation Department of the Royal Engineers, and was posted to France in February 1917, remaining there until the Armistice. On his return he resumed work as a booking clerk for the railway, and Rosalie fell pregnant. On 24 May 1921, Muriel was born, but tragically her mother died whilst giving birth. Frederick was distraught, a widow at the age of 29, and needed help with the baby. Rosalie's sister, Lucy Lilian Tucker, stepped into the breach and the couple eventually

The body of June Lay on the ground where she was shot dead by Private Lee Andrew Davis. (*Courtesy of* After the Battle Magazine)

married in 1927. By 1939, Frederick was the station master at Savernake, Wiltshire, and Muriel was working in the nearby hospital.

That fateful evening the two friends were about halfway up the hill on their return journey to the hospital when a black US soldier came up to them and asked, 'How far are you going?' Muriel Fawden replied that they were going to the hospital. The soldier then disappeared, but a few moments later the two women heard a voice shout 'Stand still or I'll shoot.' They both turned around and saw the same soldier, but now he was aiming a rifle at them. June Lay screamed, 'Run, Muriel.' They began to dash quickly up the hill and as they did so, shots rang out. Suddenly, June Lay fell, struck by bullets that had penetrated her head and a lung. Muriel Fawden stopped dead in her tracks, expecting to be hit by a bullet at any moment. A few seconds later, the soldier caught up with her, took hold of her arm and pulled her through a nearby barbed wire fence. He ordered Muriel to crouch down and take off her white mackintosh, saying, 'When we run it will show up.' Muriel removed her gloves and coat, handing them to her attacker, she never understood why she did that, but she did, and he took them from her. They went further up into the nearby forest, up on the hill into the grass, and stayed there a few minutes. Muriel heard a lorry come down the hill and stop and knew June had been found. Her attacker stood over her with the gun and said, 'Either you do what I want you to do, or you die. I am going to count ten.' He began to count to ten and Muriel, terrified, had no option but to give in to him and was viciously raped. Her assailant, now a little calmer, asked her to show him the way to the railway line, which she tried to do but the undergrowth was too thick. They walked back the way they had come towards a light, which was being emitted by torches used by the police in their search for Muriel. Throughout her ordeal Muriel kept talking to her attacker, saying anything she thought might save her life. Eventually, on reaching a small wicket gate, and after having subjected her to a second rape, the soldier slung his rifle over his shoulder and let her go. Muriel fully expected at this point to be shot dead, but it didn't happen and, distraught, she began making her way towards the light, calling for help. Police Constable Albert E. Boyer, stationed at Marlborough, heard the screams coming from the direction of Savernake Forest. He searched and found Muriel, who was hysterical and in a very distressed state. She was taken to Savernake Hospital where Dr Timothy Maurice carried out an examination, confirming she had been the victim of a violet sexual assault.

On the morning of 29 September, First Lieutenant Clarence L. Villemez, commanding Company 'D', 354th Engineer Regiment, was the leader of a group of men combing the area around Barrack 28, at the Iron Gates Military Camp. About 25yd from the barrack, he discovered a carbine rifle 'sticking straight up, barrel down, in the mud', bearing the number 1594722. A clip containing live ammunition was found about 10 to 15yd away between the rifle and the barrack. The company was not armed with carbines, so it was turned over to Detective Sergeant Hill for examination by a gun expert, Robert Churchill, who identified it as the murder weapon after comparing cartridges he fired with one found near to June's body. The weapon and a US olive-drab cap that was found near the scene were identified as belonging to Private J.C. Wheeler, Company 'C', 248th Quartermaster Battalion. He explained that he had loaned the cap to Private Lee Andrew Davis of the same unit, stationed at Iron Gates Camp, Savernake. Wheeler had an alibi, which was confirmed by other members of the company. In the meantime, a pair of bloodstained uniform trousers and a greatcoat, marked D3362, were identified as belonging to Davis. A bloodstained handkerchief, and a pair of pig-skin gloves, marked 'F.A.', were also found with the clothing. Muriel's stepmother later identified this as the mark used by her laundry to identify her belongings. Major Ferris U. Foster, Chemical Warfare Service, interviewed Davis on 30 September 1943, and after having his rights explained to him, the soldier made a full confession to both the murder and the rape.

Davis appeared before a two-day GCM on 6 October 1943 at Tottenham House, Marlborough, Wiltshire. He faced charges of murder and rape and pleaded not guilty on both counts. Unusually, the president of the court at the opening of the trial included in his instructions to the press, 'there must be no reference to colour in your descriptions or any articles of the trial in this court'. Davis, a married man, was born on 8 January 1923 in Temple, Texas, and had enlisted at Fort Huachuca, Arizona, on 25 March 1941 for a period of three years. He left New York City for Europe on 14 August 1943, arriving in Liverpool a week later. He had only been in the UK for five weeks when he committed the crimes he was accused of. Davis maintained that he went to several pubs and consumed beer, wine and whiskey, as well as beer with aspirins, and didn't know what he was doing. Despite the best efforts of the defence, Davis was found guilty of both charges and sentenced to death. Lieutenant General Jacob Loucks Devers, Commanding Officer of the ETO at the time, confirmed the sentence on 13 November 1943.

At 12.55 a.m. on 14 December 1943, Major James C. Cullens, Commanding Officer of the 2912th DTC, led a group of twenty officials and witnesses to the execution chamber. A few minutes later, guards escorted the condemned man into the chamber and as he stared at the noose, he was heard to say, 'Oh, God, I'm going to die'. Thomas Pierrepoint then placed the white hood over his head and adjusted the noose around his neck, whilst his assistant, Alexander Riley, strapped Davis's ankles together. Cullen gave a silent signal to the executioners and Davis dropped to his death. Major Lewis B. Somers, the senior medical officer present, pronounced him dead some 20 minutes later. His body was taken to Brookwood American Military Cemetery in Surrey, where it was buried, marked with a temporary wooden cross, to which was attached one of his ID tags, the other being buried with him. In 1948, his body was removed and transferred to the American Military Cemetery at Cambridge. Then, in 1949, it was dug up for a second time and secretly transported to the Oise-Aisne American Cemetery, where it rests in Plot 'E', Row 3, Grave 61.

Muriel Joyce Rosalie Fawden married on 6 November 1943, and passed away in September 2008 at the age of 87, almost sixty-five years after the murder of her friend. Cynthia June Lay is buried in Marlborough Cemetery, Wiltshire. Remember them.

1943: MURDER, RAPE AND TEN HANGED

Tuesday, 7 December 1943, England

Victim   Harry Claude Hailstone, British civilian (white)
                   Age: 28
                   Murdered

Assailant   Private J.C. Leatherberry (black)
                   Age: 22
                   Service No.: 34472451
                   Unit: Company 'A', 356th Engineer General Service Regiment

In September 1939, at the outbreak of war, the Hailstone family were living in East Hill, Colchester, Essex, an English garrison town. The head of the family was Harry Edward Hailstone, who had served in the British Army for twenty-seven years and had seen action in both the South African Boer War and the First World War. Also living at the address were his wife, Gertrude (née Bantick), and their four children, one of whom was Harry Claude Hailstone. Tragically, air raids were to claim two of their lives. Firstly, on 31 August 1940, Gertrude received a serious head injury when a bomb fell at the rear of their home. After almost a year suffering from the effects of her wounds she eventually passed away on 6 August 1941 at the age of 57. By this time, their second son, Roy William Hailstone, was serving with the Royal Air Force in North Africa. He would be killed on 6 April 1942 at Landing Ground No. 5 near Sidi Barrani, Egypt, during an enemy air raid and is buried in the Halfaya Sollum War Cemetery. Harry Claude was unable to undertake military service as he had a disability. He had a contracted foot, which caused him to limp, and his hands were deformed following an accident, preventing him from stretching

Harry Hailstone, the disabled taxi driver murdered by Private J.C. Leatherberry. (*Source: Essex Police Museum*)

Private J.C. Leatherberry. (*JAG file*)

his fingers and forcing him to give up hairdressing. The family were rehoused in Maidenburgh Street and he took up work with an engineering company. In July 1943 he began taxi driving, and by September that year had taken up lodgings with Sidney and Mary Pearce at their home in nearby Maldon Road.

Late on the evening of 7 December 1943, Harry was hired to take two black US soldiers back to their base at Birch aerodrome, about 8 miles south-west of Colchester. This, however, would be the last fare Harry would ever undertake. A crime was about to take place that would leave behind a twisted web of lies and deceit on the part of both the assailants and their accomplices, which the Essex Constabulary and US Army investigators would have to unfurl and which would lead to more heartache for the Hailstone family. At midday on 8 December, a Vauxhall cab with the registration number CPU 602 was found abandoned in Haynes Green Lane, Layer Marney, about 50yd from the main road between Colchester and Maldon, and just a quarter of a mile from Birch aerodrome. The lights were on and the top was wet, indicating the cab had been outside during the night. There was blood on the rear seat and a piece of heavy rubber, used as a draught screen, had been torn down. The condition of the car suggested that a violent struggle had taken place. A bloodstained mackintosh and a blue jacket were on the rear seat, with their sleeves turned inside out as though they had been dragged off the wearer, and a pair of gloves and an empty wallet were on the floor. In the pocket of the mackintosh the police found a driver's licence and a taxi driver's plate belonging to Harry Claude Hailstone. On the same day, a member of the public found a Canadian officer's raincoat covered with bloodstains by the side of the road near the village of Tolleshunt d'Arcy. This belonged to Captain John J. Webber, who was serving with the Royal Canadian

Army Medical Corps at the 18th General Hospital based in Cherry Tree Camp, Colchester.

The following day, 9 December, after an extensive search, Constable Edgar Snowling found the body of Harry Claude Hailstone, his face smeared with blood and severely bruised. There were thumb marks on his throat, indicating he had been strangled from behind, his thyroid cartilage was fractured, his windpipe was congested and there was haemorrhaging in his eyes. The bruises on his face were consistent with blows from a fist and he had abrasions on his shins and knees, indicating the assailant had pulled him backwards over the driver's seat and his legs had smashed against the lower dashboard as he died, gasping for air. His body had then been dragged under a barbed wire fence and unceremoniously dumped in a field, and it was estimated he had been dead between 36 and 48 hours. Superintendent George Henry Rookwood Totterdell was tasked with investigating the case. He had served with the Royal Naval Air Service during the First World War, and was still mourning the loss of his two sons a year earlier. They had died at sea together aboard HMS *Firedrake*, on 17 December 1942, when the ship was torpedoed and sunk by the German submarine *U-211* whilst escorting convoy ON-153 in the North Atlantic. Totterdell concluded the killer might be an American by the way the vehicle had been discarded on the right side of the road. Additionally, given the weight of the victim's body, it appeared that at least two assailants had been involved. He tracked down Captain Webber and established the raincoat had been stolen by a black US soldier, along with a Rolex wristwatch and £5 in cash. However, the inept crook had left behind a gas-mask case belonging to a member of Company 'E', 356th Engineer General Service Regiment, stationed at Birch aerodrome. The owner, whose name was Private J. Hill, confirmed the case was his and that it was missing after he had loaned it to Private George E. Fowler of the same company. Totterdell believed he had the killer.

On 13 December, George Fowler, a 22-year-old from Peoria, Illinois, was interviewed about the crime. He claimed that on 5 December he had left Birch by bus to travel into Colchester, where he was going to visit the White Horse public house. Also on the bus that night was a soldier that Fowler later identified as Private J.C. Leatherberry. The two men got talking, then started drinking together. They decided to go into London, where they would spend their leave in the time-honoured fashion pursuing women and alcohol. The next 48 hours were passed in a variety of cafes, a seedy joint known as the West India Club and in the company of women with whom they paid to have sex. He claimed that he spent much of the time with two women, Christine Harvey and Constance Jennings, who were lodging in the home of a rather unsavoury character named Francis 'Freddie' Wettner. Leatherberry, on the other hand, spent his time with a lady suggestively named Mistress Jean Von Splang. Fowler claimed they had left London on 8 December and returned to Colchester by train. During the journey, Leatherberry, who was short of cash, suggested getting a taxi back to camp from the railway station and robbing the driver. Fowler thought that his companion was 'just kidding'. This, however, had not turned out to be the case. On arrival at Colchester railway station, Fowler had given Leatherberry a raincoat that he claimed was his because his companion felt cold. This would turn out to be the coat belonging to Captain Webber, which Fowler had stolen along with a Rolex watch. On 14 December Leatherberry was questioned at length by US Army investigator Staff Sergeant Stephen J. Graham and Detective Inspector William Draper of the Essex Constabulary, but was adamant that he had told the truth and said he had nothing more to add to his statement. He appeared in two identification parades on 16 December. In one, Fowler picked him out as the man he had accompanied on the night of the murder, and the owners of the premises where he stated he had stayed the night in London identified him as the man who had been there on 6 December but not on the following night. Both Leatherberry and Fowler were charged with murder and handed over to the US military authorities. They left Colchester police station accompanied by armed US MPs and were driven away.

It would not be until 19 January 1944 that a unique double GCM took place in the town hall at Ipswich, Suffolk. The trial of Leatherberry was presided over by Lieutenant Colonel Zeigler and nine other officers, only two of whom were African American. Fowler was the principal witness for the prosecution and once he had given his evidence, he crossed to the second court where his own trial commenced. He was charged with murder, as well as stealing a raincoat, a watch and £5 from Captain Webber, and pleaded not guilty. His evidence remained the same as he had given at Leatherberry's hearing. At 9.30 p.m. Leatherberry's court martial was adjourned until the 24 January, to allow his counsel to obtain more evidence. He then crossed to the second court to give evidence against Fowler. At first he was unwilling, but eventually stated that he had spent time with Fowler in London but denied being in the taxi at all. The defence made every effort to establish an alibi, but Hailstone's rare blood group was a telling factor, and Leatherberry was obliged to admit that he had changed his account of where in London he was supposed to have stayed on the night of the murder. There were traces of blood under one of Fowler's nails, but there was blood under all of Leatherberry's, none of it sufficient for grouping. Hailstone, unlike the two soldiers, was of the relatively rare AB blood group, and this matched dried blood found on Webber's raincoat and on Leatherberry's clothing. Following the completion of their trials, Fowler was sentenced to life imprisonment with hard labour for his part in the crime, whilst Leatherberry was sentenced to death.

The court sentence was confirmed by General Dwight D. Eisenhower, who was in the process of making the final arrangements for the invasion of Europe. It would be some time before justice would be served, during which time the Commanding Officer of the 2912th DTC at Shepton Mallet, Somerset, Major James C. Cullens, wrote to Eisenhower suggesting that clemency be allowed, given the outcome of the case for Fowler. Eisenhower was unimpressed with the request and at 1.00 a.m. on 16 May 1944, following a silent signal from Cullens, the executioner, Thomas Pierrepoint, opened the trapdoor and Private Leatherberry dropped through, being officially pronounced dead some 18 minutes later. He was buried in Brookwood American Military Cemetery, Surrey, and in 1948 his body was reinterned in the American Military Cemetery at Cambridge. A year later, it was removed and secretly buried in the Oise-Aisne American Cemetery, where it rests in Plot 'E', Row 4, Grave 86.

By 1946, Fowler had been transferred to the penitentiary in Atlanta, Georgia, his sentence reduced to twenty-five years. In 1950 his sentence was further reduced to twenty years and in 1960 he was released.

It is presumed that Harry Claude Hailstone was buried alongside his mother in Colchester cemetery. Remember him.

Friday, 17 December 1943, Italy

Victim	Private David Quick (white/Mexican)
	Age: 35
	Service No.: 32313266
	Unit: Company 'A', 387th Engineer Battalion
	Murdered
Assailant	Private Charles E. Spears (black)
	Age: 33
	Service No.: 32337619
	Unit: Company 'D', 387th Engineer Battalion

The grave of Private David Quick, Long Island National Cemetery, East Farmingdale, Suffolk County, New York.

David Quick was a New Yorker, born in North Carolina on 23 February 1908. He was inducted into the army on 11 April 1942 at Fort Jay, Governors Island, half a mile from the southern tip of Manhattan. By June 1942, he found himself in detention at Fort George Meade, Maryland, along with Private Charles E. Spears, a soldier serving with the same unit. Spears, born in Zanesville, Ohio, on 20 May 1910, one of eight children, had quickly developed a poor military record. Since being inducted into the army on 16 May 1942, he had been convicted of a variety of offences on four separate occasions, including being absent without leave, theft and escaping confinement. He spent many months performing hard labour, but this does not seem to have produced the effect the army were looking for. He was known for getting 'pretty nasty' when he was drinking, was in the habit of carrying a small pistol and he didn't get along with David Quick.

Spears and Quick's battalion arrived at Naples-Bagnoli, Italy, in October 1943, and the two soldiers again found themselves in confinement. This time they shared a pup tent at Oran, Algeria, one of the landing points in Operation Torch and where Spears claimed he had given Quick $5 and wanted repaying. Spears found himself in confinement again in November but broke out and, on that occasion, met up with Quick and went drinking with him. About a week later, he again asked Quick for the money he owed him but was again refused. On this occasion, Quick made a clear threat to Spears to the effect that he would shoot him if he continued to ask for the money. After this incident, their relationship soured significantly, and Spears was on the look-out for the man who had wronged him. On 17 December 1943, David Quick and Charles Spears were drinking at a bar in Naples at about noon. Spears was again absent without leave. An argument soon occurred over money, it seemed that every time they got together it was the same thing, the $5 Quick owed Spears. The two men walked out of the bar, and Quick made his way through the narrow streets to the home of Mattero Francesco and her husband, Rafael Di Orio, to pick up his laundry. As he was sitting in the kitchen talking to Rafael, who spoke a little English, Spears appeared. What followed was like a scene from a Western movie.

Spears, carrying a pistol in his hand that he had purchased a day or two before, said, 'Quick, I hear you have been looking for me and I am looking for you?' After Quick asked why Spears was looking for him, Spears replied, 'I have witnesses that say you have been threatening to shoot me. I think it is about time to come to a showdown.' It was alleged that Quick then said, 'If there is going to be any shooting, let's shoot', and then stuck his hand inside his jacket. Spears was faster on the draw and pulled up his own pistol, firing two shots at close range. The bullets slammed into Quick, one of which did appalling damage, entering his chest above and to the right of his heart, perforating his windpipe and destroying the principal blood vessel. Quick grasped his chest, staggered to his feet and fell down, dead. Rafael called the Military Police, who found a small Italian Beretta pistol in Quick's right-hand pocket. A witness would later testify that the dead soldier had not made any move towards his weapon, and that his arms had been folded across his chest when he was shot. Spears had fled the scene. He stayed at a place he knew as 'Lina's house'. He was apprehended at the address by agents of the Criminal Investigation Division five days later, hiding on the roof.

The case went to a GCM on 27 January 1944 at the Peninsular Base Section (PBS) in Naples. Spears pleaded not guilty to the charge and claimed he had not intended to shoot Quick when he went to the house but had fired his pistol when Quick tried to get his gun. The court did not believe him. They returned a verdict on the same day, finding him guilty of murder and sentenced him to death by hanging. Following approval and review, the sentence was confirmed on 8 March 1944 by Lieutenant General Jacob Loucks Devers, the Commanding General of the NATO. On 19 April 1944, Private Charles E. Spears was hanged at the Peninsular Base Section Stockade Number 1 by an unknown executioner. He was initially buried in the General Prisoner Section of the Naples military cemetery, but his body was secretly reinterred in 1949 at the Oise-Aisne American Cemetery, where it lays in Row 1, Grave 18.

On 30 November 1948, as part of the Return of the Dead Program, Private David Quick was reinterred in Long Island National Cemetery, East Farmingdale, Suffolk County, New York, USA, Section H, Site 8860. Remember him.

Chapter 5

1944: The Heat of Battle

Sunday, 16 January 1944, Italy
Victim   Private Wilbur Lee Bryant (white)
                 Age: 19
                 Service No.: 35660204
                 Unit: 2651st Military Police Company
                 Murdered
Assailant   Private Otis Bell Crews (black)
                 Age: 27
                 Service No.: 14057830
                 Unit: 3423rd Quartermaster Truck Company

During the Second World War, many US families would hang a Gold Star in the window of their home, denoting a family member who had died in service. James Night Bryant and his wife, Jannetta 'Nettie' Caroline Butler, whose home lay in Blue Sulphur Springs, West Virginia, a small community deep in the Appalachian Mountains, would need two Gold

Left to right: Private Wilbur Lee Bryant; Wilbur's grave in the At the End of the Trail Cemetery, Clintonville, Greenbrier County, West Virginia; PFC Miller J. Bryant; James and Nettie Bryant; Brigadier General Francis H. Oxx, Commanding General, Peninsula Base Section in Italy.

Stars. The circumstances would vary dramatically, but two of their sons would lose their lives in the same European theatre of war, Italy. Wilbur Lee Bryant was born on 9 September 1924, one of twelve children. He was inducted into the US Army on 15 May 1943 at Huntington, West Virginia, following in the footsteps of his older brother, Miller, who had joined the army six months earlier. The young Virginian would lose his life in a tragic incident, far from the front lines, which would be an example of the deep prejudices that existed amongst black and white soldiers in the US forces.

On the evening of 6 January 1944, Raffaella del Prete was sitting in front of the fireplace at her wine shop in Via San Donato, in Orto D'Atella, when three black soldiers opened the door, entered and called out '*Signorine, signorine*'. Raffaella replied, 'We have no *signorine* here', and so the soldiers drank three glasses of wine from a bottle on a mantlepiece in the dimly lit room, and then asked for more. She told them that the wine was all finished and began to get nervous when she saw that they didn't want to leave, so she sent for the Military Police. Private Milton K. Ziegler and Private Wilbur Bryant, who were serving with the 2651st Military Police Company, were on patrol nearby. Bryant was carrying a .30 carbine, whilst Ziegler was unarmed. The pair went into the wine shop and exactly what was said next remains unclear, but Ziegler later claimed he had asked the soldiers to pay for their drinks. One of them, a tall, moustached, black soldier, later identified as Private Otis Bell Crews, had his right hand inside his field-jacket pocket, and made a movement as if gripping a pistol when Ziegler moved forward to search the men. Shots rang out and Wilbur Bryant was struck by three bullets, one to the left chest, one to the spleen and kidneys and a third to the buttocks. The three soldiers fled, and Ziegler began to pursue them, after picking up Bryant's weapon, but heard his comrade crying for help and returned to assist him. Sadly, there was not much to be done for the soldier and Bryant died from his injuries 26 hours later. His parents were about receive their first Gold Star.

The MP attempted to investigate the shooting but had no leads and within a few months the case grew cold. Then, on 4 June 1944, the Criminal Investigation Division assigned Agents Victor Dobrin and Bernard Lipinski to investigate the case. They sought witnesses, developed descriptions and then sent the information to every unit containing black soldiers in the Peninsula Base Section and the entire US Fifth Army. Eventually, they produced a list of forty suspects. The pair contacted every unit with black soldiers and asked them to report the name of every soldier who was absent without leave on the day of the incident. They then requested a report on all confiscated .45 pistols over the previous six months. The intrepid officers examined all the information, which had begun to indicate that the three men were in the 3423rd Quartermaster Truck Company. The two agents drove to the unit and, after a discussion with the chain of command, fingerprinted the entire battalion, as the three soldiers in question had left the fingerprints on their glasses at the cafe. It seems a match was made and on 30 July 1944, Private Otis Bell Crews was subsequently arrested for the crime of murder.

On 1 August 1944, some seven months after the incident, the agents interviewed the surviving MP, Private Milton K. Ziegler, and he claimed that whilst on patrol an Italian man had approached him saying that three 'coloured' soldiers were in his wine shop and had refused to pay for their drinks. After they entered the shop he warned Bryant, 'Watch it', and told the black soldiers, 'Put your hands up. You've got to be searched.' Ziegler also claimed that Bryant never spoke during the incident but held his weapon at the ready, as if he expected trouble. In a final statement Ziegler wrote, 'I positively identify this soldier as the tall soldier of the three who fired at Bryant.'

Investigators then questioned Private Richard W. Coleman and Private David Morris, the other two soldiers who were with Crews that night. Coleman claimed he did not know that Private Crews was armed and that both MPs were carrying carbines over shoulders. One of the MPs did all the talking saying. 'These niggers are no good and let's shoot them', although he could not identify which one had made the statement. He added that the two MPs then took their weapons off their shoulders and Private Crews began shooting. Morris, in his statement, claimed that when the MPs came into the shop, one had a 'Tommy gun' and the other had a .45 pistol. He stated that not much was said, except that one of the MPs alleged the three men had not paid for their drinks. Then he added, that as one of the MPs stepped toward Private Crews, he gave him a little push and started firing, stating, 'I saw Crews do the shooting.' Crews claimed he had shot the MP but had fired in self-defence after he heard Bryant state, 'Let's don't argue with them. Let's kill them.' Crews also stated that Private Bryant had said, 'You got no business in these people's house; you don't go in white people's houses in the States.'

Brigadier General Francis H. Oxx, Commanding General, Peninsula Base Section in Italy, ordered a GCM, which met at Naples on 26 September 1944. Private Otis Bell Crews pleaded not guilty to the charge of murder, a violation of the 92nd Article of War. The court, having scrutinised all the evidence, found him guilty and sentenced him to death by hanging. Brigadier General Oxx approved the sentence and Lieutenant General Joseph T. McNarney signed the confirming order on 18 January 1945. On the morning of 21 February 1945, eight commissioned officers assembled at Aversa, Italy, to witness the execution of Private Otis Bell Crews. Chaplain William T. Watts provided the religious presence and at precisely 8.00 a.m. the trapdoor was opened by an unknown executioner, and Crews plummeted to his death. Captain Samuel Penchansky, a medical officer, pronounced him dead 9 minutes later. His body was initially buried in the US Military Cemetery in Naples. Sadly, on 17 September 1944, whilst the investigations were underway and Wilbur's killer was held in a stockade, his brother, PFC Miller J. Bryant, was killed in action serving with 363rd Infantry Regiment, 91st Division, as it faced stubborn resistance attacking the German Gothic Line, whilst advancing to the Santerno River.

During the Return of the Dead Program the body of Private Otis Bell Crews was removed from Naples and secretly transported to Plot 'E' of the Oise-Aisne American Cemetery, where it rests in Row 2, Grave 30. The bodies of Private Wilbur Lee Bryant and PFC Miller J. Bryant were returned to their loved ones and both are buried in the At the End of the Trail Cemetery, Clintonville, Greenbrier County, West Virginia. Remember them.

Thursday, 20 January 1944, Italy
Victim   Corporal John P. Brown Jr (white)
               Age: 28
               Service No.: 33468375
               Unit: 57th Military Police Company
               Murdered
Assailant   Private Robert L. Donnelly (white)
               Age: 19
               Service No.: 13131982
               Unit: Battery 'B', 36th Field Artillery

It is estimated, by some, that the US Army suffered 50,000 deserters during the Second World War. This is exactly what Private Robert L. Donnelly, a 19-year-old white soldier from Pittsburgh, Pennsylvania, planned to do when he abandoned his unit on 16 December 1943 at Venafro, Italy. A former labourer, he had been wounded in action on 25 September, although his injuries were light. On 10 October he

The grave of Corporal John P. Brown Jr in the Sicily-Rome American Cemetery, Italy.

was admitted to hospital suffering with jaundice, and perhaps had time to hatch a plan. After making his way to Naples, he spent the next four weeks drinking in different bars by day and living in different hotels by night. This, however, ended abruptly on 20 January 1944, when he was apprehended in the city by two MPs, Sergeant Frank J. Barresi and Corporal John P. Brown Jr of the 57th Military Police Company. Barresi was sergeant of the 'vice squad' and on that night he and Brown were working on the 'black market' in Naples. As they drove down Piazza Dante in their command car, Barresi saw Donnelly standing with five civilians just off the sidewalk. The teenager, armed with a German Luger pistol, and his group of Italian friends, were intending to rob a civilian store. When he was asked what he was doing there, Donnelly said he was waiting for a friend to take him to a hotel. Brown questioned the five Italians, who gave the same response. Donnelly refused to give his name and unit to Barresi, who drew his pistol and immediately arrested the youngster and the group as 'suspicious characters'. It was at this point that a grave error was made. The two MPs packed Donnelly and the five civilians into their command car without searching them. As they started to drive down the narrow street, Brown hollered, 'Look out, Barresi, he's got a gun!' At that moment, Barresi looked over his shoulder and saw a flash go past him. A struggle now ensued, and Donnelly hopped over the front seat and out of the door. Barresi took a shot at him and saw where he went. He took up the chase and fired at the deserter as he made his escape down an alley and then down some steps, but lost track of the gunman. Barresi made his way back to the car and

Private Robert L. Donnelly, the teenager murdered Military Policeman Corporal John P. Brown Jnr.

looked around for Brown, finding him about 20ft from the front of the command car. He looked him over for wounds, but didn't see any, so asked some *carabinieri* who were standing nearby to help take the MP into the station. Barresi arrested the five civilians, and a doctor was called, but it was too late, Corporal John P. Brown was dead. Donnelly remained at large for a further seven days until he was apprehended on 27 January 1944, at which point he made a voluntary statement admitting to the crime.

A GCM began in Naples on 14 March 1944. Although Donnelly pleaded not guilty, it didn't take the court very long to determine his guilt, given that he had made a voluntary statement admitting to the crime when he was apprehended. He refused to take the stand and the defence counsel presented no witnesses. He was found guilty of desertion and murder, and sentenced to death. Brigadier General Arthur W. Pence approved the verdict and sentence. Lieutenant General Jacob Loucks Devers confirmed the sentence on 30 April, and four weeks later, on 31 May 1944, Captain William G. Wood supervised the execution in the company of ten commissioned officers, who were present as official witnesses. At 5.20 a.m. the trapdoor was sprung by an unknown executioner and Private Robert L. Donnelly plunged downwards. It would be a full 14 minutes before the medical officer, Captain William W. Huntress, would pronounce him dead. After being taken down, his body was buried in the US Military Cemetery in Naples. In 1949, it was secretly transported to Plot 'E' at the Oise-Aisne American Cemetery, where it rests in Row 4, Grave 95.

Corporal John P. Brown Jr is buried in Plot D, Row 14, Grave 35 at the Sicily-Rome American Cemetery, Italy. Sadly, on 10 October 1944, Sergeant Frank J. Barresi was killed in Italy, as the result of an automobile accident. Under the Return of the Dead Program, his body was sent home to his loved ones and is buried in the Calvary Cemetery, Cleveland, Ohio. Remember them.

Sunday, 5 March 1944, England
Victim   Dorothy Holmes, British civilian (white)
                Age: 16
                Raped
Assailants   Private Eliga Brinson (black)
                Age: 25
                Service No.: 34052175
                Private Willie Smith (black)
                Age: 22
                Service No.: 34565556
                Unit: 4090th Quartermaster Service Company

Not unsurprisingly, teenage women in wartime Britain were often attracted to the impetuous and sometimes extravagant US servicemen based in the United Kingdom. Elaborate uniforms, higher pay, the seemingly unending supply of goods from the 'PX' and fanciful ideas generated by Hollywood movies drew girls to them like a moth to a flame in dreary wartime Britain. Amongst these was a 16-year-old English girl, Dorothy Eileen Holmes, whose home was in the Gloucestershire village of Bishops Cleeve. Born on 31 August 1927, she was the youngest daughter of Fred and Harriet Martha Holmes, one of nine children. Her father had joined the Gloucestershire Regiment in 1915, but was transferred to the Royal Warwickshire Regiment, serving with a Garrison Battalion in both the Sudan and Egypt. Perhaps he, understandably, would have been well aware of how soldiers behaved when they were overseas in wartime.

There was excitement in the air on the night of 4 March 1944, when Doris, as she was known, prepared to go to a dance in Bishops Cleeve with a young US soldier she had been 'going with' for about five months, PFC Edward 'Eddie' J. Heffernan. After the dance was over, at around 12.25 a.m., they were walking past the King's Head pub in the village and Doris noticed two black soldiers who were standing in the doorway and who began to follow the couple. They passed the Old Elm Tree pub and walked along Peckett's Piece Lane, then stopped for a while at the end of Brookside Lane, where she heard footsteps, which she later said sounded like someone wearing hobnailed boots. Whilst they were talking, two black soldiers approached them, but they passed by. A few minutes later the two solders returned. One of them asked Hefferman what he was doing, and then struck him on the nose with what was believed to be a glass mineral water bottle. The second soldier attempted to strike Hefferman again but, it seems, he got up and ran off to seek help. Dorothy was dragged and then carried, by the two soldiers into a nearby field, where her mouth was covered to stifle her screams. She was held down by her shoulders, her underwear torn off and her legs forced apart, each man taking a turn at viciously raping her. When the ordeal was over, the two soldiers ran off across the field, and Doris ran home in a distressed state, calling for her mother. She was nervous and hysterical, her clothing was 'dirty and messed up terribly' and the lower part of her body was covered with mud. Her cheeks were swollen, her lips were bruised and she complained her throat hurt.

By now, Heffernan had attempted to get help from a nearby house, where a man told him to go to the police station. After getting lost, he eventually saw a policeman but claimed he did not get any help. Heffernan then went to Doris's home where he found her crying in the street. Some 20 minutes later, now accompanied by Police Constable William G. Hale, stationed at Bishops Cleeve, and Sergeant James O. Hall, of the 255th US Military Police Company, Heffernan returned to the scene of the rape. Here, two specifically distinct types of footprints were found in the snow. One appeared to have a hobnail pattern with studs in the heels, the other had a rubber military style patten on the heel. Blood was spotted on the gate into the field and a bobby pin, a type of hairgrip, was also said to have been found. This appears to be significant detective work, given it was about 1.00 a.m., in darkness and with snow on the ground. Hall took soil samples, covered the footprints with cardboard and then the two policemen went to the nearby camp of 4090th Quartermaster Service Company, an African American unit, to investigate the attack further.

At 3.26 a.m., they awoke the Commanding Officer of the unit, and then set about searching the tents for shoes with comparable patterns on the sole and heel. Hall stated that in Tent 21 he found a pair of shoes with a similar irregular form, as it seems the studs had been driven in by hand. He marked these and took possession of them. At 5.23 a.m. as the soldiers began to get dressed, with Private Willie Smith unable to find his shoes. Hall informed him that he was an MP, asked him for his clothing, then took him to the orderly room where he was made aware of his rights. He was not informed as to the exact nature of the charge but was told that a serious crime was being investigated. Shortly after 9.00 a.m. that morning, Detective Constable Ernest Wilfrid Slade, stationed at Cheltenham, went to the junction of Peckett's Piece Lane and Brookside Lane, where he took casts of the footprints found by Hall, who was by now again present at the scene. Slade later testified that by the time he took the casts, 'the snow was melting, the sun shining brightly, and the ground muddy'. He was unable to state when the prints were made and felt that they could have been several days old. Although Police Inspector Charles E. Walkeley took photographs of the footprints, which he handed to Sergeant Hall, the US military did not take pictures of the scene until 10 March, some five days after the event.

It would not be until midday that Sergeant Hall spoke to Private Eliga Brinson, who was also made aware of his rights by Staff Sergeant Bowen. First Lieutenant Jerome Frank Kapp, 817th Ordnance Base Depot, was appointed as the investigating officer. Kapp spent only 45 minutes with either Smith or Brinson and did no more than read out the reports provided by the MP. There is no evidence to demonstrate that Kapp actually conducted an investigation. Yet, on 28 April 1944, the GCM of both Brinson and Smith took place at Cheltenham, Gloucestershire, with Captain D.J. Harman presiding as the Trial Judge Advocate, and Captain J.G. Roye acting as defence counsellor. Neither Doris Holmes nor Eddie Heffernan, who both gave evidence at the trial, could positively identify Brinson or Smith as their attackers. The outcome of detailed forensic tests carried out by Dr Edward Burdon Parks, Director of the Bristol Forensic Laboratory, sealed the fate of the two soldiers. Parks stated that various articles of clothing from both Doris Holmes and the two accused were stained with human blood, semen and soil similar in character to that found at the place where the attack was perpetrated. With regard to the shoe prints, he stated that, 'it is nearing the realm of sheer impossibility for another heel to make the cast other than those of Smith', and that it was 'a very, very unlikely possibility' that the second set of prints were made by shoes other than those belonging to Brinson. Several soldiers from their unit were called as witnesses, testifying that the two men were out drinking that night, but no one had seen them with Doris, nor saw them return to their quarters. Surprisingly, Mabel Morehen, a 53-year-old midwife, who had known Doris since birth, gave evidence that she had found scratches on her legs and a bruised and swollen lip but, in her opinion, Doris showed no signs of having been sexually assaulted. After examining the girl's private parts, her comment that, 'There was nothing abnormal to my mind' appears not to have been fully considered. The two soldiers were both found guilty of their alleged crimes and, following a 2-hour closed session, Captain Harman pronounced that a secret ballot had found them guilty of the crime and, unanimously, sentenced them to death.

There is no doubt that Dorothy Holmes was attacked and brutally assaulted by two black soldiers, but neither she nor Heffernan could positively identify Smith and Brinson as the assailants. The evidence against them, although strong, was purely circumstantial and there were clear errors in the process of investigation. Yet, the court, seemingly ordered their execution without hesitation. This is in direct contrast to the trials of other white US soldiers who, at the same time, had been found guilty of rape, with far stronger evidence, yet were only ever imprisoned for their vile crimes. Evidence of this is found in the very next case of the Opinions of the Board of Review. Miss Priscilla Lock of Thorndon, Norfolk, worked as a canteen assistant in the American Red Cross club at Thorpe Abbotts, the base for 100th Bombardment Group (H). On 3 May 1944, a detachment from 1285th Military Police Company (Aviation), 95th Bombardment Group (H), stationed at Horham, Suffolk, was resident at Thorpe Abbotts. Amongst the men of the detachment was Private Theodore White. On that night, White, who was later positively identified by Miss Lock as her attacker, forced her off her bicycle as she was cycling home, attempted to subject her to oral sex and, following her refusal, raped her, twice. Private Theodore White was found guilty of the crime and sentenced to ten years' imprisonment, something, it seems, the Board of Review thought was appropriate for the offence. Colonel Charles Matthew Van Benschoten sat on both these boards and, it could be argued, the variation in sentencing is surprisingly disproportionate, given the offences occurred just a few weeks apart.

On the 9 June 1944, with the invasion of Europe firmly at the front of his mind, General Dwight D. Eisenhower confirmed the sentences. Despite the cordial interventions of US Senator Claude Pepper to review the sentence, the judicial process rolled on and on 4 August 1944 Brigadier General Edwin Colyer McNeil set the execution date. Just before 1.00 a.m. on 11 August 1944, the small execution chamber at Shepton Mallet Prison was occupied by Major James C. Cullens, Commanding Officer of the 2912th DTC, along with a group of seventeen officials and witnesses. In what would be a simultaneous hanging, Private Willie Smith and Private Eliga Brinson were marched into the chamber between two guards. Thomas Pierrepoint placed a hood over their heads, whilst his assistant strapped their legs together. Following a silent signal from Cullens, both men dropped through the trapdoor and were pronounced dead a short time later. Their bodies were transported to Brookwood American Military Cemetery, Surrey, for burial. In 1948, they were both removed from this location and transferred to the American Military Cemetery in Cambridge. Then, a year later, in secrecy, they were dug up for a second time and transported to Plot 'E' at the Oise-Aisne American Cemetery, France, where Brinson lays in Row 4, Grave 93 and Smith in Row 3, Grave 69.

Doris Holmes married in 1956, and would mother four children, sadly passing away in 1979 at the age of 52. Undoubtedly, the events of that night never left her thoughts. Remember her.

Sunday, 5 March 1944, England

Victim   First Sergeant Thomas Evison (white)
                  Age: 43
                  Service No.: 6806955
                  Murdered
Assailant   Private Alex Flores Miranda (white)
                  Age: 20
                  Service No.: 39297382
                  Unit: Battery 'C', 42nd Field Artillery Battalion,
                        4th Infantry Division

On the same night that 16-year-old Dorothy Holmes was attacked and raped in Gloucestershire, First Sergeant Thomas Evison would be murdered as he slept in his bunk at Broomhill Camp, Honiton, Devonshire, and 20-year-old Alex Flores Miranda from Santa Ana, California, would be destined to become the first US serviceman to suffer death by firing squad in the ETO.

Thomas Evison was a professional soldier and an Englishman. He was born on 29 May 1901 at Hindley Green, near Wigan, Lancashire. By the time he was 10 years old, he and his brother, Robert, were living with their grandparents, Thomas and Meryl Ann Evison. After leaving

First Sergeant Thomas Evison, an Englishman in the US Army who was murdered by Private Alex Flores Miranda.

school, he started working as a coal miner with the Wigan Coal & Iron Company, a tough life underground. However, a new life beckoned and in August 1922, he, along with his mother, brother and two sisters, boarded the White Star liner *SS Cedric* at the port of Liverpool destined for the United States. After arriving in New York, the family went to live with a relative, Blanche Atkinson, in Garrett, Pennsylvania. Intent on obtaining permanent US citizenship, Thomas enlisted in the US Army in Harrisburg, Pennsylvania, on 6 July 1928. Now a regular GI, he served with Battery 'D', 6th Field Artillery at Fort Hoyle, Maryland. Thomas became a naturalised citizen on 10 May 1940, the day the German Army invaded Belgium and France, and by then had married a divorcee, Sallie Simmons. The couple had two children, Terrence and Evelyn. Although his career as a soldier had ended before the outbreak of war, the Japanese attack at Pearl Harbor on 7 December 1941 changed all that, and Thomas re-joined the US Army. Now it was only a question of time before he would be engaged in combat. As the Allies prepared for the invasion of Europe, the US Army was busy shipping more troops into the United Kingdom as part of Operation Bolero, and First Sergeant Thomas Evison would once again set foot on English soil on 4 February 1944, but he would never leave the country alive.

Just four weeks later, on the evening of 4 March 1944, 20-year-old Private Alex Miranda, who was serving with the same unit, went into Honiton on a drinking spree. Just after midnight, two policemen, Sergeant William Durbin and Police Constable North, found him urinating in the doorway of a shop in the High Street. His speech was thick, his breath smelled of alcohol and, after they told him that his behaviour was unacceptable, he became nasty and abusive. Amongst other things, he described Durbin as a 'fine, fat sergeant', which did not go down too well with the policemen. As a result, they arrested Miranda and took him to the local police station. When a group of policemen left the station to assist some sergeants who had been involved in an accident, Miranda was heard to remark, 'I hope they rip their guts out.' He then told Durbin, 'I was not pissing in the street, you are lying and I will rip your guts out' and it appeared he had a marked dislike of sergeants in general and that this may have been the catalyst for what subsequently occurred. Two MPs, T/5 James W. Wesley and Corporal Joel R. Wehking, were sent to collect the drunken soldier and after being driven back to camp, he was placed in the guardhouse.

At about 12.30 a.m., Miranda was released back to his hut, which he entered in a noisy, boisterous manner, cursing in the direction of First Sergeant Thomas Evison, who was asleep. Staff Sergeant James

A. Merklein told Miranda not to worry about the incident and go to bed, but he kept muttering about what had happened in the town. Miranda then went up to Evison's bunk and grabbed hold of him, shook him until he woke up, then told him to stop snoring and making so much noise. Evison simply told the soldier to go back to his bunk, and went back to sleep, but continued to snore. Miranda, now enraged, and concerned what action Evison, a strict disciplinarian, might take against him, picked up a carbine from a rack at the back of the hut, pressed it against the sergeant's forehead and pulled the trigger. A bullet entered Evison's forehead, passed through his brain and exited from the back of his head. It then passed through a wooden part of the bed and a carton of cigarettes, before becoming buried in the wall. Brain matter was exuded from the hole in his forehead and spinal fluid was leaking out of the exit wound. Sergeant Thomas Evison died within minutes of being shot. Private Alex Miranda, now giggling hysterically, cried, 'Your worries are over now, boys, I have shot the First Sergeant and I will turn on the lights so I can show you.' He turned on the lights and was seen standing about 2ft feet from Evison's bunk. Another soldier took the gun from Miranda and handed it over to Staff Sergeant Merklein. He was now under arrest for something infinitely more serious than urinating in a shop doorway.

On 20 March 1944, Miranda appeared before a GCM in Exeter, Devon, charged with the murder of Sergeant Thomas Evison. Born on 28 July 1923 in El Monte, California, Alex Flores Miranda had enlisted on 15 May 1943 at Los Angeles, California. He refused to give evidence or to be cross-examined. The only defence his counsellor could provide was based entirely upon the contention that he was so drunk that he did not know what he was doing. However, many witnesses formed the opinion that he was not incoherent because of alcohol, in fact, he appears to have had rational conversations, and all the indications were that he was in full control of himself. This was simply a cold-blooded and deliberate murder. The court wasted very little time on the case, and he was found guilty by secret ballot and sentenced to death by shooting, and not hanged, which was the preferred method used by the US military as it was considered a more ignominious death than shooting. It has been suggested that the court may have been racially prejudiced against Miranda because he was Hispanic, and that it was this which brought a verdict of murder rather than manslaughter, for which he would be imprisoned rather than executed. In deciding what penalty Miranda should face after his conviction, a member of the court, Lieutenant Colonel White E. Gibson, apparently made derogatory comments about Hispanics, saying that they 'are undemonstrative and uncommunicative, as well as being inclined to violence when drinking'. Perhaps not the best way to demonstrate judicial impartiality.

At 1.00 a.m. on 30 May 1944, Miranda was strapped to a wooden post in the yard of Shepton Mallet Prison. A large number of officials, witnesses and a firing squad were present. The order to 'Fire' was given, and a number of bullets slammed into his chest, death being almost instantaneous. His body was removed and taken to Brookwood American Military Cemetery, Surrey, for burial. In 1948, as with all those who were buried at Brookwood from Shepton Mallet, his body was removed and reburied in the American Military Cemetery at Cambridge. Then in 1949, he was secretly removed from this location and transported to Plot 'E' at the Oise-Aisne American Cemetery, France, where he was buried for a third time in Row 2, Grave 27. But this was not the end of the story. In 1988, Louis Martinez Jr, a 47-year-old cement worker from Santa Ana, California, said he 'was always bothered' by his family's story of how his uncle had died. On behalf of other family members, Martinez decided to find out what really happened. After sending for a copy of the court-martial transcript he became convinced that his uncle had been too intoxicated at the time of the shooting to realise the consequences of his action and thus should not have been executed. Louis filed a formal request that his uncle's murder conviction be reversed and that he be found guilty of the lesser charge of manslaughter. He also requested that his uncle's remains be exhumed and returned to his family. On 15 November 1990, Miranda's remains were exhumed from Plot 'E' and are now buried in Santa Ana Cemetery, Placentia, California. His conviction was not overturned.

The body of First Sergeant Thomas Evison rests in the American Military Cemetery, Cambridge, England, where it can be found in Plot C, Row 5, Grave 52. Sallie Evison never remarried. She remained a Gold Star wife for the rest of her life, raised her children in the best way she could and would live to see the arrival of grandchildren and great-grandchildren, passing away on 21 November 2006 at the age of 95, still with Thomas in her heart and mind. Remember him.

Monday, 6 March 1944, Northern Ireland
Victim   Harry Coogan, Irish civilian (white)
               Murdered
Assailant   Private Willey Harris (black)
               Age: 25
               Service No.: 6924547
               Unit: 626th Ordnance Ammunition Company

The first US troops to arrive on the shores of Northern Ireland disembarked at Belfast docks on 26 January 1942. The presence of so many Americans changed this small corner of Ireland forever, but along with the elation that accompanied the advent of Allied support the local population would also experience heartache and homicide. The following story is a disturbing one. The victim was a white Irishman who, it was claimed, was a pimp, using local girls, often by force, to provide sexual comfort to whoever was prepared to pay for it in a part of the city known as Sailortown, a well-established red-light district much visited by soldiers and sailors.

The killer, Private Wiley Harris Jr, was a black soldier born in Greenville, Meriwether County, Georgia, on 12 June 1918. In his early years he suffered with a severe stutter and, after he abandoned school, he became a labourer. His life was tumultuous and although he had married and fathered a daughter, he found nothing positive in life. On 21 May 1937, Harris entered service with the army in Fort Benning, Georgia. He was serving with the 626th Ordnance Ammunition Company which, by March 1944, was based at Dromantine House, Poyntzpass, Co. Down. Its key role was to manage ammunition supply points and prepare for its part in the D-Day invasion. Far from being behind the scenes or away from battle, these companies, usually manned by African Americans, were often in the thick of the action during 1944 and 1945. Their men were highly trained, combat ready and more than capable of reacting swiftly and violently if required.

On the evening of 6 March 1944, Harris and his friend, Private Robert Fils, were on a 24-hour pass. After taking the train into the city, they made their way to the American Red Cross Club, situated on James Street, which was specifically for black service personnel. After drinking in several public houses, they found themselves in the Diamond Bar in North Queen Street, a working-class enclave close to the docks, known for its rough and ready nature and at the heart of the red-light district. It was here that Harris started a conversation with Eileen Megaw, a local girl who had been drinking in the bar all afternoon. He started speaking to her but, as he did so, a man approached him and said, 'Do you want a woman?' When Harris confirmed he did, the man pointed at Eileen Megaw and said, 'There she is.' By now, it was about 10.00 p.m., and Eileen said she was 'available' for the sum of £1, which Harris agreed to, paying with a variety of coins. The man, later identified as Harry Coogan, then escorted the pair to an air-raid shelter in nearby Earl Street, which ran between North Queen Street and Garmoyle Street, an area that had been badly bombed in the Blitz of 1941, leaving many buildings in ruins. Harris and Eileen went inside the shelter, where he took off his greatcoat and laid it on the floor for her, and Eileen raised her dress. Coogan stood by the shelter doors claiming that he would keep a look out for the police. Harris had no reason to suspect Coogan or Megaw because it seems his colleague, Sergeant John W. London, had been in the air-raid shelter with her only half an hour earlier.

However, after just a minute or two, before anything had occurred between the couple, Coogan shouted that the police were coming. Eileen jumped up and dashed outside, with Harris following. The soldier began to shine his flashlight up and down the darkened street but could not see anyone about. He asked Eileen to go back into the shelter with him, but she refused and so, not unsurprisingly, Harris asked for his money back but was again refused. At this point, Coogan said, 'She can't give you the money back.' Eileen then started to run, and Harris became acutely aware he was the victim of an age-old trick, he was being ripped off. As Eileen fled the scene, she dropped some of the money, which Harris stopped to pick up. Annie Murdock, who lived in Earl Street, was one of a number of witnesses to what occurred next. She had been at home listening to her wireless when her sister-in-law, Bridget Murdoch, called out and told her to come outside to 'see the carry on'. She heard two men arguing over money in Earl Street and Coogan shouted to the gathering onlookers, 'This nigger is going to stab this woman, but I'll not let him!' He then took a swing at Harris, catching him under his right eye. Bridget grabbed Coogan's arm at this point and tried to restrain him, telling him not to hit the soldier. Harris, a highly trained soldier, now had adrenalin pumping through his veins and, knowing exactly what was happening, pulled out what was later described as a 'Boy Scout-type' knife and, in retaliation, jumped on Coogan and stabbed him in the stomach, chest and head. As more witnesses began to appear at the scene, Harris then fled on foot, pursued by another witness, James Tynan. Harris managed to evade Tynan and, after taking a tram and a horse cart, made his way back to the American Red Cross Club, where he began to wash the blood from his uniform, something that his friend Private Robert Fils witnessed. At about the same time Head Constable James Armstrong and Sergeant William Herron of the Royal Ulster Constabulary attended the scene. There was nothing they could do for Coogan by the time they arrived. He was placed in an ambulance and taken to the Mater Hospital, Belfast, where Dr James Crilly performed a lengthy examination of his body. He determined there were a total of seventeen stab wounds, made by a sharp blade at least 4in long. The injuries ranged from superficial cuts to deep wounds. The knife had been wielded with such force it had entered Coogan's skull, pierced his diaphragm and caused some of his organs to protrude.

The police soon determined that a black US soldier was responsible for this crime and quickly established who was on a pass that night. The following morning, members of the MP arrested Wiley Harris at his camp. He was taken to Belfast Prison, where he was interviewed and, allegedly, confessed to the crime. On 17 March 1944, Harris appeared before a GCM at Belfast's Victoria Barracks, which backed onto Lepper Street, where Coogan had lived, and he was charged with murder. He pleaded not guilty to the charges against him but remained silent throughout the hearing. Captain Earl R. Garner, Commanding Officer of the 626th Ordnance Ammunition Company, gave evidence that Harris performed his duties efficiently, had received no company punishment nor had he been court-martialled, and was effectively a good soldier. The defence argued that Harris had initially been questioned, without legal representation, by Sergeant James O'Connor of the United States Army Criminal Investigation Division, where he allegedly admitted everything. Four eyewitnesses, Bridget Murdock, Annie Murdock, Kathleen McGinness and Kathleen Dickey, testified that they did not hear Harris use threatening language towards Eileen Megaw prior to the fight with Coogan, something that Megaw herself confirmed. None of them were able to identify Harris as the soldier involved in the fight. It was quickly becoming apparent that this was nothing more than robbery on the part of Coogan and Megaw, and that Harris had reacted violently in an attempt to recover his money. The only real question raised was, at what point did Harris produce a knife? Was it at the time the money was dropped and was Coogan, therefore, attempting to defend Megaw, or was it when he was punched by Coogan, which might mean it was a case of self-defence? A manslaughter charge would see the private jailed for between eight and fifteen years in a US state penitentiary, but it is clear from all the case papers that are available that an example was being sought. At least three civilians in Northern Ireland had perished at the hands of US servicemen by this time, all the assailants being white and all been imprisoned for their actions. After the hearing, the court, made up of seven US Army officers, sentenced Private Harris to be hanged by the neck until dead. The records do not show, however, that the vote was unanimous. Interestingly, the Northern Ireland Coroner, Dr H.P. Lowe, said at a public inquiry that, in his opinion, the whole thing was done in a moment of passion and his impression was that Harris had no premeditation in the crime and no malice. He felt sorry for deceased's relatives and for the predicament the soldier had put himself in through the unfortunate incident.

Dramatic eleventh-hour efforts were made to save the life of Private Wiley Harris. Brigadier General Leroy P. Collins, Commanding General of the Northern Ireland base section, who had confirmed the sentence, received numerous telegrams pleading for the commutation of the sentence to one of imprisonment. Leaders of the local Catholic, Presbyterian and Methodist churches made a joint appeal the night before Harris was due to be hanged, asking for a stay of execution, but it was all to no avail. At 12.53 a.m. on 26 May 1944, as the Allies made their final preparations for the invasion of Europe, Major James C. Cullens, Commanding Officer of the 2912th DTC, led a group of officials and witnesses into the execution chamber at Shepton Mallet Prison. Two guards, Corporal Andre Creed and Corporal George W. Pressey, escorted Private Harris into the chamber a minute later. After reading out the court verdict and ensuring Harris had no last statement to make, Thomas Pierrepoint quickly placed the white hood over the soldier's head and adjusted the rope around his neck. The executioner's assistant, Alexander Riley, strapped Harris's ankles together. Major Cullens gave a silent signal, and Private Wiley Harris Jr dropped to his death and was pronounced dead 15 minutes later. His body was handed over to First Lieutenant Lynford Chase, the Graves Registration Officer. Harris was initially buried in Brookwood American Military Cemetery, Surrey, where one of his identification tags was fixed to a small provisional wooden cross whilst the second one was buried with his body. In 1948, the army transferred Harris' remains to the American Military Cemetery at Cambridge. A year later they were secretly removed and reinterred in the Oise-Aisne American Cemetery, Plot 'E', Row 4, Grave 92.

A month after Harris was executed Major Theo F. Cangelosi requested that the Office of the JAG in Washington provide a certificate showing what the actual vote was in the Wiley Harris case. No such evidence appears to have been provided. A Portland stone memorial, sculpted with the crests of the US military forces, stands in the grounds of the Belfast City Hall, erected in 1943, in recognition of the first anniversary of the arrival of US service personnel who served in Northern Ireland. A further reminder can be found in the city's war memorial building, a part of which was renamed the Hall of Friendship in honour of the close bonds struck between locals and the US soldiers who passed through the province during the conflict. There are no memorials to the women who bore the heartache of the huge increase in illegitimate births, arrests for prostitution and cases of venereal disease that occurred in a tight-knit and highly conservative society.

Spare a thought for those who pass unnoticed.

Saturday, 15 April 1944, Italy
Victim   Private John Henry Brockman (white)
                   Age: 22
                   Service No.: 32452761
                   Unit: 112th Military Police Prisoner of War Detachment
                   Murdered
Assailant   Private Ray Watson (black)
                   Age: 24
                   Service No.: 33139251
                   Unit: Company 'B', 386th Engineer Battalion

On 15 April 1944, PFC Philip Tobeas and Private John Henry Brockman, serving with the 112th Military Police (Prisoner of War) Detachment, were on foot patrol in Secondigliano, a suburb of Naples. Brockman, who hailed from New Jersey, was born on 23 September 1921, the son of John and Julia Brockman, one of eight children. He had worked at the Picitinny Arsenal in New Jersey, an armaments development facility that employed over 18,000 people, producing bombs and artillery shells, and joined the US Army in Newark on 28 July 1942. At the same time, members of the 386th Engineer Battalion were drinking in a nearby bar, amongst whom was Private Ray Watson, who was serving with Company 'B' and who had been drinking Strega, an Italian herbal liqueur. Watson, born on 9 August 1921 in New Jersey, was living in Allegheny County, Pennsylvania, when he enlisted in the US Army on 7 February 1942. As he became more intoxicated with the liquor, one of his comrades realised Watson was armed with a revolver and was beginning to make threats about shooting someone, so he left the bar to report the matter to the MP.

On being told about what was going on, Brockman and Tobeas entered the bar, where Watson was pointed out to them. Brockman was carrying a 12-gauge pump riot shotgun and Tobeas was armed with a Thompson .45 submachine gun. They were then joined by Private James Stewart and Private James Nichols, who were both carrying sawn-off shotguns. Before there was a chance for the MPs to converse with Watson, pandemonium ensued. He produced a revolver and began firing at the policemen, who were just feet away. He then backed out of a door, followed by the MPs, whom he continued to face as he left the room. Once all of them were on the pavement, Watson began to fire rapidly with the revolver. Tobeas was hit first, a bullet breaking his left leg and knocking him to the ground. Then, Brockman was struck, the bullet entering the left side of his chest, passing through the left lung, ripping into the aorta and penetrating the fourth thoracic vertebra.

Watson, still firing his weapon, was now in a shoot-out with Privates Stewart and Nichols. He began to make an escape down the street, and the two MPs pursued him firing their shotguns, striking him in the right hand and leg. A British airman, Leading Aircraftsman Ivan Hope, witnessed the incident from a nearby balcony and watched as Watson stopped a weapons carrier of the 316th Service Group being driven by Private Stephen Fredcricks with Corporal Ray Griffith as a passenger. Watson shouted, 'Hold it, Joe' and jumped on the right-hand fender, with the pistol still in his hand, then said, 'Drive away and drive away fast', instructing Fredericks to 'drive as he directed'. After travelling a short distance out of town, Watson jumped off and the weapons carrier crew drove back towards Secondigliano. On the way they met PFC Earl M. Smith, of the 56th Military Police Company, and reported what had happened. Smith returned with them to the place where Watson had jumped off the truck, and he was spotted running in the grass about 50 or 60yd from the road, stooped over and crouching. Smith then ordered the soldier to halt and fired two shots. Watson fell and Smith approached him, asking for the pistol, but it had been disposed of by then. Watson, with blood on his leg and one of his hands bandaged, was placed under arrest and transported to a nearby hospital for treatment, where he remained for eight days.

On 30 May 1944, Watson appeared before a GCM, held at the PBS in Naples. He took the stand in his own defence and pleaded not guilty to murdering Brockman, on the basis that he was intoxicated and 'just started firing' when the MPs came into the bar. An investigating officer, who interviewed Watson shortly after the shooting, stated that he had made the prisoner aware of his rights, but that Watson stated, 'I did the shooting and I'll take my medicine.' Private Obediah Johnson, who was drinking that day with Watson, claimed that the soldier was 'pretty well intoxicated', but when he was pressed by the prosecution stated, 'I couldn't say he was drunk because I can't distinguish a drunk person.' The court did not accept Watson's defence, finding him guilty of the charges and sentencing him to death. On 17 July 1944, Lieutenant General Jacob Loucks Devers signed the confirmation of sentence, and

THE PLOT OF SHAME

on 29 August 1944 at Aversa, Italy, Private Ray Watson was hanged by an unknown executioner. He was temporarily buried at the US Military Cemetery in Naples. In 1949, his remains were secretly removed and transported to France, where they were reinterred at the Oise-Aisne American Cemetery in Plot 'E', Row 2, Grave 25.

The body of 22-year-old, blonde-haired, blue-eyed Private John Henry Brockman is buried amongst the honoured dead in the Sicily-Rome American Cemetery, Italy in Plot F, Row 4, Grave 54. Remember him.

Wednesday, 14 June 1944, France
Victim   Aniela Skrzyniarz, Polish civilian (white)
                Raped
Assailant   Private Clarence Whitfield (black)
                Age: 20
                Service No.: 34672443
                Unit: 240th Port Company, 494th Port Battalion,
                    Transportation Corps

A platoon of black troops surrounds a farmhouse as they prepare to eliminate a German sniper holding up an advance, Omaha Beachhead, near Vierville-sur-Mer, France, 10 June 1944. (*Source: NARA Identifier: 531188*)

Despite the long and desperate wait the people of Europe endured, the invasion by Allied forces on 6 June 1944 did not detract from the needs of everyday life, even when it was just a stone's throw from the landing beaches. As the fighting forces moved forward, support troops were left in the rear to ensure that supplies were maintained, keep the Allied armies equipped and help consolidate any ground that had been liberated, ground that remained occupied by civilians. It is in these circumstances that an incident occurred that would see a black American hanged, the first US soldier to be executed after the D-Day landings, and an extraordinary event ensue.

There appears to be no explanation as to why a Polish man, his wife and her sister were living on a farm at Vierville-sur-Mer, Normandy, just behind Omaha Beach, but this was the case, just eight days after the Allies had landed. On 14 June 1944, Aniela Skrzyniarz and her sister, Zofia Sondej, were pulling a wagon along a road towards a field where they were going to milk cows. As they did, four black soldiers, who had been drinking in a nearby bombed-out church, approached them and helped push the wagon into the field. One of the soldiers, who spoke some French, indicated they wanted some milk, but it appears that this may not have been their real intention. As Aniela started to milk a cow, her sister went into an adjoining field to round up more of the animals. As she did so, one of the soldiers pointed a rifle at her head, knocked her down and attempted to rape her. Zofia put up a fierce struggle and did not give in to her attacker. Aniela, concerned as to where her sister was, began to look around for her and saw her on the ground with the soldier. She cried out, 'What are you doing?' and Zofia replied, 'They put a rifle to my head.' At this point, another of the soldiers fired a shot, Aniela dropped to her knees and Zofia managed to escape from her attacker. She then ran home and informed Aniela's husband about the incident.

In the meantime, Aniela was left alone with the soldiers. There appears to have been a squabble amongst them as to who was going to 'have her', and it would be Private Clarence Whitfield who was successful.

Aniela testified that Whitfield threw her to the ground and fell on top of her. He then laid his rifle down close beside her, lifted her dress and raped her. Every time she tried to escape, Whitfield reached for his rifle. Frightened for her life, Aniela could do little to resist the efforts of her attacker. By now, her husband and her sister had reached the location of the 3704th Quartermaster Truck Company, where they informed Captain Roland L. Tauscher, First Lieutenant James P. Webster and

Second Lieutenant Walter S. Siciah of the attack. The officers sprang into action and took two jeeps to the scene, some 300yd away. Here they found Aniela struggling on the ground with a black soldier, quickly identified as Private Clarence Whitfield, who was serving with the 240th Port Company. The husband promptly struck the soldier in the face and Second Lieutenant Siciah, who spoke Polish, asked Whitfield what he was doing. He replied, 'I am not doing anything here. I was passing through.' First Lieutenant Webster then questioned the soldier, who said he 'was getting something' and made a 'back and forth' motion with his hand in front of his crotch. The officers took Whitfield to the battalion headquarters for further questioning where, it seems, no rights warning was given, nor would it be. He was then taken before his executive officer, and his battalion commander, who found a loaded round in his rifle which was 'cocked and on safe'. Then the soldier was questioned about who was involved. Initially, he was evasive with his answers but, after some straight talking, Whitfield finally admitted that two men from his unit, Private Leroy Welch and Private Morris Tarver and 'another coloured boy' who he did not know had been present at the farm. Within 48 hours of the crime being committed, charges were preferred against Whitfield.

At this point some questions must be addressed. On 20 June 1944, a First Army GCM was convened at the Château Sisl in Vierville-sur-Mer, just 100yd from the scene of the crime. Whitfield pleaded not guilty and, at his own request, took to the stand, where he said he tried to convince the victim to have intercourse with him, but had never touched her when she rejected his advances. First Lieutenant Webster and Second Lieutenant Siciah testified for the prosecution, as did the victim and her sister. Private Leroy Welch and Private Morris Tarver testified for the defence, implicating a third soldier, who had never been identified. There was no medical evidence taken or provided. Put simply, Aniela stated that Whitfield had intercourse with her and he denied it. During the proceedings, Aniela claimed that she attempted to call out to passing vehicles, yet, when questioned about this, admitted that she had not called out as she was too frightened. Equally, she 'could not say exactly how it was' when asked if she had made any efforts to prevent Whitfield from having intercourse with her. There resulted, therefore, questions of fact and of the credibility of the witnesses which were left to the sole determination of the court. The jury believed the victim, found Private Whitfield guilty of carnal knowledge, a violation of the 92nd Article of War and voted for the death penalty. Colonel Ernest M. Brannon, the Judge Advocate General for the US First Army reviewed the case on 22 June 1944. He said the matter boiled down to two issues: 'first whether the accused and Aniela Skrzyniarz had sexual intercourse and, second, if so, whether she consented'. He believed the victim had been raped and that Whitfield had done it. He later wrote:

> In my opinion the accused's conduct merits the extreme penalty imposed by the court. His act was vicious and without any extenuating circumstances. Such conduct not only brings disgrace on our Army but, if not checked will interfere with the good relations that must be maintained between our forces and the local populace. Under existing conditions, with a large force of troops congregated in a relatively small area where there are few women, stern measures are necessary to deter others.

Four days later, Lieutenant General Omar Bradley approved the results and on 17 July 1944, General Eisenhower signed an order confirming the sentence. Eventually, in the late afternoon of 14 August 1944, Private Clarence Whitfield was escorted to temporary gallows in the grounds of the Château de Canisy, near Saint-Lô. After being asked if he had any last statement to make, which he did not, the chaplain asked if he had anything to say to him. Whitfield replied, 'What will you tell my mother?' The chaplain replied that she would be told that he died in France. Whitfield then asked if his mother would get his insurance. Colonel Wright said that she would. It appears that, in fact, she would not receive her son's GI life-insurance death benefit.

What followed next was highly unusual. The US First Army did not have an official hangman at this stage, something that would need to be fixed quickly. To address the immediate needs, the staff at Eisenhower's headquarters arranged for Thomas Pierrepoint to be flown into the combat zone, in order that he could perform the execution. Now, in the grounds of a French chateau, an English executioner was about to hang an American for a crime committed against a Pole. Pierrepoint placed a hood over the soldier's head followed by the noose. At exactly 5.00 p.m., Colonel Wright gave a silent signal and Clarence Whitfield dropped like a stone through the opening. He was pronounced dead 15 minutes later. His body was then buried at the US Military Cemetery in Marigny, Normandy, in a separate area reserved for General Prisoners. In 1949, his remains were secretly removed and reinterred at the Oise-Aisne American Cemetery in Plot 'E', Row 2, Grave 37.

Little is known about Aniela Skrzyniarz but there is little doubt she never forgot her terrible ordeal that day. Remember her.

Saturday, 17 June 1944, England

Victim	PFC James Edward Alexander (black)
	Age: 19
	Service No.: 38507839
	Murdered
Assailant	Private Benjamin Pygate (black)
	Age: 35
	Service No.: 33741021
	Unit: 960th Quartermaster Service Company

On 27 February 1944, the 960th Quartermaster Service Company, consisting of 3 officers and 222 enlisted men, sailed from New York aboard the troopship UST *Frederick Lykes*, arriving in Glasgow, Scotland, on 11 March. The unit then travelled by train to Westbury, Wiltshire, where the officers were billeted in a private home, whilst the enlisted men stayed in barracks. Amongst the troops was 19-year-old PFC James Edward Alexander, who was born in Jefferson County, Arkansas, on 16 October 1924, the son of Mashula and Martha Alexander. A teenager who had little opportunity to savour life, he was inducted into the US Army on 24 May 1943 at Little Rock, Arkansas, and from there he joined the 960th Quartermaster Service Company. Private Benjamin Pygate on the other hand, was a 35-year-old hardened criminal, a man with vast life experience. Born on 2 February 1909, in Dillon, South Carolina, he had left school at an early age and moved to various locations in the United States, working wherever he could, seemingly a magnet for trouble. Standing at just 5ft 1½in in height, he enlisted at Fort Myer, Virginia, on 5 May 1943. He was a man short on stature and, seemingly, even shorter in temper, one that would ultimately lead him to be the second, and last, US soldier to be executed by firing squad in the United Kingdom.

On 17 June 1944, Pygate left his barrack, Hut 17, and went to the Drill Hall, which had been set aside for recreational purposes, and where beer was served. On that evening PFC James Edward Alexander, PFC J.M. Blackwell and Privates C.A. Dempsey, A.L. Graves and Roy Easley were also drinking at the bar. A soldier, Private Booker, was acting as bartender and when he announced it was closing time, it seems that PFC Alexander became irate, calling out, 'If I come in again and can't get any beer, I will turn the place out.' An argument then started between Private Dempsey and the drunken teenager. The disagreement continued outside the Drill Hall and in front of Hut 2, but began to escalate as some of the soldiers started to arm themselves. At this point, PFC Alexander tried to quieten the argument. Pygate, who had not been the aggressor up to this point, said, 'You fellows all in the same company should be friends'. It seems that he then lost control, first telling Alexander, 'Get back in that hut before I kill you.' Then he stepped back and kicked Alexander in the right groin, and as Alexander fell back against the door, Pygate pulled a knife out from his rear pocket and stabbed the teenager in the neck. Alexander would not last long, he grasping his throat he was quickly taken to the camp infirmary but died a short time later. Pygate was immediately arrested, and an investigation commenced.

On 30 June, Brigadier General Charles O. Thrasher ordered a GCM to be held and Pygate was brought before a court martial at Tidworth Barracks, Wiltshire, on 15 July 1944 where he pleaded not guilty. He testified that after arguing with the other soldiers, including Alexander, he tried to act as a peacemaker, but that his mind went 'dark' at the time of the stabbing and he didn't remember anything, including how he got back to his hut. Captain George Schwartz, Medical Corps, testified that on 25 April he had treated Pygate for a large scalp wound, which required ten stitches, after a box fell on his head as he was working. However, Schwartz thought that there had not been any brain injury, although it was probable that the blow might be behind any lapses of memory. What the court was not aware of, until after Pygate had been executed, was that he had a string of over fourteen offences behind him, including several arrests for assault with a deadly weapon, a man who was known to the FBI. Despite his protestations, Private Benjamin Pygate was found guilty and sentenced to death by shooting. On 28 November 1944, he was led into the yard at Shepton Mallet Prison, where he was strapped to a wooden post, a black hood was placed over his head and a 4in-diameter white target placed over his heart. A large number of officials and witnesses were present as the officer in charge of the nine-man firing squad, Captain Philip J. Flynn, gave the commands, 'Ready, Aim, Fire.' One of the rifles contained a blank round, as with all firing squads, but the remainder sent a volley of bullets slamming into Pygate's body and he died almost instantly. His body was first buried in Brookwood American Military Cemetery, Surrey, where one of his identification tags was fixed to a small provisional wooden cross whilst the second one was buried with his body. In 1948, the army transferred the remains to the American Military Cemetery at Cambridge. A year later they were secretly removed and reinterred in the Oise-Aisne American Cemetery in Plot 'E', Row 4, Grave 85.

PFC James E. Alexander is buried amongst the honoured dead in the American Military Cemetery, Cambridge in Plot B, Row 3, Grave 39. Remember them.

Tuesday, 20 June 1944, France

Victims	Jeanne Martin, French civilian (white)
	Age: 28
	Raped
	Louise Bocage, French civilian (white)
	Age: 26
	Raped
Assailants	Private Roy W. Anderson (black)
	Age: 27
	Service No.: 35407199
	T/5 James Buck Sanders (black)
	Age: 27
	Service No.: 34124233
	Private Florine Wilson (black)
	Age: 24
	Service No.: 34124246
	Unit: Company 'B', 29th Signal Construction Battalion

Neuville-au-Plain is a small village, just a few miles north of Sainte-Mère-Église, and in June 1944 men of the German Grenadier-Regiment 1058 were stationed here. The capture of the village on D-Day was entrusted to the 2nd Battalion, 505th Parachute Infantry Regiment, 82nd Airborne Division, commanded by Lieutenant Colonel Benjamin Hayes Vandervoort. Over the next two days, a bitter battle was fought as the two sides struggled for possession of the village. Finally, on 8 June, the Americans forced the Germans out of the village and the civilian population was liberated.

One of the homes in the village was occupied by Madame Louise Bocage. She shared her house with two married couples, Alphonse and Marguerite Lehot and Auguste and Jeanne Martin, as well as the Martins' young daughter. Although there was an air of relief at the liberation, tension remained as the Allies fought to take the Cotentin Peninsula. The intense air bombardments prior to the Allied landings and the subsequent land battle hugely damaged the area and communications had to be firmly re-established. The 29th Signal Construction Battalion arrived in Normandy on 17 June 1944. Its purpose was to erect telephone poles, wooden telephone towers and lay telephone lines. The role was an arduous one and was still well within the combat zone and so the troops involved had to be fully armed and ready for action.

At about 11.00 a.m. on 20 June, three black US soldiers called at Madame Bocage's house and asked for cider. She filled their canteens and the soldiers departed, but returned about 7 or 8 minutes later, accompanied by four or five other black soldiers. Madame Bocage, happy at the liberation, again served them cider, which they drank as they stood and sat about in the yard. She also cut roses which she gave to the three soldiers who first appeared at her home and they, in turn, showed her photographs as she passed pleasantries with them. However, things would quickly start to turn ugly. Her gesture of goodwill was seen as an invite to a sexual encounter as the soldiers began to ask for women and indicated a desire for sexual intercourse. They showed her a French-English phrase book and pointed to the French expression for 'I want to pass the night'. They also offered her money in exchange for sexual favours, having previously paid her for the cider. Louise Bocage became frightened by their demeanour and sought the help of her neighbour, Monsieur Dubois. He collected up the women and took them to his house, after which the group of Americans departed, and the civilians returned home.

At about 12.30 p.m., three of the Americans returned to the house, Private Roy W. Anderson, T/5 James Buck Sanders and Private Florine Wilson. On this occasion, their intention was to take what they had been asking for. They entered the kitchen, pointed their rifles at the women and ordered all of them into the courtyard, apart from Louise Bocage. Alphonse Lehot was also forced into the yard and then one of the soldiers, later identified as Roy Anderson, fired a shot from his carbine between the legs of Lehot, the bullet striking the ground and ricocheting behind him. Louise Bocage, who had managed to escape and join the other women, was forced back into the house where she was subjected to a vicious rape by both Anderson and Sanders. Having finished with her, Sanders went into the courtyard and at gunpoint forced Jeanne Martin into the house and the two soldiers then took turns in raping her. At this point, a third soldier, believed to have been Private Riggle McCutcheon, entered the house and raped Louise Bocage. Private William L. Pope, of the same unit, arrived at the house and on asking what was going on was told plainly that he should leave. As Pope left, he ran into Private Patrick R. Keely, a friend of Anderson's. Keely could see what was happening and told the soldiers that they had better leave quickly as officers had got wind of what was going on and would soon be there to investigate. Unrelenting, the two men continued to assault the women, whilst Florine Wilson held the remaining occupants of the house at gunpoint until the ordeal was over, when the men all returned to their bivouac area. Neither of the rape victims spoke English, but the alleged crime was reported and US Army officials began an investigation. However, the situation soon became confused as each of the women were unable to fully identify their attackers, whilst Sanders and Anderson both admitted taking part. Anderson claimed he had paid Louise Bocage for sex with both women, but the circumstances of the alleged assault did not seem to tally with his claim.

A GCM was held in the town of Sainte-Mère-Église on 17 July 1944 when all three appeared at a three-day trial. In what has been described as a confusing circumstance, T/5 Robert J. Railland acted as an interpreter for the case. This is something that was later highly criticised. The witnesses, in an extremely excited state, gave evidence, some of which has been described as 'lost in translation' and allowing for the 'possibility of error'. Despite this, the eleven voting members of the court found all three men guilty of the charges against them, sentencing Anderson and Sanders to death and sending Wilson to a US state penitentiary for life. Unusually, they submitted a recommendation for clemency, but despite this, on the advice of the Board of Review, Brigadier General Plank approved the sentence and on 2 August 1944, General Dwight D. Eisenhower confirmed the sentence, but withheld the execution date until the US Army in France had employed an official hangman. As a result, both Anderson and Sanders were detained until the Seine DTC, in Caserne Mortier, Paris, was opened. They were moved there to await their fate.

By 25 October 1944, the Theatre Provost Marshal had agreed that Private John C. Woods, soon to be Master Sergeant, assisted by PFC Thomas S. Robinson would act as official hangmen. On this day, seemingly the first in which Woods acted as the executioner, Private James Buck Sanders was led into the execution room at Seine DTC, the first to be hanged. After the court decision had been read out to him, he dropped through the trapdoor and it seems dangled on the rope for a full 14 minutes before he eventually choked to death, mainly due to the inexperience of Woods as a hangman. Roy Anderson was next, taking a little less time to die, and was declared dead just 11 minutes after falling through the trapdoor. Both men were then buried at the US Military Cemetery at Solers, France. In 1949, as with many others featured in these pages, the bodies were removed from their resting place and transported to the Oise-Aisne American Cemetery, to be buried in Plot 'E'. Sanders was buried in Row 3, Grave 58 and Anderson in Row 2, Grave 29.

There is little doubt the victims never forgot their ordeal that day the liberators came to their home. Remember them.

Tuesday, 27 June 1944, Italy
Victim   Anna Zanchi, Italian civilian (white)
                Murdered
Assailants   Private Fred A. McMurray (black)
                Age: 25
                Service No.: 38184335
                Private Louis Till (black)
                Age: 23
                Service No.: 36392273
                Unit: 177th Port Company, Transportation Corps

On 27 June 1944, Ernesto Mari, with his wife and their daughter, Freida, along with Benni Lucretzia and her daughter, occupied a small shack near a US water point in Cisterna, a suburb of Civitavecchia, northwest of Rome. At about 10.30 p.m., they were all asleep when an anti-aircraft barrage commenced. Freida got up and opened the door of the shack, possibly to watch the spectacle or perhaps because she heard an unusual noise. As she did so three men, wearing black masks, pushed past her and entered the shack. What took place next was an horrific assault on innocent Italian civilians. Ernesto was grabbed from behind, a hand placed over his mouth, and was then struck on the head twice with a pistol, knocking him unconscious. Benni Lucretzia and Freida, who were both pregnant, were then subjected to a violent sexual assault. Benni, whose clothes had been torn off by her initial attacker, was raped at least twice. Both she and Freida fought gallantly to protect themselves against their assailants, one described as tall and the other two as short, but they were too powerful, overcame the women and raped them both. Although

Private Louis Till, who murdered Anna Zanchi on 27 June 1944.

their faces were covered, their hands were not and the women could see, from the light created by the barrage, the searchlights and from the matches the intruders struck, that these were black soldiers. The assailants shouted, 'We are not coloured, we are white', which appeared to be an odd and highly suspicious act. When they had finished, the assailants ran out of the shack.

About half an hour after the attack, there was a knock on the door of a house a short distance from the Mari home. This was occupied by Anna Zanchi, her son, her daughter and her daughter's fiancé, John Masi. A voice said, 'Un poco di vino, per favore', a request for wine. John Masi, who had lived in Brooklyn, New York, for fifteen years, went to the door and replied in English, 'I am sorry, we don't have no wine. Go back to the camp because it is late.' The door was then forced open and Masi was confronted by two masked men, one tall and one short, each holding pistols pointed at his chest. Masi tried to reason with the men, who were wearing US Army working uniforms, but one of them, described as tall, pushed a pistol into the Italian's chest and told him, 'Listen, if you don't go inside, I am going to bust your head. I'll give you a count to three, and if you don't get inside, I'll kill you.' Masi knew there was going to be trouble and told everyone in the house to lay on the floor in case shots were fired. Everyone dropped to the floor, but Anna Zanchi then got up, went out and said to the two men, 'Go, or otherwise tomorrow morning I go to the MPs and tell them who you are. I am not scared of you', whereupon the two men then began firing their weapons. The tall one, later identified as Private Louis Till, fired twice and the other one fired once. Anna Zanchi said, 'They got me, they got me' and fell to the floor bleeding heavily from a wound. The attackers ran off and a US MP was summoned. Anna was rushed to a US stationary hospital where her wound was dressed and morphine administered. She was then taken to a US evacuation hospital, where she sadly died from her injuries.

On the night of the shooting, US MPs found three bullet holes in the door of Anna Zanchi's home, as well as three cartridge cases. One was from a .38 pistol, the others from a .45 pistol. About 5m from the house a soiled air-mail envelope was discovered, addressed to Private Fred McMurray of the 177th Port Company. The word 'laundry' was written in pencil on the back of the envelope. This would be the first man that the MPs would need to speak to, but there was to be a revelation in the case. Private James Thomas, from the same unit as McMurray, was about to confess to being one of the attackers, along with Private Fred McMurray, Private Louis Till and an unknown British soldier. He provided a detailed statement indicating that the four men, after meeting at the water point, drank a sizable amount of wine and then planned a 'raid' on the little shack, where they knew some women lived. He provided a detailed account of the assault, claiming that he was present, but did not have sex with either of the women, and how McMurray and Till had fought over who was going to have sex with Benni Lucretzia first, with McMurray backing down to Till. He also stated that McMurray was armed with a .38 pistol and Till a .45 automatic pistol. McMurray was interviewed by a member of the US Criminal Investigation Division and claimed that after the attack on the women in the shack the four soldiers began to make their way back to the US camp, but en route Till stated that he wanted to make another 'raid' and said he was going back to the water point, and his companions should go with him. However, Thomas and the British soldier continued to the camp, and he agreed to go with Till, as he was frightened of him. He had taken the pistol back from the British soldier, who had carried it on the first attack, so both men were now armed. They had carried out the attack described by John Masi and McMurray claimed he had only fired one shot and that Till had fired two from his weapon. This was sufficient evidence for the investigators and the case was put forward to senior commanders, but their report was delayed, so it was not until 27 December 1944 that Brigadier General Francis H. Oxx called for a GCM. This commenced at 9.45 a.m. on 17 February 1945 at Livorno, Italy. No evidence was introduced by the defence, and both accused elected to remain silent. A US Navy sailor, James E. Carter, gave evidence that he was at an Italian civilian's house doing his laundry when he had been approached by four men. One, about 6ft tall, struck Carter three times in the face, shoved a small pistol into his back and robbed him, taking a .45 calibre Model 1911 US service pistol from him. Carter was badly knocked about, when his assailant yelled, 'I'm going to kill the mother-fucking son of a bitch.' The attacker, identified as Private Louis Till, then fired a shot, but the pistol jammed and the shocked sailor jumped into his jeep and escaped. He reported the incident to the MP, who escorted him through several all-black units in the area, but he did not find his assailants. It would be this pistol that was used in the attack on Anna Zanchi's home.

Both men had poor military records. Fred A. McMurray was born on 25 February 1920 in Ruston, Louisiana, and, like Till, was married. He was inducted into the US Army in Camp Livingston, Louisiana, on 30 June 1942, and had appeared before four previous Summary Courts Martials. Till, born on 7 February 1922 in New Madrid County, Missouri, worked for the Argo Corn Company near Chicago, Illinois, and married Mamie Carthan on 14 October 1940, when they were both 18 years old. They would have one son, Emmett, but by 1942 had separated due to his violent treatment of Mamie. He was inducted into the US Army on 9 July 1942 and, like so many black soldiers, was destined to serve in a supply unit, being posted to the 177th Port Company, where he met McMurray. Both men were unanimously found guilty of their crimes and sentenced to death. Lieutenant General Joseph T. McNarney confirmed the sentences, and the two soldiers were transferred to the Peninsular Base Section Stockade No. 1 near Aversa, Italy, where, just over a year after their crime, on 2 July 1945, they were executed. McMurray would be the first to be hanged, followed swiftly by Till. The bodies of both men were first buried in the American Military Cemetery in Naples. Then, in 1949, they were secretly removed from this location and reburied in Plot 'E' at the Oise-Aisne American Cemetery. McMurray was in Row 1, Grave 2 and Till in Row 4, Grave 73.

The British soldier who took part in the horrific assault and raped both women was never identified. Although Benni Lucretzia survived the ordeal, her unborn child did not, with her suffering a miscarriage the day after the attack. Freida Mari's child was born prematurely some twenty days after the assault. The body of brave Anna Zanchi was removed from the US Army General Hospital on 28 June 1944 and buried the following day. Emmett Till, Louis's son, went on to become an internationally recognised figure regarding human rights after he was abducted, tortured and lynched on 28 August 1955 by two white men during a visit to his relatives in Mississippi. His body was identified by a silver ring he was wearing, which had belonged to his father and bore the initials 'LT'. Remember them.

Wednesday, 12 July 1944, France
Victims   Marie Lepoittevin, French civilian
                Age: 62
                Raped
                Louise Lagouche, French civilian
                Age: 15
                Raped
                Louis Leveziel
                Raped
Assailants   Private William Clifton Downes (black)
                Age: 29
                Service No.: 33519814

> Private James Robert Parrott (black)
> Age: 23
> Service No.: 32483580
> Private Grant U. Smith (black)
> Age: 23
> Service No.: 35688909
> Unit: 597th Ordnance Ammunition Company

Some of the sex crimes committed by Allied soldiers in France during the Second World War bear a disconcerting similarity. Often under the influence of, or in search of, alcohol homes would be invaded by a small group of troops. On establishing who occupied the premises, women would be approached for sexual favours and if these were not agreed to, or paid for, they would simply be taken by force. Victims, if they felt able to report the crime, would often be required to attend an identification parade or relive their assaults in a courtroom filled with military officials and faced by their alleged assailant.

At about 11.30 p.m. on 12 July 1944, three black US soldiers knocked at the door of Paul Jeanne's house in Etienville, a small commune about 7 miles south-east of Sainte-Mère-Église. Failing to gain immediate entrance, they knocked the door down with their rifles, entered the house and lit a candle on the mantelpiece. The three soldiers discovered Jeanne's two sons and pointed their rifles at them, claiming they were 'American Police' looking for 'Boche'. After about 5 minutes, they decided to leave the property and asked Paul Jeanne for cognac, but their request was refused. As they left, they asked if there were US soldiers in the area and were told that some were nearby, whereupon they left. Paul Jeanne watched as the men began to walk in the direction of 'this American camp', but then they turned around and headed in the direction of a nearby house, the home of Ernest Lepoittevin, his 62-year-old wife, Marie, and her granddaughter, Louise Lagouche, who was just 15 years of age. Ernest had his bed in the kitchen, whilst Marie and Louise slept in the bedroom. The soldiers, calling out 'American Police' and 'Boche' knocked at the door. Lepoittevin opened it, and the three soldiers entered the house, lit matches, looked in his bed and then proceeded to the bedroom. Here, Lepoittevin would not open the door, so one of the soldiers grabbed him around the throat and 'mastered' him into the kitchen, whilst the others broke the door open. Both women were in bed and the largest of the three soldiers threw himself upon Louise, and a second seized Marie. Each soldier took it in turns to restrain Ernest Lepoittevin, whilst the others each raped both women, who were frightened and crying in the darkened bedroom. When the ordeal was over, the soldiers left, and Ernest Lepoittevin reported the incident to the mayor of Etienville.

Two weeks later, at about 2.00 a.m. on 26 July, three black soldiers broke into the home of 74-year-old Just Hebert, in the village of Renouf, just 2 miles from Etienville. In the house with him at the time were his widowed daughter, Madame Louis Leveziel, and her two sons, aged 6 and 8. The soldiers climbed in through a window which contained no glass, and their voices disturbed Louis Leveziel, so she hid behind a closet in her bedroom. Just Hebert managed to persuade the soldiers to leave the property, but they returned 15 minutes later, and this time one of them discovered Madame Leveziel in her hiding place. She was dragged out, thrown on the floor and raped. Her efforts to resist her attacker were met with blows to her head. Just Hebert took his youngest grandson and ran to a neighbour for help.

At about 3.20 a.m., First Lieutenant Michael Sorbello of the 795th Anti-Aircraft Artillery Automatic Weapons Battalion, stationed near Pont-Labbe, was awakened by two French children who ran to his Command Post calling for help. Sorbello, along with Staff Sergeant Edward J. Cravens and two enlisted men, accompanied the children along the road toward Etienville. As they did so, they discovered three black soldiers close to the Hebert house and began to question them. They claimed they were looking for friends of theirs who were somewhere on the road searching for calvados, a brandy made from apples. At this point, Madame Leveziel appeared on the scene, she was frightened and in a dishevelled state. Using Sorbello's flashlight she emphatically identified one of the soldiers, a taller one, who was Private William Clifton Downes serving with 597th Ordnance Ammunition Company. Leaving Staff Sergeant Cravens in charge of the three soldiers, Sorbello accompanied Madame Leveziel to the Hebert home where he was shown the damage the soldiers had apparently caused.

On the morning of 27 July, Captain Vadie P. Pyland, 1293rd Military Police Company, took the three soldiers to the Hebert house in his jeep. As they approached the home, Ernest Lepoittevin was standing in the road with his wife and Louise Lagouche. Marie Lepoittevin positively identified Downes as the soldier who attacked her on 12 July but was unable to identify the others. Her granddaughter was unable to identify any of her assailants. After a thorough investigation, the Commander of the Normandy Base Section determined that the three men would be tried jointly, and they were brought before a court in Cherbourg on 22 November 1944. All three men pleaded not guilty to the charges against them. The court considered the statements of the victims, particularly the degree of certainty with which they could, or could not, positively identify the three soldiers. Eventually, Private William Clifton Downes, from Copeland, Virginia, was found guilty of all the charges against him and was sentenced to death. Private James Robert Parrott and Private Grant U. Smith could only be found guilty of breaking and entering but were also sentenced to death. However, a US Army judicial review recommended to General Dwight D. Eisenhower that the sentences of Parrott and Smith should be commuted to life imprisonment. Downes would hang in isolation.

On 26 February 1945, Master Sergeant John Clarence Woods, T/3 Thomas F. Robinson and T/5 Herbert A. Kleinbeck travelled to the scene of the first crime in Etienville. Here they erected portable gallows in a field just south of the village. Two days later, at 10.00 a.m. on 28 February 1945, Private William Clifton Downes was hanged in front of twenty-two officials and witnesses, including one of the rape victims. They would stand in the chilly winter rain for almost 20 minutes before he was pronounced dead. His body was transported to the US Military Cemetery in Marigny. In 1949, his remains were removed and secretly transferred to the Oise-Aisne American Cemetery, where they are buried in Plot 'E', Row 1, Grave 16.

Thursday, 20 July 1944, France
Victim   Marie Dupont, French civilian (white)
                Raped
Assailant   T/5 Richard Bunney Scott (black)
                Age: 28
                Service No.: 38040012
                Unit: 229th Quartermaster Salvage Collecting Company

On 20 July 1944, Marcel Dupont, a house painter, was living in a small ground-floor apartment in Hue Sadi-Carnot, Octeville, a suburb of Cherbourg, with his wife, Marie, and their three children. At the time, Marie was heavily pregnant with their fourth child. At about 10.30 p.m. that night, there was a knock at their door and a voice called out, 'Police'. Marcel immediately opened the door and as he did so a black US soldier pushed past him and entered the bedroom. He pointed at a small hole in the shutter, through which light was shining, which Marcel quickly stuffed with paper. The soldier then walked into the kitchen, sat down at the table, pointed at a bottle of cider and demanded a drink. He then produced a small blue dictionary, containing some photos, which he showed to Marie. Oddly, he then placed his head on the table and promptly fell asleep. Marcel woke him after a few minutes and the soldier got up, laid on the kitchen floor and fell asleep again. Marie Dupont went to the home of Joseph Chatel to ask for help. As he came down the stairs, the soldier jumped up, pulled out a bayonet and shouted, 'Boche, Boche.' Appearing to be terribly angry and unnerved, the soldier held the bayonet against Joseph's waist, piercing his shirt and causing his skin to bleed. He then ordered Joseph to return to his home, which he did immediately. The soldier, now seemingly even more angry, pushed the Duponts into the kitchen, where he turned the light out, but Marcel switched it back on again. The couple were made to enter the bedroom, where the three children were sleeping. He forced Marcel into a corner of the room and then, holding the bayonet to her throat, he forced Marie onto the floor, pushed up her clothes and raped her. Throughout the whole ordeal he kept his eyes on Marcel, and each time the Frenchman moved the soldier picked up his bayonet. When he had finished, the soldier ran out of the house like a 'madman' and disappeared into the night.

The assailant may have gotten away with the crime if it weren't for one small thing, he left the dictionary behind, containing his details. This was handed to the civil affairs authorities and, by 2.00 a.m. on 22 July, Agent Jack Goldsmith, of the US Army Criminal Investigation Division, sat down to interview 28-year-old T/5 Richard Bunney Scott, who had been inducted into the US Army on 7 March 1941 in Dallas, Texas, and had been serving with his unit since that date. He then made two statements to the agent. In the first he claimed that he knew the family, and on the afternoon of the crime he had left his camp to go for a walk, where he met the Dupont children. After giving them chocolate and candy, he was invited into their home and after his visit he had simply left his dictionary behind. This might have proved difficult for the Duponts to deny if Scott had not made a second and more bizarre statement. In this he claimed that the first statement was not true and that he had visited the Dupont home on the night of the crime, after having a glass of cognac in a bar. He had knocked at the door of their home, believing it to be a bar. Marcel Dupont had welcomed him and given him some cider and cognac, after which he fell asleep with his head on the table in the dark. Marie Dupont was with him and he didn't realise Marcel was in the room, so when he appeared, Scott claimed he was frightened. He then claimed that Marcel Dupont had taken him to the bedroom and invited him to have sex with his wife, which he did. When he left, Marie Dupont had kissed him on his jaw, he had not used the words 'Police' or 'Bosche' and he was not carrying his bayonet that night. Scott was brought before a GCM in Cherbourg on 7 September 1944. He took to the witness stand and claimed that he had consensual sex with Marie Dupont, which was strongly denied. She maintained that she was pregnant at the time, had three small children and had been 'forced' by Scott at bayonet point, whilst her husband was held at bay. The court did not believe Scott, found him guilty of the charges against him and sentenced him to death. Scott felt he had not been given a fair trial and that the French witnesses had lied. A later review would have this to say about the case, 'The story of the accused, that the husband of a pregnant woman would, after trying to prevent the accused from sleeping on a table, or on the floor, invite him to have intercourse with his wife on the floor and in his presence, is too incredible for belief.'

General Dwight D. Eisenhower confirmed the sentence and on the morning of 18 November 1944, in an area of flat ground behind buildings at Fort Du Roule, Cherbourg, Scott was hanged on temporary gallows before a total of forty-eight officials and witnesses by Major Mortimer H. Christian. He was pronounced dead some 13 minutes later. His body was initially buried in the US Military Cemetery at Marigny, France. In 1949, it was secretly removed from this location and transported to the Oise-Aisne American Cemetery, where he was and reburied in Plot 'E', Row 2, Grave 45.

Wednesday, 26 July 1944, England
Victim   Beatrice Maud Reynolds, British civilian (white)
                  Age: 59
                  Raped
Assailant   Private Madison Thomas (black)
                  Age: 23
                  Service No.: 38265363
                  Unit: 964th Quartermaster Service Company

Of all the cases described within these pages, this is perhaps amongst one of the most disturbing. Not only was it an attack on an ageing woman, but the victim was a British war widow who had spent most of her life caring for her disabled brother and raising money for the British Legion. Beatrice Maud Roberts was born on 23 February 1885, the daughter of Richard James and Emily Roberts, who lived in Goschen Street, Devonport, Devon. She was one of nine children, although four had not survived infancy. Little is known of her early life, but by 1911 she was still living at home with her parents and working as a

Private Madison Thomas.
(*JAG File*)

dressmaker. In 1916 she met a sailor, Chief Writer Thomas Henry Reynolds, a 34-year-old Irishman who had been serving in the Royal Navy since 1901. The couple married on 11 May 1916, and just a few days after their marriage, Thomas was ordered to sea. His ship, HMS *Defence*, was the flagship of Rear Admiral Sir Robert Arbuthnot, who was leading the First Cruiser Squadron. Thomas Reynolds never returned from this voyage, the ship having been sunk by the German battlecruiser SMS *Derfflinger* on 31 May 1916, during the Battle of Jutland. They had been married for just three weeks. Following the death of her husband, Beatrice became an active supporter of the British Legion and eventually became chairman of the British Legion Hall at Gunnislake, Cornwall, a small village where she lived with her brother, Alfred James Roberts.

On 26 July 1944, with the invasion of Normandy in full swing and no doubt thoughts of her husband in her mind, Beatrice left the British Legion Hall at about 10.40 p.m. to return home, after having organised a dance for service personnel based in the area. As she did so, a young black soldier appeared, walking by her side, and asked her if she had far to go. She replied, 'No,' and suggested that he had better hurry up to catch his ride back to his camp as she did not care for his company. Beatrice, thinking the soldier would continue onwards, stopped to talk to 16-year-old Jean Elizabeth Blight, who was sitting outside her home. However, the soldier returned and started to speak to Jean, asking for a goodnight kiss, which was declined. Beatrice waited until he was out of sight, then continued on her way home. As she came to the loneliest part of her walk, the soldier reappeared, again asking her if she had far to go. She gave a definite, 'No', but the soldier suddenly grabbed her, picked her up and threw her over a hedge. She pleaded with him, saying she was old enough to be his mother, but his answer was, 'That don't make any difference.' Her attacker wrenched a gold wristwatch from her arm and said he would return it when she gave him all he desired and when she replied, 'That will never be boy', he then struck her a heavy blow on the side of the head, knocking her senseless. She pleaded, prayed and reminded him of his own parents, but he said he had none. He then dragged her, still struggling, further into the field. She tried to scream for help, but he clutched her throat and she thought she was dying, falling into semi-consciousness. The soldier produced a knife, which he held up to her throat, then subjected her to a severe sexual assault and rape. After the attack was over, he showed her a .30 carbine bullet and said, 'You see this bullet, if you make any attempt to run, you'll get it.' He pulled her to her feet and quickly disappeared.

The following day, Dr Frederick Albert John Woodland examined Beatrice, finding her in a very shocked condition, her clothes dishevelled, her hair down, a contused wound over the right eye and a small cut on her nose. Pieces of grass were stuck to the back of her neck, there was mud on her knees and both stockings were badly torn. The left side of her neck showed extensive bruising with marks normally caused by fingernails. He took a sample of her blood, which was identified as belonging to group A. At the same time, Police Constable James Herbert Elliott, accompanied by Jean Blight, travelled to nearby Whitchurch Down Camp, the base for the 964th Quartermaster Service Company, an African American unit. The whole company was summoned to an identification parade and Jean Blight picked out a soldier, the one she had seen with Beatrice. He was identified as 23-year-old Private Madison Thomas, from Arnaudville, St Landry Parish, Louisiana, who had only been with the unit for three weeks. His tent was searched and a pair of blood-stained trousers were found in his kit bag, along with a .30 bullet in the hip pocket. A knife, matching the description given by Beatrice, was found under his pillow. Thomas claimed the stains were paint but a forensic test by Dr Frederick D.M. Hocking, of the Royal Cornwall Infirmary, Truro, determined this was human blood from group A, the same blood group as Beatrice. Thomas himself was blood group O.

Thomas was interviewed on 2 August by Special Agent Michaelson, of the US Army Criminal Investigation Division, who was based at Raglan Barracks, Devonport. Thomas denied the accusation made against him, although he admitted being at the dance in Gunnislake and not leaving until 11.00 p.m. On 21 August 1944, he was brought before a GCM, held in Plymouth, where Thomas pleaded not guilty to the charges against him and chose to remain silent. During the hearing, a darker piece of information was revealed. Private Madison Thomas had attempted a similar crime during the time he had been in England. Earlier in the year he had been brought before a Special Court Martial for using threatening language against an English woman, telling her, 'I'll shoot if you don't stop', and offering her money for sex, which she refused. On this occasion it did not lead to rape but was a clear indicator of his character. The evidence was overwhelming, and he was quickly found guilty and sentenced to death by hanging.

Brigadier General Charles O. Thrasher approved the sentence and General Dwight D. Eisenhower confirmed it on 12 September 1944. At 1.00 a.m. on 12 October 1944, Private Madison Thomas was marched into the execution chamber at Shepton Mallet Prison where, before a group of officials and witnesses, Thomas and Albert Pierrepoint quickly prepared him for execution. Following a silent signal from Major Herbert R. Laslett, he dropped through the trapdoor, being pronounced dead 7 minutes later. His body was first buried in Brookwood American Military Cemetery, Surrey, where one of his identification tags was fixed to a small provisional wooden cross whilst the second one was buried with his body. In 1948, the army transferred his remains to the American Military Cemetery at Cambridge. A year later they were secretly removed and reinterred in the Oise-Aisne American Cemetery, Plot 'E', Row 4, Grave 76.

Beatrice cared for her brother until his death and herself lived until the age of 85, passing away in 1970, hopefully her last thoughts being of the brief time she had with her husband. Remember her.

Chapter 6

1944: August – Summer Madness

Throughout August 1944, during the Allied campaign in France, there was scorching hot weather, heavy fighting and a great many casualties amongst the opposing forces. In addition, members of the liberating powers committed acts of violence and sexual assault against French civilians who were desperate for liberation and peace. Some of the offending troops would suffer the ultimate penalty at the hands of an executioner, whilst others would face life imprisonment. However, there were a few who would, occasionally, slip through the net of justice, as the result of nothing more than procedural error. The following is a list of those members of the US forces who were charged with capital crimes committed during that month and who were apprehended and brought before a GCM but were not sentenced to death. It is not exhaustive but should provide some perspective on the subject.

US General Courts Martial, France, August 1944

Date	Name	Crime	Location	Sentence
3 Aug. 44	Private Joe Lewis	Murder	Tessy-sur-Vire, France	Death by shooting, commuted to life
3 Aug. 44	Private O.K. Odom	Attempted murder	Fierville, France	5 years' imprisonment
5 Aug. 44	Private Fred	Murder	La Haye-Pesnel, France	Death – legally insufficient, released
7 Aug. 44	Private W.D.	Murder	Avranches, France	10 years' imprisonment

Date	Name	Crime	Location	Sentence
9 Aug. 44	Private William F. Bigrow	Murder	Vannes, France	15 years' imprisonment
11 Aug. 44	Private O.B. Ward	Attempted Rape	Le Chêne Gurin, France	20 years' imprisonment
13 Aug. 44	Private Eugene Houston	Rape	Yvré l'Évêque, France	Life imprisonment
13 Aug. 44	Sergeant John J. Rosinski	Murder	A-35 Airfield, France	10 years' imprisonment
15 Aug. 44	Private Peter Blake	Rape	La Baconnière, France	Life Imprisonment
15 Aug. 44	Private James E. Clemons	Rape	La Baconnière, France	Life imprisonment
15 Aug. 44	PFC Eugene Haney	Rape	La Baconnière, France	Life imprisonment
15 Aug. 44	Private William R. Rose	Rape	La Baconnière, France	Life imprisonment
15 Aug. 44	Private Bob West	Rape	La Baconnière, France	Life imprisonment
15 Aug. 44	Private Searcy Howell	Rape	Arzano, Finistère, France	Life imprisonment
15 Aug. 44	Private Clarence L. Franklin	Rape	Arzano, Finistère, France	Life imprisonment
18 Aug. 44	Private Charlie Whitehead	Attempted rape	Cheville, Normandy, France	Life imprisonment
18 Aug. 44	Private Jerry Key	Attempted rape	Cheville, Normandy, France	Life Imprisonment
18 Aug. 44	Private Harry L. Wilson	Attempted rape	Cheville, Normandy, France	Life imprisonment

1944: AUGUST – SUMMER MADNESS

Date	Name	Crime	Location	Sentence
20 Aug. 44	T/4 Sanders C. Hartsell	Rape	Bricquebec, France	Life imprisonment
20 Aug. 44	Private W.H. Manning	Attempted rape	Almeneches, France	5 years' imprisonment
30 Aug. 44	T/5 James R. Thurman	Double murder	Les Orme, Yonne, France	Life imprisonment
30. Aug. 44	Private Robert W. Post Double	Murder	Les Orme, Yonne, France	Life imprisonment

Tuesday, 1 August 1944, France

Victims   Auguste Louis Clement Lebarillier, French civilian (white)
Age: 19
Murdered
Marie Osouf, French civilian (white)
Age: 19
Raped

Assailants   Private Waiters Yancy (black)
Age: 21
Service No.: 37499079
Private Robert L. Skinner (black)
Age: 20
Service No.: 35802328
Unit: 1511th Engineer Water Supply Company,
     US Third Army

The home of Xavier and Renée Hèbert was in the village of Hameau au Pigeon, Quettetot, which is some 15 miles north of Sainte-Mère-Église. The couple employed a maid, 19-year-old Marie Osouf, and a hired hand, Auguste Lebarillier. As the Allied forces began to consolidate and reinforce the Cotentin Peninsula, support units were stationed in the area to maintain supplies to the military forces. An African American unit, the 1511th Engineer Water Supply Company, which had arrived in France on D-Day + 2, was amongst these. Its role was to maintain supplies of fresh water to the fighting forces as they expanded across Normandy.

Auguste Louis Clement Lebarillier, the 19-year-old Frenchman murdered by Private Waiters Yancy and Private Robert L. Skinner on 1 August 1944.

On the evening of 1 August 1944, Xavier and Auguste were working in a field close to the house and Marie was helping Renée with household chores. Two young black soldiers suddenly arrived at the house and asked for cider, which Renée gladly gave them. After drinking about five glasses, they left the house, but returned just a few minutes later asking for more. Renée protested, claiming that it had all gone, but the soldiers were insistent, so she sent Marie to the cider cellar to fetch some more. One of the soldiers, a taller one, followed Marie towards the cellar and the second soldier pointed his carbine at Renée, who realised what was about to happen. She called Marie to come back, but now all hell broke loose. Marie attempted to run away but was quickly caught and dragged into the courtyard. Renée, after a struggle with the second soldier, managed to wrestle his carbine from him and ran towards the home of a neighbour, Auguste Mace. She was wearing wooden shoes and the soldier soon caught up with her, knocking her to the ground, and began to hit her with his fists and a steel helmet. Renée dropped the rifle and managed to reach her neighbour's house. As Auguste Mace opened the door to his home, a shot rang out, striking him in the right arm. Hearing the shooting, and his wife's cries for help, both Xavier and Auguste ran to the Mace home. As they approached, four more shots rang out, two hitting Auguste in the stomach and two striking Xavier in the back as he turned. Xavier was then struck on the head and arm with the butt of a rifle. The blows were so severe, the weapon broke into three pieces. In the meantime, Marie had managed to escape and was running towards the Mace home. The soldier, who had been hitting Xavier, then approached her and struck her in the face with the stock of the broken rifle. With a knife drawn to her throat, she was dragged into a nearby apple orchard, where she was raped. When they had finished, Marie escaped and ran to her neighbour, Madame Laisne. The soldiers disappeared, and Auguste Mace sought help from the 4th Special Service Company, which was bivouacked nearby. The victims were taken to the 101st Evacuation Hospital, stationed at St Sauveur, where Major Joseph D. Whalen did all he could for them. Auguste had severe wounds to his abdomen and died, in a great deal of pain, on 3 August. Xavier's arm had been broken in the attack and Marie had suffered a fractured skull as well as a sexual assault.

MP investigators, Captain Henry Rollman and Staff Sergeant John V. Nesfield, examined shell cases found in the vicinity of the Mace home bearing the marks 'EC-43'. It was discovered, after a check of about 1,500 troops in the vicinity, that the only unit using such a marking on its ammunition was the 1511th Engineer Water Supply Company. Parts of a broken carbine were also found in a garbage rubbish area near the unit's location, wrapped in a pair of OD trousers which were marked in indelible ink with the name 'Yancy'. On 3 August, Captain Rollman interviewed Private Waiters Yancy who admitted being at the farm on the night of the assault with Private Robert L. Skinner, but denied the attacks. Finally, as the interview progressed, Yancy was told a blood-covered field jacket had been found in his kit bag. The soldier admitted that both he and Skinner had carried out the attacks and the rape. Yancy, who hailed from Van Buren County, Arkansas, and Skinner, who came from Paris, Henry County, Tennessee, were tried separately on 7 November 1944 at Cherbourg, France. Yancy pleaded not guilty to the crimes, despite his earlier confession. A psychiatric report found he had an average mental age of 9 years and 8 months. However, this did not help the soldier, who admitted to having previously committed other sex crimes and had also been the subject of previous courts martial. His trial was suspended until Skinner's could take place. The following day, Skinner, described as having an arrogant and flippant attitude, appeared in court. He pleaded not guilty but refused to take to the witness stand. He was found guilty of rape and Yancy was found guilty of rape and murder. Both men were then sentenced to death. The sentences were approved by Colonel Eugene M. Caffey, the Normandy Base Section commander and confirmed by General Dwight D. Eisenhower on 23 December 1944. Skinner wrote to General Eisenhower claiming he did not meet with his defence counsel until the night before his trial and that the sex was consensual. He further alleged that the witnesses had lied in court and he was not guilty of rape. A subsequent investigation found no grounds for these claims and that Skinner was to suffer the same fate as Yancy.

The morning of 10 February 1945 was cold and rainy in the little village of Bricquebec, where engineers had erected temporary wooden gallows in an orchard named La Ferme des Galeries, off the Avenue Matignon. Here twenty-eight officials, witnesses and spectators were gathered as Private Waiters Yancy was led by three guards up the steps. Lieutenant Colonel Henry L. Peck, Commanding Officer of the Loire DTC, gave a silent signal and Master Sergeant John Clarence Woods sent the prisoner to his death. A short time afterwards, the small crowd watched as the process was repeated for Private Robert L. Skinner. The bodies of both men were transported to the US Military Cemetery at Marigny, where they were buried side by side. In 1949 they were both secretly removed and reinterred in Plot 'E' at the Oise-Aisne American Cemetery. Yancy in Row 2, Grave 31 and Skinner in Row 3, Grave 64.

Xavier Hèbert and Marie Osouf spent nearly six weeks in hospital recovering from their injuries but eventually returned home. Auguste Lebarillier was buried on 5 August 1944 in an isolated grave at Quettetot. Remember them.

Tuesday, 1 August 1944, France
Victim   Julia Herbaut, French civilian (white)
                Raped
Assailant   Private William Drew Pennyfeather (black)
                Age: 24
                Service No.: 32801627
                Unit: 3868th Quartermaster Truck Company

On the night of 1 August 1944, just as rape and murder had been committed in the village of Hameau au Pigeon, four black soldiers knocked at the street door of 1 Rue Emmanuel Liais, in Cherbourg, and called out, 'Is there any girls?', 'Is there any Boche?' Emile Lobbrecht opened the window of his apartment and was told by the soldiers to come downstairs. When the door was opened, they forced their way in. Also in the apartment was Georgette Lobbrecht, the sister of Emile, her fiancé, Roger Berton, and a friend, Marcel Chevereau. A knife was held against Berton's chest and one of the soldiers enquired, 'There are Germans here?' The three Frenchmen were ordered back into the apartment, followed by the soldiers, one of whom was Private William D. Pennyfeather. He searched the premises whilst two other soldiers remained by the door. His penis was hanging out of his trousers and Georgette Lobbrecht, who was sitting on the bed, became frightened. She went over to her fiancé and as she did so, Pennyfeather tried to catch hold of her, but his companions prevented him from doing so and took him out of the room. Julia Herbaut lived in the third-floor apartment and was laying on her bed when Pennyfeather burst in, with his penis still hanging out. Julia got up and ordered him to leave, but he refused and locked the door behind him. She managed to open it again and saw two other black soldiers on the stairs. She screamed for help and Chevereau and Berton ran to her apartment. They found Julia screaming and struggling with Pennyfeather whilst the two other soldiers looked on. The Frenchmen tried to stop the soldier from raping Julia, but his companions were armed with knives and looked on as Pennyfeather dragged Julia to her bed, threw her violently upon it, got on top of her and raised her clothing. She resisted with all her might and, finally, the soldier bit her on the left cheek, loosened her arm and told her, by making signs with his head, to perform oral sex. When she refused, he tried to bite her on her other cheek. She continually tried to get away from him but eventually became so weak she 'could do no more' and Pennyfeather raped her.

Two MPs, Corporal Donald L. Sharshel and Private Arthur J. Thomas, noticed two black soldiers standing in front of the house, attempting to hide behind two Frenchmen. They claimed they were waiting for their 'buddy' who was upstairs. The policemen ordered them to return to their barracks as it was after 11.00 p.m., the curfew hour, and then went to the apartment of Julia Herbaut, where they found Pennyfeather on top of Julia, on the bed. The soldier was, apparently, having intercourse and 'was really going to town'. The lady seemed to be putting up no resistance but was sighing or groaning. When the policemen forcibly removed Pennyfeather, he said, 'I'm getting myself some pussy.' Julia was adamant that this was not consensual and that she had been raped. In a later statement, Pennyfeather said, 'She struggled a bit, but I held her down and had intercourse with her.'

On 2 September 1944, Pennyfeather, who had been serving in the ETO since 7 October 1943, appeared at a GCM in Cherbourg, France. The soldier, born in New York on 21 July 1921, was a married man and a hardened criminal who had seen the inside of prison on more than one occasion, having been arrested for a variety of offences, including armed robbery. The evidence against him was strong, as he had been caught in the act of rape in the victim's apartment. The court wasted no time and he was found guilty and sentenced to death. Colonel Benjamin B. Talley, the Normandy Base Section commander, approved the sentence and General Dwight D. Eisenhower confirmed the death penalty on 4 October 1944. On the morning of 18 November 1944, in an area of flat ground behind buildings at Fort Du Roule, Cherbourg, Pennyfeather was hanged on a temporary gallows before a total of forty-eight officials and witnesses by Major Mortimer H. Christian. Just 15 minutes before, T/5 Richard Bunney Scott had been hanged for rape on the same gallows. Pennyfeather's body was initially buried in the US Military Cemetery at Marigny, France. In 1949, it was secretly removed from this location and transported to the Oise-Aisne American Cemetery and reburied in Plot 'E', Row 3, Grave 66.

Julia Herbaut may have witnessed her attacker's life come to an end that morning, but the terror of her ordeal was a constant companion for the rest of her days. Remember her.

Sunday, 6 August 1944, England
Victim   Agnes Cope, British civilian (white)
                Age: 74
                Raped
Assailant   Private Aniceto Martinez (white)
                Age: 22
                Service No.: 38168482
                Unit: Headquarters Detachment, Prisoner of War
                    Enclosure No. 2

Agnes Lilian Sammons was born on 15 March 1870, the daughter of John and Elizabeth Sammons of Longdon, Staffordshire, one of seven children. On 4 July 1889, she married Alfred Henry Cope, a railway employee, and the couple would have at least three children. For many years, the family lived in Sandy Lane, Rugeley, Staffordshire. Her husband passed away in 1943 and by summer 1944, Agnes was living alone, a frail, 74-year-old woman, in a small cottage surrounded by a 6ft hawthorn hedge. Close to her home was a prisoner of war camp, where German soldiers captured in the Normandy campaign

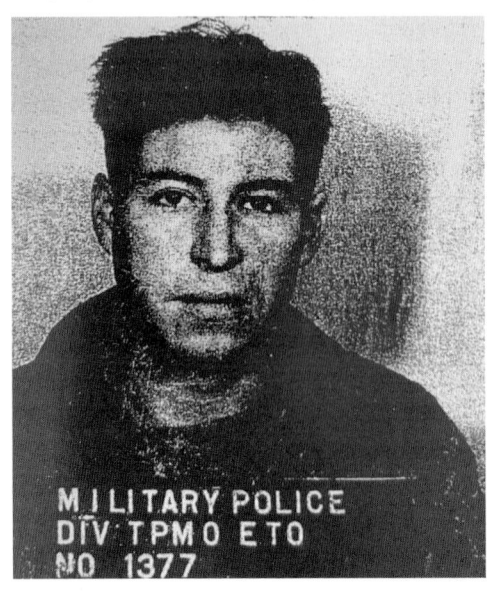

Private Aniceto Martinez, who raped 74-year-old Agnes Cope on 6 August 1944. (*JAG File*)

were sent. The local population had nothing to fear from the captives as the camp was guarded by members of the US Army.

At about 3.15 a.m. on 6 August 1944, Agnes Cope was woken from her sleep when she heard someone on the stairs of her home. Suddenly, a man appeared in the doorway. She said, 'Oh dear master, whatever do you want. If it is money you want, I haven't got it.' The man, whose speech sounded American, replied, 'I don't want money. You know what I want. It be a woman I want.' He was a big man, wearing khaki clothes and a hat with a black peak, but Agnes could not see his face. After placing his hat on her bed and moving her to one side, he lifted her nightdress and raped her. She did not consent to his actions, and resisted him as best she could, but he struck her in the face with his fist. After he left, she made her way to the police station and reported the incident. The police surgeon, Dr L.D. Roberts, examined the elderly woman, and found she had sustained a sprained thumb and minor bruises on her face and neck, and showed injuries consistent with recent intercourse. Both the civil and military police now focused their enquiries on the nearby prisoner of war camp. On the night of the attack a bed check had been carried out and the only soldier missing was Private Aniceto Martinez, a 22-year-old from Vallecitos, Rio Arriba County, New Mexico, who had been inducted into the US Army on 19 October 1942. Upon further investigation, an enlisted man's service cap was found, which Martinez admitted he had borrowed from a friend and worn the previous night. A thorn sticking in the cap was like the ones on the bushes that surrounded Agnes Cope's home, and blue fibres adhering to it were like those found on a quilt on her bed. Fibres were also found on the soldier's shirt and trousers that corresponded with those from Agnes's nightdress. The following day Martinez was interviewed by Special Agent Harold F. Ford, from the Criminal Investigations Division, and claimed that on the night of the assault he had visited two or three pubs in the area, where he had quite a few beers. He was feeling 'high' but not drunk. After the pubs closed at 10.00 p.m. he had walked around for a while and finally came to a group of houses, where on two previous occasions he had talked to a lady in one of the houses. He later entered a house that he believed was a place of 'ill repute'. Martinez claimed that when he told a lady on the premises what he wanted, she said, 'Let's get it over so you can go back home.' He placed his peaked hat on the bed, sat down and pulled her down beside him. He was on top of her only for a second and could not recall hitting her. He continued by claiming, 'It wasn't any good', so he got up, grabbed his hat and went out of the back, jumped over the hedge onto the road and proceeded back to camp. At the conclusion of the investigation, all the interview notes and relating material were sent to the Theatre Provost Marshal in London via train. The case file was lost during the journey and was never recovered, forcing the authorities to repeat the investigation. As a result, a GCM could not take place until 21 February 1945, which was held at Wittington Barracks in Lichfield, Staffordshire. Martinez pleaded not guilty to the crime, but the evidence was overwhelming, so the Mexican was soon found guilty and sentenced to death by hanging. The sentence was approved by Brigadier General Harry B. Vaughan Jr, the commander of the UK Base Section, and confirmed by General Dwight D. Eisenhower on 15 April 1945.

At 10.20 p.m. on 15 June 1945, Martinez was marched into the execution room at Shepton Mallet Prison, where he was met by Major Philip J. Flynn and a group of nine witnesses. Also waiting in the room, now crammed with people, were Thomas and Albert Pierrepoint. The soldier was quickly prepared by the executioners as he spent the last agonising moments of his life waiting for the trapdoor to open. A silent signal by Major Flynn sent him hurtling downwards, the last man to be hanged for the crime of rape in the UK. His body was first buried in Brookwood American Military Cemetery, Surrey. In 1948, the army transferred the remains to the American Military Cemetery at Cambridge. A year later they were secretly removed and reinterred in the Oise-Aisne American Cemetery, Plot 'E', Row 2, Grave 39.

Agnes Cope passed away in 1952 at the age of 82, and one can only hope that her last thoughts did not include those of that terrible night in August 1944. Remember her.

Tuesday, 8 August 1944, France
Victim	Marie Josef Gourdin, French civilian (white)
	Age: 33
	Raped
Assailants	Private Joseph Watson (black)
	Age: 26
	Service No.: 39610125
	T/5 Willie Wimberly (black)
	Age: 32
	Service No.: 36392154
	Unit: 257th Signal Construction Company

The capture of the naval bases at Lorient, St Nazaire and Brest was vitally important for the invading Allies, in order that they could land the vast number of supplies required as their armies advanced across France. American forces, under the command of Lieutenant General George S. Patton, were tasked with capturing these crucial objectives, as well as liberating the people of the region.

Amongst those waiting patiently for the arrival of friendly troops were 66-year-old Pierre Gourdin and his 33-year-old, unmarried daughter, Marie, whose home was in the tiny commune of Le Pas en Ferre. At about 8.00 p.m. on 8 August 1944, two Americans arrived in the form of Private Joseph Watson and T/5 Willie Wimberly Jr, both of whom were serving with the 257th Signal Construction Company. But the liberators were not thinking about ridding the civilian population of Nazi tyranny, they had other things on their mind.

Marie had poor eyesight and wore glasses, but she could see that one of them, Watson, was large in stature, whilst Wimberley was much smaller. The two black soldiers understood no French, but made it known they wanted some apple cider. They were told to return the next day, but became insistent, so were given a litre of the alcohol. They then left, but Pierre was nervous about their intentions, and so he barricaded the farmhouse door and went upstairs to his bedroom. Marie remained downstairs where she usually slept. About 5 minutes later the soldiers returned, shook the door, broke a windowpane and then forced open the door which was nailed shut with a plank of wood. Terrified, Marie called for her father's help. He came downstairs and reproached Wimberly about the broken window but the soldier struck the old man on the back of the head with the butt of his Thompson submachine gun, causing a gaping wound from which blood flowed down his neck. Watson then seized Marie by the shoulders and pushed her into a chair. Oddly, the two soldiers then departed, and the shaken civilians opted to sleep on the upper floor. At midnight, the two soldiers again returned, stormed up the steps and began firing their submachine guns through the door, one bullet fracturing Marie's left tibia and another entering Pierre's right foot. In a panic, he began crying out asking what they wanted. Marie, who could only drag herself across the bedroom floor, managed to reach the foot of the bed. The soldiers burst into the darkened bedroom, Watson grabbed hold of Pierre and Wimberley approached Marie. The old man broke free and hobbled quickly down the steps and rushed for help. Marie, who was somewhat ignorant about sexual matters, cried out for help but one of the soldiers put his hand over her mouth, whilst the other held a gun to her chest. She was left alone with the assailants who, grabbing her by her injured leg, began a vicious rape upon her slight body, an ordeal that lasted for more than an hour. When the torment was over, Wimberly had enough presence of mind to leave the scene of the crime, but Watson fell asleep on the blood-stained bed. Marie took the opportunity to slip out of the room and then made her way to the house of a neighbour, Alexandre Henry, who lived almost a kilometre away. She made the entire escape and subsequent journey by dragging herself along on her elbows.

In the meantime, Pierre, his head and foot bleeding, had managed to make contact with the Americans, being brought before Colonel Thomas A. Nixon, of the Ordnance Department, Third US Army. Nixon led a group of officers and MPs to the farmhouse, where he found a US helmet liner on the steps marked 'W2154', the initial and four digits identifying the owner as Wimberley. On climbing the stairs, he found Watson, still asleep on the bed, and a second helmet liner on the floor, surrounded by two-dozen expended cartridges. He grabbed the soldier, jammed the helmet liner on his head and ushered him out of the room. Over the next few hours, MPs interviewed Watson on three occasions. Each time he changed his story. At first he claimed he had been sent to the house by a sergeant to investigate a shooting. Then he claimed he had been at the house with one or two other soldiers. Finally, he stated he had never been in the house at all. However, the evidence was too strong and linked both men to the scene of the crime. Wimberly, who had now been arrested, attempted to blame Watson for the assault, claiming he was only trying to get back to the company.

On 17 August 1944, the soldiers were brought before a GCM at St Sabine. It was clearly established that Marie had been raped by one or both of them. Despite her poor eyesight, she knew that the two men who broke into the bedroom were the same soldiers who had visited the house earlier in the evening. She saw their faces during their first visit and, although it was dark in the bedroom, she knew they were the same two because of their speech, clothes and their inability to speak French. The GCM took no time in finding the pair guilty and sentencing them both to death. Following the approval and review stages, their death sentences were confirmed by General Dwight D. Eisenhower on 23 September 1944. They were both transported to the Seine DTC in Paris where, on 9 November 1944, before a small group of officials and witnesses, they were individually hanged by Major Mortimer H. Christian, assisted by Master Sergeant John Clarence Woods. Wimberly was executed first and, having dropped through the trapdoor, took a full 15 minutes before he choked to death. Watson, however, died quickly and was pronounced dead just a few minutes after the trapdoor was sprung. Following their execution, the bodies of both men were buried at the Solers American Military Cemetery, France. In 1949, they were secretly removed from their resting place and reinterred in Plot 'E' in the Oise-Aisne American Cemetery. Private Joseph Watson is buried in Row 1, Grave 17. Private Willie Wimberly Jr is buried in Row 2, Grave 34.

Some days after their execution, Lieutenant General George S. Patton ordered that a letter be sent to the rape victim. The dispatch ended with the following paragraph: 'The Commanding General wishes to express his sincere regret that the unfortunate incident occurred and that a member of the United States forces was guilty of such disgraceful conduct.' These words were, no doubt, expressed with genuine compassion for Marie but it is unlikely the events of that terrible night ever left her thoughts. Remember her.

Thursday, 10 August 1944, France

Victim	Aimée Hellondais Honore, French civilian (white)
	Age: 37
	Raped
Assailant	Private Charles H. Jordan (black)
	Age: 24
	Service No.: 14066430
	Unit: 3327th Quartermaster Truck Company
	Private Arthur Eddie Davis (black)
	Age: 25
	Service No.: 36788637
	Unit: 3326th Quartermaster Truck Company

The crime against Aimée Hellondais Honore, the 37-year-old wife of Amand Honore, is one that would be repeated time and time again by members of the US forces, particularly throughout the early months of the liberation of Europe. She lived with her husband and two children, a daughter, also named Aimée, aged 19, and a son Henri, aged 17, on a farm near the village of La Rouennerie en Montour, France.

At about 6.30 p.m. on the evening of 10 August 1944, two black US soldiers arrived at the farm and asked for cognac. Aimée sent her daughter into the house and told the soldiers there was no cognac to be had. They left after one of them had showed her a rabbit he had in his shirt, but the two men returned at about 8.30 p.m. that evening. Her husband was present and her daughter was in bed. This time the soldiers repeatedly asked 'for cognac and for young unmarried women'. When they were told there were none, they began to fire a rifle over Amand's head. When they repeated the shot, Aimée gave them some cognac, hoping it would make them leave. One of the soldiers then seized her arm, whilst the other held her husband, and she was forced to lie down in a haystack. Amand managed to escape and soon returned with Joseph Taburel, a neighbour from an adjoining farm. One of the soldiers pointed his carbine at Aimée's back, and the other fired his rifle directly at the two men, both of whom ran to call the police. The soldiers then took her to a nearby field, forced her to lie down and, despite her resistance, each man raped her multiple times. When she attempted to resist, they placed their rifles against her forehead, each taking turns holding the gun over her. During her ordeal, the magazine fell out of a carbine and could not be found. The assailants then threw Aimée's shoes away and left her alone, having been in the field with her for at least 2 hours. In the meantime, Amand Honore had contacted the US Army, and members of the MP found the two soldiers a short distance from the farm. Aimée was able to identify her attackers, as one of them was wearing two unusual bracelets, this was Private Arthur Eddie Davis. He wore a bracelet bearing his name and a second one made of English copper farthings. The next morning, Aimée had to endure an examination by a US medical officer, who confirmed that she had recently had sexual intercourse. The two soldiers were identified by Amand Honore, Joseph Taburel and another witness, Marcel Berthelot. Her son found the missing rifle magazine in the field where the rape had taken place and later testified that his mother had returned home at about 11.00 p.m., alone, barefoot and crying. First Lieutenant Edward C. Heyue, 503rd Military Police Battalion, interviewed Davis on 12 August, and he admitted going with Private Charles H. Jordan to seven or eight farmhouses in the area, looking for cider and cognac, and to a small town. On their way back to camp they had bought a rabbit from a boy. Jordan was then questioned and, at first, his story was like that of Davis, but then he became confused and told a different story, denying they had been to any town.

As soon as he was made aware of the case, Lieutenant General immediately ordered a GCM to take place. On 16 August 1944, both men were tried simultaneously at Poilley, and both chose to remain silent throughout the proceedings. Private Charles H. Jordan, born on 9 October 1920 in Monticello, Georgia, was a married man with three children and worked as a truck driver. He had enlisted in the US Army on 6 January 1942 at Fort McPherson, Georgia, and had an overall poor service record. Private Arthur Eddie Davis, born on 8 August 1919 in Cleveland, Ohio, was also a truck driver who was separated from his wife and child and inducted into the US Army on 8 November 1943, in Chicago, Illinois. Given the brutality of their assault, there was little room for sympathy. Both soldiers were found guilty of the rape, although not of attempted murder, and were sentenced to death. The sentences were reviewed and approved by Brigadier General Edward Chambers Betts, and confirmed by General Dwight D. Eisenhower. On 22 November 1944, Jordan and Davis, who had been transported back to the area where they had committed their crime, were hanged, one after the other, on a temporary gallows near the village church at Montour, Ille-et-Vilaine, before a total of thirty-nine officials, witnesses and spectators. Their bodies were then taken to the US Military Cemetery at Marigny for burial. In 1949, the were secretly removed from this location and taken to the Oise-Aisne American Cemetery and reburied in Plot 'E'. Private Charles H. Jordan is buried in Row 2, Grave 40. Private Arthur Eddie Davis is buried in Row 4, Grave 82.

For Aimée, as with so many other rape victims during the Normandy campaign, it is unlikely the events of that terrible night ever left her thoughts. Remember her.

Saturday, 12 August 1944, France

Victim	First Sergeant Loyce M. Robertson (white)
	Age: 26
	Service No.: 32102530
	Murdered
Assailant	PFC Paul Mauritz Kluxdal (white)
	Age: 37
	Service No.: 36395076
	Unit: Headquarters Battery, 200th Field Artillery Battalion, V Corps

(My deepest thanks to Sandford Chandler and Jill Boatwright for their assistance with this story)

'Getting even' with an NCO is something that many soldiers thought about during their service, particularly when older men found themselves taking orders from a much younger man. In most cases, it came to nothing, but in a few, the animosity would eventually lead to murder.

Loyce M. Robertson was born on 22 August 1917, the son of William Francis Robertson and Willie Mary Edwards, one of nine children. The family were farmers, living in Gadsden, Alabama, a small community balanced on the edge of the Coosa River. Raised at a time when the

Left: First Sergeant Loyce M. Robertson. (*Source: Sandford Chandler and Jill Boatwright*)

Below: First Sergeant Loyce M. Robertson posing with his football team after a practice session at Glencoe High School, 1936. He is seen on the front row, far right. (*Source: Sandford Chandler and Jill Boatwright*)

nation was in the midst of a sustained economic recession that shaped the lives of many Alabamians, he attended the Glencoe High School, where he was on the football team. By 1940, his family were living in Hokes Bluff, and it was from here he left to join the US Army on 9 April 1941. Loyce soon found himself promoted through the ranks, and by the time his unit hit the beaches of Normandy on D-Day + 2, he was a First Sergeant serving with the 200th Field Artillery Battalion.

One of the men he was responsible for was PFC Paul Mauritz Kluxdal. Born on 17 July 1907, in Merrill, Lincoln County, Wisconsin, he was the son of John Anton Kluxdal and Ingeborg Anderson. An educated man, he had attended the University of Wisconsin, had seen service with the Wisconsin National Guard between 1924 and 1927, worked as a construction foreman building commercial chimneys and, by 1939 was working and living in Chicago, Illinois. It was here that he was inducted into the US Army on 17 March 1942. In July of that year, Kluxdal wrote to the staff of the *Charlotte News*, thanking them for a donation of over 1,800 books, which had been donated to the library at Camp Sutton, North Carolina, where he was acting as the librarian for the 73rd Field Artillery Brigade. By the time his unit arrived in France, he was 37 years old, and well above the average age for a combat soldier. A man used to giving orders, it seems he not only had some difficulties with authority, but he also had a chronic drinking problem, one that had got him into trouble in the past, and which brought him into conflict with First Sergeant 'Robbie' Robertson. Described as a man with a volatile nature, Kluxdal could be argumentative and had been involved in a number of fights with other members of the

PFC Paul Mauritz Kluxdal who murdered First Sergeant Loyce M. Robertson on 12 August 1944. His execution at the hands of Staff Sergeant John C. Woods went horribly wrong and Kluxdal died by strangulation.

battery. On several occasions, usually under the influence of drink, he is known to have told his comrades that some day he would get even with the First Sergeant.

On 12 August 1944, as General Bradley ordered Patton's Third Army to stop at Argentan, giving the German armies in the Falaise Pocket a chance to escape encirclement, Kluxdal, a radio operator, was riding in a truck with a group of soldiers, including Staff Sergeant Leroy Reber and First Sergeant Robertson. Apparently smelling of alcohol, he slapped Reber on the head a few times and attempted to get into conversation with Sergeant Robertson, but it seems that the sergeant had no desire to converse with him. On arrival at their bivouac position near Vire, Robertson ordered his men to dig foxholes to help give them protection in the event of enemy attack. As it began to get dark, Kluxdal, who was still in the process of digging a foxhole, was found to have a bottle of alcohol with him. Robertson ordered him to surrender it, advising him that he could not have it back until the job was done and only if the battery commander, Captain Horace L. Hall, gave permission.

By 10.30 p.m., the bivouac area was in darkness, and Captain Hall was in conversation with Sergeant Robertson. Kluxdal, who had finished his foxhole, asked another NCO, Sergeant James E. Jones, to get his bottle of alcohol back from Robertson, but Jones refused, saying 'It's best for you not to have the bottle, you have a job to do.' Kluxdal, not satisfied with this, picked up his carbine and opted to approach Robertson himself. Several witnesses then saw the two men standing face to face, about 2yd apart, and heard Kluxdal making threats, then a shot rang out. Several men rushed to the scene, disarmed Kluxdal and attempted to save the life of Sergeant Robertson, but it was too late. He had taken a bullet to the chest at point-blank range. Captain George W. Marsh, Medical Officer, went to the scene and examined Robertson, who was bleeding from a wound in front of his heart. Robertson took six final breaths, then ceased. Marsh then pronounced him dead. Following his arrest, Kluxdal made a written statement claiming he did not know the weapon was loaded and that he had been talking to Robertson and, as he started to turn away, he 'sort of stumbled' and as he began to fall the carbine accidentally went off.

A GCM took place on 4 September 1944 at Moussy-le-Vieux, France. Kluxdal pleaded not guilty and maintained his stance that the whole thing was an unfortunate accident. A battalion standing order, issued prior to 12 August and in effect at the time of trial, was produced that stated, 'No cartridge would be carried in the chamber of any weapon.' His battery commander, Major Charles D. Stoops, submitted an evaluation of Kluxdal saying, 'Because of his lack of control when drinking intoxicating beverages, his suitability for military duties is limited. His standing in the Army is satisfactory, and unsatisfactory, depending on his sobriety.' Kluxdal was found guilty of murder and sentenced to death. On 31 October 1944, Private Paul Mauritz Kluxdal was escorted into the death chamber in the Seine DTC, Paris. The executioner's assistant, Master Sergeant John Clarence Woods, placed a black hood over the prisoner's head and slipped a noose around his neck. Major Mortimer H. Christian, the executioner and officer in charge, cut the rope and Kluxdal hurtled through the trapdoor, but disaster struck. The condemned man's feet struck the floor before the rope was fully taut, and he began to choke to death. Standing at 6ft tall, it seems his height had not been sufficiently allowed for during the execution preparations, a significant error by Woods, and one that would be repeated on more than one occasion. It would be a full 18 minutes before the doctor, Captain Edward M. Sullivan, would pronounce Kluxdal dead. He was buried in the US Military Cemetery at Solers, France, and in 1949 his body was secretly removed from that location and reinterred in Plot 'E' at the Oise-Aisne American Cemetery, France, buried in Row 2, Grave 35.

On 23 January 1948, under the Return of the Dead Program, the body of First Sergeant Loyce M. Robertson arrived at the Brooklyn Army Base aboard the US Transport *Corporal Eric G. Gibson*, along with twenty-eight other Alabamians. It would be several weeks before the army could make arrangements to return him to his loved ones. but eventually he was buried in the Union #3 Baptist Church Cemetery, Ballplay, Etowah County, Alabama, USA. Remember him.

Tuesday, 15 August 1944, France
Victim	Lucy Collomp, French civilian (white)
	Age: 22
	Raped
Assailants	Private Curtis L. Maxey (black)
	Age: 22
	Service No.: 34554198
	Private L.B. Hollingsworth (black)
	Age: 25
	Service No.: 34429655
	Unit: 3277th Quartermaster Service Company, Seventh Army

On the morning of 15 August 1944, the 3277th Quartermaster Service Company, part of the US Seventh Army, landed at 'Yellow Beach' in the vicinity of Saint-Tropez, on the southern coast of France, as part of Operation Dragoon. The assault, which had originally been planned to coincide with Operation Overlord, the Allied landing in Normandy, was designed to secure the vital ports on the French Mediterranean coast and increase pressure on the German forces by opening another front.

At about 5.00 p.m. that day, two black soldiers appeared at the home of Cesar Collomp, a farmer living about 2km from Saint-Tropez. They asked for wine, which Collomp gave them, and after about 10 minutes they began to leave. As they did so the farmer's wife, 22-year-old Lucy Collomp, appeared. One of soldiers asked her, 'Are you madame or mademoiselle?' The question may not have been understood due to the language difficulties, and no more was said. Later the same evening, the two soldiers returned to the farmhouse, knocked noisily on the door and fired their rifles. Cesar Collomp, wakened by the sound, opened the bedroom window and asked who was there, 'Americans' was the response. The farmer opened the door to the two soldiers who said, *'Tedeschi'*, which is Italian for Germans. Apart from the Collomps, and their infant son, the house was also occupied by a lady named Madame Niel. The soldiers began to search the house on the pretence of looking for Germans, but this was not their true mission. One of the soldiers grabbed Lucy Collomp by the arm and dragged her outside. She screamed and her husband tried to intervene but was struck on the shoulder with the butt of a rifle. Whilst one soldier kept his rifle pointing at the husband, another raped Lucy. She then got up and ran back into the house, where her husband closed and bolted the door and carried her upstairs. The two soldiers remained outside for 30 minutes, firing their weapons. They left at about 11.00 p.m. and made their way to a small chateau about 300yd away, owned by Michel Nehme, and entered asking for wine. When they saw the owner's young daughter, one of them said, 'Sleep, sleep.' Thinking this meant they wanted a place to rest, Nehme led them to a small house adjacent to the chateau, where other US soldiers were sleeping. As dawn broke, the two men returned to their unit, arriving at about 8.30 a.m.

The farmer reported the incidents to authorities, and it was soon established that two soldiers, Private Curtis L. Maxey and Private L.B. Hollingsworth, had been missing from their company during the time the crimes were committed. First Lieutenant Lewis Burnstein, 504th Military Police Battalion, was appointed as the investigator and interrogated Hollingsworth, who admitted that he and another soldier had been at both locations on the night in question. On 20 August, Burnstein organised an identification parade containing six men from their unit, all wearing a helmet or helmet liner. Hollingsworth was immediately picked out by the Collomps. They stated that Maxey had worn unusual gold rings on his fingers, and these were found on the soldier. Additionally, Maxey had shown them some photographs of his family, a white woman who he claimed was his wife and a black child. Burnstein found the photographs in Maxey's wallet and Lucy Collomp identified them.

The soldiers were brought before a joint GCM in Saint-Tropez, on 4 September 1944, when they both pleaded not guilty to the charge brought against them. Maxey opted to stay silent and did not take the stand. Hollingsworth, however, testified that he tried to stop Maxey, but he had cut him by hitting him with his rifle. He also claimed that Maxey had an MP insignia on him during the night in question and was trying to pretend that he was an MP. Private George Boston, of 4133rd Quartermaster Company, confirmed the soldiers were the same men who had slept at the home of Michel Nehme. Hollingsworth was sentenced to a dishonourable discharge, forfeiture of all pay and allowances due or to become due and confinement at hard labour for the term of his natural life, three-fourths of the members of the court present concurring. The reviewing authority approved the sentence, and designated the United States Penitentiary, Lewisburg, Pennsylvania, as the place of confinement. Maxey, born in Deatsville, Elmore County, Alabama, on 16 June 1922, and inducted into the US Army in Fort Benning, Georgia, on 9 November 1942, was sentenced to death. All members of the court present concurred in the findings and in the sentence. These were approved by Lieutenant General Alexander M. Patch, Commanding Officer of the US Seventh Army, and confirmed by Lieutenant General Jacob Loucks Devers on 17 October 1944. Private Curtis L. Maxey was hanged at the Peninsular Base Section, Stockade No. 1, Aversa, Italy, by an unknown executioner, on 18 November 1944. Initially he was buried in the US Military Cemetery in Naples and in 1949, his body was removed and secretly transported to the Oise-Aisne American Cemetery, France, and buried in Plot 'E', Row 3, Grave 71.

The facts of the case were all too familiar, armed soldiers, away from their company, often fuelled by alcohol, were able to act in any way they chose, often terrifying innocent civilians who had welcomed them as liberators. Rape victims, often severely traumatised by what had happened to them, were required to testify before a military court and were often subjected to an interrogation by the defending officer who would ask, 'Why didn't you resist?' Perhaps, on this occasion,

Lucy Collomp provided a response that spoke for many such victims, particularly those who could not bring themselves to report the crimes against them. 'At the time I thought if I ran away or yelled, he was going to kill me. I wanted to live for my baby and husband. I was scared, I didn't know what I was doing, I was shaking with fright. When he pushed my shoulder, I laid down. I was so scared; I didn't want to resist.' Remember them.

Sunday, 20 August 1944, France
Victim   Eugene Tournellec, French civilian (white)
                   Age: 47
                   Murdered
Assailant   Private William Mack (black)
                   Age: 34
                   Service No.: 32620461
                   Unit: Battery 'A', 578th Field Artillery Regiment, US Third Army

In summer 1944, the US Third Army attempted to capture the port of Brest, reaching the formidable outer defensive lines on 7 August. Unable to penetrate the German fortifications, the next two weeks passed slowly as US forces encircled the city, and the Germans further improved their defences. The 578th Field Artillery Regiment, one of the earliest activated African American artillery units of the war, was stationed about 500yd from a three-storey farmhouse in the village of Pentreff, Le Drennec, about 12 miles north of Brest. This was the home of the Tournellec family, consisting of 47-year-old Eugene Tournellec, his wife, Louise, and their six children, Catherine, aged 16, Pierre, aged 15, François, aged 13, Michael, aged 10, Jeanne, aged 9, and Agnes, who was just 4 months old. The bedrooms in the farmhouse were on different floors and there was no electricity in the property.

On 20 August, Private William Mack, a cook, was seen drinking cognac. At about 8.00 p.m., he was in the mess tent when he announced to the kitchen personnel, 'I'm going out and get me a piece of tail, and I don't want any of you to try to stop me or follow me.' The mess sergeant reminded him of the fact that no one was allowed to leave the area and ordered him not to go out. Mack said, 'he was going anyway' and that 'he was grown, and no one could tell him anything'. He then left, walking across the field towards the farmhouse, carrying his M-1 carbine. By 11.00 p.m. it was very dark, and the family had retired for the night. Pierre, who slept in the attic, was woken by a knock on the front door. His father told him to get up, and Pierre took his flashlight and descended from the attic to the corridor which led to the front door. Before he had reached the bottom of the stairs he saw a large-built, black, US soldier, who lit a match. Pierre shone his flashlight on the intruder, who said, '*Pas Boche, pas Boche*', and grabbed the flashlight from the boy. The soldier began to search the house, eventually returning to the ground-floor kitchen, where he asked for wine, cognac and cider. By now, the whole household had been woken by the sound of his voice and had dressed themselves and gathered in the corridor leading to the front door. The soldier again demanded wine, cognac and cider, and became angry when he was told there was none to be had. He pointed his carbine and shouted, 'Boom, boom', frightening the parents, who then climbed out of a window in a bid to escape, and causing the children to burst into tears. Mack, by this time, had made several unsuccessful attempts to kiss 16-year-old Catherine, who tried to persuade him to leave. Things now began to turn ugly. Eugene Tournellec came to the entrance of the front door and told the soldier he was going to lock him in the house and fetch help. As he did so, Mack dropped the flashlight, raised his carbine and fired at the door. Opening it, he went outside and fired several more shots. The children managed either to escape or hide and, eventually, Catherine was left alone in the house with baby Agnes. William Mack then attempted to rape Catherine, tearing at her clothes and groping her breasts. However, under her dress and night clothes she was wearing a swimsuit that Mack was not able to remove, despite his best efforts. Catherine fought bravely, eventually passing out but when she regained consciousness, Mack was attempting to make her perform oral sex. Having also failed at this he left the house, telling the girl he would return the next day. Catherine was so terrified she could not bring herself to leave the house, even though she had seen her father outside. Eventually, she ran to a neighbour's house, where she remained for the rest of the night. In the meantime, 9-year-old Jeanne ran to the nearby 578th Field Artillery Regiment, screaming that the Germans were killing her parents. Second Lieutenant Alfred E. Kayes had heard shots and was aware that German patrols were in the area. He opted to wait until it began to got light before going to the farm. As soon as he could, Kayes made his way to the farmhouse with Lieutenant Colonel Gilbert C. Barnes, who was in command of the battalion. Here they found Eugene Tournellec dead, shot through the forehead. Close to the body, Kayes discovered four expended .30 calibre cartridge cases and one live round, which were then gathered up for examination. As a former ordnance man whose hobby was small arms, Kayes noticed that the mark caused by the impact of the firing pin was a little off centre, and there was a little defect on the base of the cases, caused by an imperfection on the face of the bullet. He was sure he would be able to find the weapon that fired the cartridges.

Private William Mack appeared before a GCM at Morlaix, Brittany, on 23 November 1944. The soldier, born on 21 September 1910 in Saint George, Dorchester County, South Carolina, and married with three children, pleaded not guilty to the charges against him, but opted not to take to the witness stand. An expert witness, ordnance officer Second Lieutenant Raymond A. Dortenzo, testified that he fired Mack's weapon the night prior to the trial and that the expended rounds appeared to him to be the same as those found at the scene of the crime. The defence counsel inferred that Mack had been drinking heavily on the night of the murder and was not responsible for his actions. The court did not accept this suggestion, and Mack was found guilty of the crimes and sentenced to death. Following approval and review, the sentence was confirmed by General Dwight D. Eisenhower and, on 15 February 1945, Mack was transported to a small sports field in the village of Plabennec, about 2 miles from where he had committed his crime. Here, on a bright sunny day, he was escorted up the steps of a temporary gallows which had been erected by engineers. A total of forty-two officials, witnesses and spectators, including the victim's daughter and grandmother, watched as Master Sergeant John Clarence Woods placed the hood over Mack's head and secured the rope around his neck. Following a silent signal from Lieutenant Colonel Henry L. Peck, Mack dropped to his death. His body was taken to the US Military Cemetery at Marigny for burial. In 1949, it was secretly removed from this location and taken to the Oise-Aisne American Cemetery and reburied in Plot 'E', Row 3, Grave 63.

Eugene Tournellec, a simple farmer, who had been trying to protect his family from a drunken US soldier, left behind a wife and six children at a time when there was still great uncertainty as to the outcome of the battle that continued around them. Remember him.

Monday, 21 August 1944, France
Victims   Victor Bignon, French civilian (white)
                Murdered
                Noémie Bignon, French civilian (white)
                Attempted rape
Assailant   PFC James E. Hendricks (black)
                Age: 21
                Service No.: 33453189
                Unit: 3326th Quartermaster Truck Company

1944: AUGUST – SUMMER MADNESS

The day after Eugene Tournellec was murdered, a similar incident occurred just over 100 miles to the east, in the village of Plumaudan, Côtes du Nord. Here, in a one-room house, with nothing more than a cellar, lived Constint Bouton and his family, consisting of his wife, Marie-Louise, and their three sons, Raymond, Charles and René. Across the road from the Bouton home, lived Victor Bignon with his wife, Noémie, their daughter, Jeannine, aged 18, and a farm hand, Roger Robert, who was just 12½ years old. Both homes were without electricity, and the village remained under wartime conditions, so after sunset everywhere was in complete darkness.

At about 11.00 p.m. on 21 August, a black US soldier, wearing a raincoat, helmet, yellow shirt and carrying a rifle, opened the single front door to the Bouton home and, uninvited, entered the little room, asking for 'Madame' or 'Mademoiselle'. Receiving a negative response, he tried to kiss Madame Bouton, but was stopped by her husband and sons. To appease the soldier, one of the sons, Raymond, handed the invader two eggs, which he promptly placed in his raincoat and left the house. The soldier then crossed the road and banged loudly on the door of the Bignon home. The family were all asleep and were woken by a voice, demanding that the door be opened and repeatedly shouting, '*Ouvrir, ouvrir, Mademoiselle.*' When he was told that he could not come into the house, the soldier fired a shot through the door and began to pound on it with a rifle butt. Afraid of what might happen, Victor and Noémie Bignon got out of bed and leaned and pushed against the door. After 5 minutes, a second shot was fired, the bullet passing through the door and striking Victor in the head, spilling blood and brains across the floor of the little room, and killing him outright. The bullet also injured Noémie, causing her to step away from the door, allowing the soldier the opportunity to burst in. As he entered the property, he made a grab for Jeannine Bignon, but she managed to get away and, along with her injured mother and Roger Robert, they ran across the road to the home of the Bouton family pursued by the soldier. Whilst Jeannine hid in the cellar, the soldier encountered Charles Bouton and pointed his rifle at him, but although he managed to escape and conceal himself in a nearby field. Upon entering the house, where there were separate beds in three corners of the room, the soldier made the remaining occupants lay down at gunpoint. He then turned his attention to the wounded Noémie Bignon, forcing her to lay down and attempting to rape her, but despite her wound, she fought fiercely to keep him at bay and, eventually, he left the house without achieving his aim.

Lieutenant Donald F. Tucker, a black officer, commanding the 3326th Quartermaster Truck Company, bivouacked on the outskirts of the village, had been woken by the sound of shooting and screaming. Taking a detail of eight men, they made their way towards the darkened village, where the screams could still be heard. A noise came from an adjoining hedge and Lieutenant Tucker challenged twice but received no answer. A man then appeared, shots were fired and he took cover in the ditch. One of the corporals recognised him as PFC James E. Hendricks. They were now just 10yd from the Bouton house, and Lieutenant Tucker asked the soldier why he was out of camp. Hendricks claimed that he was 'on the water detail, and he had gone to take a leak, and the truck had gone off and left him, and he was trying to find his way back to camp'. Tucker knew this was false, so repeated his question. Hendricks then claimed that 'he was walking on the road with Privates Nichols and Earls, and he was endeavouring to get back to camp'. As the detail was about to leave, one of the soldiers looked in the door of the Bignon house and saw the body of a man, with a hole in the top of his head, and what appeared to be brains on the floor. Lieutenant Tucker inspected the M-1 rifle Hendricks was carrying and found it had recently been fired and only contained five rounds, whereas the orders of the day were that seven rounds should be held in the rifle. Hendricks was taken to MP headquarters in Dinan, where he was examined and searched. He was wearing a scruffy raincoat that appeared to be blood-stained on the left-hand side of the collar and lapel. There was also a round of ammunition and an egg in one of the pockets. At the Bignon house, Lieutenant Tucker, in conjunction with the French police, found two empty .30 calibre machine-gun cases close to the front door, which were later found to match those carried by Hendricks.

Colonel Cyrus H. Searcy, Chief of Staff for the US Eighth Corps, ordered a GCM, which took place on 6 September 1944 in the town of Morlaix, Finistère. Hendricks pleaded not guilty to the crimes, even though the evidence was overwhelming, and did not take to the witness stand. However, a key part of the hearing was the fact that the French witnesses could not positively identify Hendricks as the assailant. Despite this important fact, the court unanimously found Hendricks, born in Drewry, Vance County, North Carolina, on 29 April 1923, guilty of the crimes and sentenced him to death. Two of the court members wrote to Major General Troy H. Middleton asking for clemency, suggesting the sentence be commuted to imprisonment, but their plea was ignored and Middleton approved the sentence. General Dwight D. Eisenhower confirmed the death sentence on 27 October 1944.

Hendricks was transported back to the village where he had committed the crime and, on 24 November 1944, was taken to the Château La Vallée where a temporary gallows had been erected by engineers. A group of forty-three officials, witnesses and spectators gathered in the courtyard in the cold pouring rain and watched as he was led up the steps. After being asked if he had any last words, the guards, Sergeant Earl F. Mendenhall and Sergeant Richard A. Mosley, strapped his legs together and secured his hands. A hood was placed over his head and the rope secured around his neck. Following a silent signal from Major Mortimer H. Christian, Hendricks dropped to his death. His body was taken to the US Military Cemetery at Marigny for burial. In 1949, it was secretly removed from this location and taken to the Oise-Aisne American Cemetery and reburied in Plot 'E', Row 1, Grave 13.

Another innocent French civilian had perished at the hands of a US serviceman, for which the assailant paid the ultimate price. His name, although dishonoured, is recorded in many locations and is, in effect memorialised, unlike Victor Bignon who was snatched from his family, never to return. Remember him.

Tuesday, 22 August 1944, France

Victim	Germaine Marie Françoise Pouliquen, French civilian (white)
	Age: 23
	Murdered
Assailants	Private William E. Davis (black)
	Age: 29
	Service No.: 33541888
	Private J.C. Potts (black)
	Age: 19
	Service No.: 34759592
	Unit: 3121st Quartermaster Service Company, 563rd Quartermaster Battalion

In Locmenven, about 10 miles south of Pentreff, where Victor Bignon had been murdered the previous day, Germaine Marie Françoise Pouliquen (née Cornou) was at home with her daughter, Jacqueline, who was just 2½ years old. Germaine had been happily married to her husband, Jacques, aged 28, since November 1941. He was working on a nearby farm, owned by François Gestin. At about 5.00 p.m., four black soldiers visited the farm, where they helped the civilians with carrying hay and taking seeds into a barn loft and in return for this they were given cider to drink. The four men, who were later identified as PFC Leroy Bowles, Private Ira Isabelle, Private J.C. Potts and Private William E. Davis, then left the farm, apparently making their way back to camp. On the way they came to the Pouliquen house where they saw Germaine in the yard. Potts went and spoke to her and, it appears, attempted to bribe her into having sex with him in exchange for 'K' rations, but Germaine spoke no English and did not understand what he was talking about. She attempted to leave the house and was seen by her neighbour, Madame Roue, being threatened by one of the soldiers, who had a rifle pointed at her. Germaine cried out, 'They are about to kill me', and asked Madame Roue to fetch her husband. On hearing what was happening, Jacques, along with Ernest Keruzec, Louis Quiviger and Michel Gestin, ran to the house. Jacques found his wife lying across the bed, her legs hanging over the edge and her dress pulled up exposing the upper parts of her legs. Private Davis was standing between her legs, holding her left arm under her back as she tried to push him away with her right hand. Another soldier held her feet, whilst a third soldier held their daughter by the hand and a fourth soldier stood near the door. Crying out to be saved, Jacques pulled the soldier off his wife, and the second soldier released his hold on her feet. Davis then aimed a gun at Jacques, who fled from the house followed by his wife and daughter. As they ran towards their neighbour's house, shots rang out and two bullets struck the wall close to where Jacques was. He heard his wife scream, and on returning to the corner between the two houses, saw her lying on the ground, but she had not been shot at that time. Fearing for his life, Jacques jumped over a hedge into the road and ran towards the village crucifix. Just before he reached it, he heard two more shots, stopped and saw Davis aim his rifle at Germaine and fire. She fell into a nearby ditch, mortally wounded. Jacques went to her aid and, with the help of Michel Gestin, carried her to the home of Ernest Keruzec. She was in great pain, having been wounded in the abdomen, and told Jacques that she was 'done for'. Germaine was taken to a hospital in Morlaix, where an operation was performed, but she was beyond medical aid, so the incision was closed. She was taken to her mother's house in Guiclan, where she died on 23 August 1944.

On 28 August, Corporal Richard Booker, 511th Military Police Battalion, took three of the French witnesses, separately, to three different quartermaster companies in the vicinity of the crime. Each witness picked out Davis, Potts and Bowles as the men who had been helping with the farm work, and who had carried out the attempted rape and murder of

Germaine Pouliquen. Potts and Davis were arrested and brought before a GCM at Morlaix on 23 September 1944. Davis claimed that when Jacques entered the house, Potts ran out and he was left in a struggle with the angry husband. To scare him off, he had fired his rifle and did not mean to kill Germaine. This explanation was not accepted by the court, and Davis was found guilty of the crimes of murder and attempted rape, and sentenced to death. Potts was found guilty of attempted rape and sentenced to life imprisonment. Some efforts were made to have the death sentenced reduced to life imprisonment, but these were not successful. Following approval and review, the sentence was confirmed by General Dwight D. Eisenhower. Davis was transported back to the village where he had committed the crime and, on 27 December 1944, was taken to a field a few hundred yards from where he had murdered Germaine Pouliquen. Here, a temporary gallows had been erected by engineers. A group of nineteen officials, witnesses and spectators gathered and watched as he was led up the steps. After being asked if he had any last words, Master Sergeant John Clarence Woods placed a hood over his head and secured the rope around his neck. Following a silent signal from Lieutenant Colonel Henry L. Peck, Davis dropped through the trapdoor to his death. His body was taken to the US Military Cemetery at Marigny for burial. In 1949, it was secretly removed from this location and taken to the Oise-Aisne American Cemetery, where it was reburied in Plot 'E', Row 1, Grave 19.

Germaine Pouliquen, described as a wonderful mother and of good character, died in agony at the hands of a US serviceman who was seeking momentary pleasure. Jacques remarried in 1947. Jacqueline married Hervé Nicol in 1961, and passed away in July 2011, at last joining her mother. Remember them.

Tuesday, 22 August 1944, England
Victim   Betty Dorian Pearl Green, British civilian (white)
            Age: 15
            Raped and murdered
Assailants Corporal Ernest Lee Clark (white)
            Age: 24
            Service No.: 33212946
            Private Augustine Miranda Guerra (white)
            Age: 20
            Service No.: 38458023
            Unit: 306th Fighter Control Squadron, IX Air Defence
                Command

On the same day that 23-year-old Germaine Pouliquen would lose her life in France, an English teenager would perish at the hands of two US airmen. Betty Dorian Pearl Green was born on 1 April 1929, in Ashford, Kent, the daughter of William Ernest and Sylvia Alice Kate Green (née White), one of three children. Her father, a railway worker, had served in the British Army during the First World War and by summer 1944 the family was living in New Town Road, Willesborough, Kent. Betty had finished her education and, like so many teenagers, was working for a living. She was employed by Norman's Cycle Works at their factory in Beaver Road, Ashford, where small motorcycles were produced for the use of paratroopers. Described by her father as a 'vivacious girl, but a good girl', he feared she made friends too easily and had warned her about mixing too readily with strangers. On 22 August 1944, Betty had returned home from work at about 5.45 p.m. There was a fair in town, and she was looking forward to a trip there with her workmate, Peggy Blaskett. She left home an hour later, for the last time. The two girls, who had told their parents they were going to the cinema, went into town where they met two US soldiers, George Williams and one named Eddy, who spent the evening with Betty. The girls were followed by the two soldiers to a local park, but they became tired of their company and at about 9.45 p.m., they headed for home, whilst the soldiers returned to town. After going their separate ways near Peggy's home, Betty was spotted by Harry Champion, a railway worker who knew her, running towards her house and singing. He called out, 'Goodnight, Betty', to which she replied, 'Goodnight, Harry.' She was now just a few hundred yards from home and safety, but never arrived.

At about 7.15 a.m. the next morning, a railway worker walking along the embankment noticed something in the old cricket field, near the corner of New Town Road and Black Path. He called out to Arthur Tournay, who was closer to the scene, 'Look, there's a girl in that field.' Tournay went to take a look and saw that it was a dead body, which he did not touch. He contacted the police, and Superintendent Francis Herbert Smeed arrived within a few minutes. The police took photos of the body and the surrounding area. As they began to try and identify the body, they found a silver cross at her side, a brooch about 4ft away and a hair-slide about 24ft away. Dr Frederick J. Newall, a medical practitioner, made a preliminary examination of the body and felt she had been dead for 6 to 12 hours. He found that her skirt was lifted to the waist band, her knickers were raised up to her waist, the left seam being torn, and the crotch was torn away in front. The crotch region and adjacent private parts were exposed and bloodstained. Betty's father identified her at about 7.45 a.m. that morning and again at 3.15 p.m., confirming that she was wearing the cross, brooch and hair-slide when she left home. Dr Keith Simpson, the pathologist at Guy's Hospital, London, later examined Betty's body at the mortuary, where he found a single deep-seated bruise on the right side of her neck and four rounded or oval bruises on the left side, very much in keeping with the tight application of a right hand from in front. Her voice box was not fractured but some bruising was present behind it because of it being pressed against her spine, in keeping with asphyxia due to manual strangulation. There were many other bruises and scratches on her body and a vaginal swab showed evidence of semen. Several hairs from various locations on the body were recovered and sent to Dr Henry J. Wall of the Metropolitan Police Laboratory, Hendon, for analysis.

It appears that there were not too many US airmen in town that night, so the police decided to begin their investigation in Ashford, at the base of 306th Fighter Control Squadron, part of the Ninth Air Force Service Command. In a stroke of luck, William and Sylvia Green had taken an evening stroll on the night of Betty's death, and William had stopped off at the Smiths Arms for a drink. There, he saw a US airman who often frequented the pub, Private Augustine Miranda Guerra, and William identified him after accompanying the police to the squadron base. Another suspect had already been named as Corporal Ernest Lee Clark. Both men were arrested and samples of their hair taken. It was quickly established that the hairs found upon the body of Betty Green came from both Clark and Guerra. Initially, the army decided to try both men together, however the defence requested two separate trials. Both trials took place in Ashford, Kent, with Private Augustine Miranda Guerra appearing before a GCM on 22 September 1944. Born on 4 May 1924 in San Antonio, Bexar, Texas, he was the son of Demascio Guerra and Vicenta Miranda, one of at least twelve children. His past was littered with minor criminal offences, and he had been arrested for drunkenness, theft and vagrancy. Since joining the army on 5 April 1943, things had improved, and he was determined to be an efficient soldier of excellent character. The trial of Private Clark began on 6 October 1944, lasting three days. He was born on 10 August 1920 in Clifton Forge, Alleghany County, Virginia, the son of James William Clark and Euna Rosa Pollock, one of five children. His mother had died from tuberculosis when he was 11 years old, and his father passed away eighteen months later from acute heart failure. The family split up after this and he went to live with his aunt, Nora Clark, in Covington, West Virginia, where he later worked at the Naval Ordinance Plant in

South Charleston. On 17 September 1942, Clark enlisted in the army in Roanoke, Virginia, serving with the Army Air Corps and assigned to the 306th Fighter Control Squadron, based in Ashford, England. Both men faced three charges: the murder and rape of Betty Dorian Pearl Green and aiding the other soldier to commit rape. The evidence at both trials was, in the main, identical. According to their testimonies, they had both achieved a pass to leave camp that afternoon and headed into town, determined to enjoy themselves. They went to a movie, and from there to several pubs where they drank considerably, ending up at the Smith Arms. On leaving the pub they went through the Black Path and walked near the railroad bridge. They saw a girl approaching and Clark went over and asked where she was going. She told them 'home'. They talked for about 5 minutes, and he asked her to go for a walk. He put his arm around her and proceeded with her towards the gate of the cricket field. Clark then picked her up and carried her through the gate, with Guerra following. After Guerra covered her mouth with his hand, she struggled, trying to say something. Whilst this was happening, Clark carried her further onto the field and laid her down whilst she was still struggling. Guerra raised her dress and tore her knickers apart. She started to scream so Clark covered her mouth whilst Guerra raped her. After he had finished, they swapped places and whilst Clark was finishing, he suddenly felt her relax her resistance. Clark claimed he lifted her blouse and felt her heart beating, and believed she was simply unconscious. He also asserted that as they were leaving, he went back and checked on her again, and her heart was still beating, so he figured she had fainted and would be fine after a rest. Although there were some minor differences in detail that could be attributed to two drunken men trying to relate one event from their perspectives, their stories were remarkably similar. The courts wasted no time and both men were sentenced to death.

The sentences were approved and reviewed with General Dwight D. Eisenhower confirming the execution order. A Board of Review examined the court proceedings and determined that the GCM had been conducted appropriately and in accordance with US military law. At 1.00 a.m. on 8 January 1945, Major Herbert R. Laslett, the Commanding Officer of the 2912th DTC, stood in the cramped execution room at Shepton Mallet Prison before seventeen other witnesses. Both soldiers were led onto the gallows in what would be a double hanging. Thomas and Albert Pierrepoint prepared both men as quickly as they could for execution. A silent signal was given from Major Laslett and both men dropped through the trapdoors. Clark was pronounced dead 13 minutes

1944: AUGUST – SUMMER MADNESS

later, Guerra 2 minutes after that. Their bodies were initially buried in Brookwood American Military Cemetery, Surrey. In 1948 they were reburied in the American Military Cemetery in Cambridge and a year later they were removed from the ground for a second time and secretly transported to the Oise-Aisne American Cemetery, where they were buried in Plot 'E'. Corporal Ernest Lee Clark is buried in Row 3, Grave 68. Private Augustine Miranda Guerra is buried in Row 2, Grave 44.

The execution room at Shepton Mallet Prison. Corporal Ernest Lee Clark and Private Augustine Miranda Guerra were jointly hanged here for the murder of 15-year-old Betty Dorian Pearl Green on 22 August 1944. Fourteen other US servicemen were executed here during the Second World War. (*Paul Johnson*)

Betty Dorian Pearl Green, the vivacious teenager who was murdered for momentary pleasure, is buried in an unmarked grave in Willesborough, Kent. Remember her.

Wednesday, 23 August 1944, France
Victim			Adolphe Paul Drouin, French civilian (white)
			Age: 47
			Murdered
Assailant		Private Walter James Baldwin (black)
			Age: 22
			Service No.: 34020111
			Unit: 574th Ordnance Ammunition Company

Adolphe Drouin lived quietly with his wife, Louise, and their 21-year-old daughter, Yvette, in the hamlet of Rigauderie, near Beaufay, France, about 10 miles north-east of the city of Le Mans. On 23 August 1944, he left the house on his bicycle to inspect a turnip field and had only been gone for about 10 minutes when Louise and Yvette heard footsteps in their yard. They had the shutters to their home closed and, suddenly, a black soldier looked through the glass at the top of the bedroom door. Yvette watched as the soldier shook the bedroom door and then tried the shutters and cellar entrance. Eventually, he sat down on a garden bench and began to talk to himself and manipulate the bolt on his rifle. This lasted for over an hour, by which time her father had returned to the house, leaned his bicycle against the wall and opened the gate. Yvette watched as the soldier approached her father, then she heard them talking, and suddenly her father said, 'No, no!' There was a gun shot, and Yvette and Louise rushed out of the bedroom. When they reached the yard, they found Adolphe lying on the ground, with the soldier standing nearby holding his rifle. Adolphe called for help and Louise ran toward him, but the soldier shot her in the left thigh and she fell near to her husband. Yvette could now see the soldier, and realised he was an American because of his uniform. She ran around the house and across a field where she met a neighbour, Basile Evrard, who was running toward her home. When Evrard got to the yard, he found the wounded couple lying on the ground, and the soldier standing and holding his rifle in a horizontal position. Evrard attempted to help the victims, but the soldier pointed his rifle at him and said something he did not understand, so he was forced to withdraw and shelter at the end of a wall. A brief time later he saw that the soldier had gone and went to fetch Dr George Perimony. At 4.00 p.m. that afternoon,

Private Walter James Baldwin, who had been absent from his unit for five days, returned to his camp and informed an officer, First Lieutenant Russell Frank Flanders, 'I have just shot a Frenchman in the leg.' Flanders immediately dispatched T/5 Harold A. Cooley and Corporal William H. Morton to render first aid. They found Louise on the ground, begging for help, her leg bleeding badly. The medic applied a tourniquet but she passed out, not waking up until she found herself in hospital at La Blancheirdiere. Cooley treated Adolphe and observed a small hole above his abdomen and blood on his back and foot. Sadly, when they reached the 101st Evacuation Hospital at Le Mans, he was pronounced dead. Baldwin was taken into custody by the MP, seemingly not drunk, but very excitable and incoherent. In the coming days, he would provide investigators with a variety of explanations, some quite bizarre, as to where he had been for the five days of his absence and why he had shot the couple. Eventually, he claimed he fired at Adolphe in self-defence when he was attacked with a pitchfork.

Walter James Baldwin was brought before a GCM convened at the Palais de Justice, Le Mans, on 7 October 1944. He pleaded not guilty to the crime, maintaining his actions were self-defence. Baldwin was born on 8 October 1922 in Shellmound, Mississippi, the oldest of four children. His mother had left home when he was 3 and his father had died of a heart attack at the age of 49. He had worked as a truck driver and was inducted into the US Army on 10 March 1941, at Camp Shelby, Mississippi, and had no history of hereditary mental disorders. However, in October 1942, his superiors noted his mental deficiency and ordered a psychopathic evaluation. The report stated, 'It is my impression that this patient is constitutional psychopath with emotional instability and inadequate personality and should be discharged from the service under the provisions of Section Vill as he is too inadequate to ever become a soldier.' He was not discharged, but instead was posted to France with his unit. The soldier, who stood at 6ft 2in tall and weighed 210lb, had the mental age of 14 and had faced at least five other courts martials. The court wasted no time, finding him guilty of the charge and sentencing him to death by hanging. Following approval and review, the sentence was confirmed and Baldwin was transported back to Rigauderie, Beaufay, where, on 17 January 1945, he was taken to a snow-covered field on the farm of Adolphe Drouin, close to where he had murdered the Frenchman. Here, a temporary gallows had been erected by engineers and a group of fifty officials, witnesses and spectators gathered and watched as Baldwin was led up the steps. Master Sergeant John Clarence Woods placed a hood over his head and secured the rope around his neck. Following a silent signal from Lieutenant Colonel Henry L. Peck, who was commanding the proceedings, Baldwin dropped through the trapdoor to his death. His body was taken to the US Military Cemetery at Marigny for burial. In 1949, it was secretly removed from this location and taken to the Oise-Aisne American Cemetery, where it was reburied in Plot 'E', Row 2, Grave 43.

Adolphe Drouin, who was just trying to protect his family, lays in a cemetery close to his home. Remember him.

Wednesday, 23 August 1944
Victim   Madeleine Quellier, French civilian (white)
              Raped
Assailant   Private Tommie Davison (black)
              Age: 30
              Service No.: 34485174
              Unit: 427th Quartermaster Troop Transport Company

It seems almost inconceivable that, before the week was halfway through, US soldiers had murdered and raped four French civilians and an English teenager, but this was the reality and it was set to continue. Madeleine Quellier and her husband were living with her sister on her farm near the hamlet of Prise Guinment, Manche, France. Henri Duqueroux, his wife and their two children were also living at the property. None of the residents spoke any English, so communication with passing soldiers was made by gestures or the use of a phrase book that many troops had been issued with. On 23 August 1944, four black soldiers arrived at the property and asked Madeleine for cognac. She said they had none, so one of the soldiers, Private Tommie Davison, demanded a chicken. At this moment, the other residents, who had been working in the field, returned and one of them caught a chicken, but Davison refused it claiming he wanted a pullet. He began talking about 'zigzig' and making suggestive gestures, then asked Henri Duqueroux for a 'mademoiselle' and offered 500 francs in US invasion currency. The residents were frightened by Davison's demeanour and Duqueroux told the women and children to run and hide, but then the soldiers left. Madeleine, her husband and the Duqueroux family ran into the house, locked all the doors and went up to the second floor. The others who had been working in the field, ran across the road to a barn and hid in the hayloft. Davison then returned and circled the house, knocking on the back door, then breaking open the front entrance. Henri Duqueroux came downstairs with his 2-year-old daughter in his arms, Davison pointed his pistol at him, patted down his pockets and pushed him out the door. Henri then made his way to a nearby military camp to report the intrusion and, as he did so, he heard a shot fired. Madeleine, her husband and Duqueroux's 10-year-old son remained upstairs. Davison pushed the husband aside, kicked the boy, then took Madeleine by the arm and forced her downstairs. Her husband ran to the window and shouted for help, whilst she ran out of the house to an apple-crushing machine, where she saw another black soldier and begged for his help. Davison, grabbing Madeleine by the shoulder, forced her to accompany him down a path into a meadow some 60yd from the house. She called out for help many times, but Davison pressed his pistol against her cheek and breast, threw her to the ground and raped her, stifling her cries for help by covering her mouth with his hand. By this time Henri Duqueroux had notified Chief Warrant Officer Earl E. Lane Jr of the incident. He took the battalion surgeon with him to the farm, where Madeleine was given a shot to help calm her down. Lane then set up an identification parade and brought the French witnesses to the camp later that evening. As they began, Davison stepped out of the line with his hands in the pockets of his raincoat. Lane ordered him to show his hands, but he refused. Lane then asked him what he was holding and Davison replied, 'I have a gun', which he partially withdrew and pointed through his coat. A struggle then took place to remove the weapon from Davison's possession, during which he struck Lane on two separate occasions. He was later identified by Madeleine and Henri Duqueroux as their attacker.

Private Tommie Davison was brought before a GCM at Granville, France, on 9 December 1944, charged with rape and assault. He pleaded not guilty, but testimonies from the French witnesses and men in his company confirmed he was the soldier who had committed the crimes. Born on 10 August 1914 at West Point, Clay County, Mississippi, he was painted as a nasty individual who had been inducted into the US Army on 2 December 1942 at Camp Shelby, Mississippi. His unit had arrived in England in September 1943 and landed in Normandy on 10 June 1944. The court soon found him guilty of all charges and sentenced him to death. The sentence was approved by Brigadier General Henry S. Aurand and confirmed by Brigadier General R.B. Lord on behalf of General Dwight D. Eisenhower. Davison was transported back to Prise Guinment on 29 March 1945 and taken to a field surrounded by hedgerows, where a temporary gallows had been erected by engineers.

A group of twenty-five officials, witnesses and spectators gathered and watched as Davison was led up the steps. An executioner placed a hood over his head and secured the rope around his neck. Following a silent signal from Lieutenant Colonel Henry L. Peck, who was commanding the proceedings, Davison dropped through the trapdoor to his death. His body was taken to the US Military Cemetery at Marigny for burial. In 1949, it was secretly removed from this location and taken to the Oise-Aisne American Cemetery, where it was reburied in Plot 'E', Row 3, Grave 60.

Amongst the spectators that day was Henri Duqueroux, who Davison had shot with a German P-38 pistol he had picked up. Madeleine Quellier did not attend, but doubtless those terrifying moments in summer 1944 remained with her forever. Remember her.

Thursday, 24 August 1944, France
Victim   Julienne Fontaine, French civilian
                Murdered
Assailant   Private Willie Johnson (black)
                Age: 23
                Service No.: 38270465
                Unit: 3984th Quartermaster Truck Company

A US Army fuel truck similar to the one driven by Private Willie Johnson and which he used to crush Julienne Fontaine to death on 24 August 1944.

On the same day that Madeleine Quellier was raped, three French women, Therese Souillet, Julienne Fontaine and Julienne's daughter, Denise Fontaine, had decided to make the journey from the city of Rennes to their home in Antrain, a distance of some 25 miles, on foot. Shortly after they began walking, a US Army fuel truck came along, which they flagged down, and asked the driver, Private Willie Johnson, for a lift. He told them he was going in their direction and all three women squeezed into the tiny cab. As they neared Antrain, Johnson began repeatedly placing his hand on the knees of Therese Souillet and Denise Fontaine, but both women sought to reject these advances by brushing his hand aside. When they reached their destination, the women asked Johnson to stop in order that they could get out, but he ignored their requests and continued. All three women began to scream and Therese Souillet attempted, unsuccessfully, to bring the vehicle to a stop by taking hold of the steering wheel. About a mile past the small town, Johnson stopped the truck, grasping Therese Souillet's arm as he did so. Denise Fontaine jumped out and her mother also tried to escape, but paused on the running board to search for a small bag she had with her. Therese Souillet managed to free herself from Johnson's grasp and started to get out but was obstructed by Julienne Fontaine's presence. Before either of the women could reach the ground, Johnson started the truck in motion. Therese Souillet then jumped from the moving truck, which continued with Julienne Fontaine still aboard, now all alone.

The following morning, a woman's body was found on the road near the village of Équilly, some 30 miles from Antrain. Jean Bodiles of the Gendarmerie Nationale was called to the scene, and found the woman with terrible head injuries and her legs crushed. He quickly established that she had been raped. A prolonged investigation eventually pointed to Johnson as the man who had driven the truck. PFC Leon P. Reed, another driver with the same unit, explained that Johnson's truck was part of a convoy on 23 August, but that he had left the column and was not seen until the following morning. He then showed Reed a small red bag with white flowers on it, containing six or seven jars of face cream. Johnson told Reed that the night before he had 'clipped a woman'. Later that day, on their way toward Rennes, they passed the body of a dead woman on the road, guarded by MPs. Reed noticed blood on the trousers and sleeves of Johnson and when they arrived at their new location, he inspected the entire vehicle and found blood on the running board gas can, the rifle rack and the passenger's seat. He passed this up to his company commander. Second Lieutenant Paul E. Pauly of the Criminal Investigation Division received the case and by the end of September, through solid detective work, had established which unit was most likely to be involved in the incident. Pauly finally located Private Johnson, who after being advised of his rights, made a statement on 7 October 1944, confirming he had picked up the three women, but that they had all jumped off his truck and he returned to his unit. Johnson said he discovered the little red bag in the cab of his truck, but he could not explain the blood found on the vehicle. Two days later, after having been advised of his rights, he made a full written confession. In this, he said that about 10 miles beyond where Therese Souillet jumped from the truck, Julienne Fontaine exited the moving vehicle as well. When she did, he stopped, picked her up, and placed her back in the truck. Her head was bleeding at the time, and she was moving around, after which she quietened down. After driving for about 2½ hours, he stopped, placed her left leg on the seat and her right leg near the brake pedals and had sex with her. In order that she could not tell anyone what had happened, he dragged her out into the road, placed her in front of the right rear wheel and drove over her with the truck, then drove back to his unit. Johnson was not certain if she was dead before he placed her under the wheels, but stated she 'was warm' at the time.

Johnson appeared before a GCM at Granville, France, on 27 January 1945. But now there was a major problem. Private Johnson was officially a moron. Psychological tests had determined that he had a mental age of 8 years and that, whilst legally sane, he was mentally abnormal, had a psychopathic personality and possible encephalopathy. Born on Christmas Day 1921 in Idabel, McCurtain County, Oklahoma, he had only attended school for six months, could not read or write and suffered with enuresis until he was 21. He had been inducted into the US Army in September 1942 but was unable to complete the road marches and could not qualify with a weapon. Although he was slow and dull, he was cooperative and rational, did not have a criminal record and his character was described as excellent. However, his mental disabilities meant that he struggled not only to tell the difference between right and wrong but understanding the ramifications of making a full confession to the crime. The court, after a good deal of consideration, determined that Johnson had the ability to understand orders, and had always appeared capable of carrying out normal military duties and responsibilities. On this basis, they found him guilty of the crime and sentenced him to death. The sentence was confirmed by General Dwight D. Eisenhower on 29 March 1945.

With the war in Europe now over, Private Willie Johnson was transported to a rock quarry at Le Haye Pesnel, some 4 miles south of Équilly on 26 June 1945. Here a temporary gallows had been erected by engineers. A group of seventeen officials, witnesses and spectators gathered and watched as Johnson was led up the steps. Master Sergeant John Clarence Woods placed a hood over his head and secured the rope around his neck. Following a silent signal from Lieutenant Colonel Henry L. Peck, who was commanding the proceedings, Davison dropped through the trapdoor to his death. His body was taken to the US Military Cemetery at Marigny for burial. In 1949, it was secretly removed from this location and taken to the Oise-Aisne American Cemetery, where it was reburied in Plot 'E', Row 2, Grave 28.

What was meant to be a short ride home for Julienne Fontaine and her two companions ended in terror, rape and murder. Remember her.

Chapter 7

1944: The Year Ends

Saturday, 2 September 1944, France
Victim   Alexina Vingtier, French civilian (white)
                  Age: 24
                  Raped
Assailants   Private Amos Agee (black)
                  Age: 29
                  Service No.: 34163762
                  Private John Cleveland Smith (black)
                  Age: 27
                  Service No.: 33214953
                  Private Frank Watson (black)
                  Age: 21
                  Service No.: 34793522
                  Unit: 644th Quartermaster Troop Transport Company

The tiny commune of Le Noyer is some 16 miles to the north-east of Alençon, France, the first city liberated solely by French troops when it was captured on 12 August 1944 by General Philippe Leclerc's 2nd Armoured Division. Raoul Vingtier, his wife, Alexina, and their 2-year-old child lived in Le Noyer on an isolated farm, which was the home of his uncle, Leon Boet. A few weeks after their liberation, on 30 August, the 644th Quartermaster Troop Transport Company, an African American unit, was bivouacked near the farm. On that day, three new recruits reported for duty in the form of Private Amos Agee, Private John Cleveland Smith and Private Frank Watson. Just three days later, on the afternoon of 2 September, Agee, Smith and Watson went to the farm and asked for something to drink and were given cider. As they drank, Watson took a notebook from his pocket and each man wrote his name in

The tiny commune of Le Noyer where Alexina Vingtier was raped on 2 September 1944 by Private Amos Agee, Private John Cleveland Smith and Private Frank Watson. All three were brought back to a location near here and executed on 3 March 1945.

it, then the Vingtiers signed their names, after which the soldiers left. The three men had been seen by Edouard Lorieux, a neighbour, and by Gisele Lupernant, a maid at the nearby Hotel Vassel, where they had gone for more drinks that afternoon. She was also asked to write her name in the notebook, and when she did, she saw the names of the Vingtiers.

At 11.00 p.m. that night, the three soldiers returned to the farm and knocked on the door repeatedly. Raoul believed the door would eventually give way, so he told his uncle to get up and his wife to get dressed and then opened the door. As he did so, one of the soldiers, Watson, pointed his rifle at Raoul and ordered him out of the house, but he refused to leave. Alexina picked up the baby from the cradle and attempted to leave, but Agee and Watson seized her by the arm and took her out to a building in the yard. Watson then carried the baby back to the house and gave it to the uncle at the door before returning to the outhouse. Agee pushed Alexina to the floor, lifted her dress and raped her, covering her mouth with his hand as he did so. When he had finished, his place was taken, firstly by Watson, then by Smith. Alexina screamed and struggled throughout her ordeal but was held down by one soldier as the others took their turn in violating her. Leon Boet and Raoul Vingtier were held at gunpoint throughout the ordeal and robbed of their money by Watson. The three assailants then left the farm. The following day, after reporting the attack, Raoul and Alexina were taken to the nearby camp where Captain Isidor Lazar, commanding officer, held a line-up of the soldiers. The Vingtiers identified Watson, but Agee and Smith were not amongst them. Lazar brought the French couple back to the camp the following day, along with Edouard Lorieux and Gisele Lupernant. This time they identified all three rapists and, to be certain, Lazar had the witnesses removed, scrambled the line-up, then had the witnesses return, and they quickly identified the same three men, who were then arrested by MPs and on 9 September, Captain Abraham J. Swiren, the investigating officer, took statements from each of them, all telling a similar story, claiming they had gone to the farm in the afternoon, but never returning that evening, and that none of them were armed.

On 18 October 1944, all three soldiers appeared before a joint two-day GCM at Rambouillet, on the outskirts of Paris. They each pleaded not guilty to the crimes. Private Amos Agee, born on 16 February 1916, came from Linden, Alabama, and was inducted into the army in Fort McClellan, Alabama, on 19 November 1941. Private John Cleveland Smith, born on 20 September 1917, was from Bedford County, Virginia, and was inducted into the army in Fort Meade, Maryland, on 14 October 1942. Private Frank Watson, born in 1923, hailed from Oneil, Florida, and was inducted into the army in Camp Blanding, Florida, on 29 September 1943. Only Agee had previous military convictions, and he begged the court for mercy, saying, 'Let me live, sir.' The court was unsympathetic to the pleas and all three men were convicted and sentenced to death by hanging. General Dwight D. Eisenhower confirmed their death sentences on 14 January 1945 and on 3 March, described as a cool crisp day, the soldiers were transported to an orchard bordered by hedges in La Saussaye, just east of Le Mêle-sur-Sarthe, close to where they had committed the rapes. Here a temporary gallows had been erected by engineers. A group of twenty-nine officials, witnesses and spectators, including Raoul Vingtier, gathered and watched as they were led up the steps, where Master Sergeant John Clarence Woods placed a hood over each man's head and secured a rope around each of their necks. Lieutenant Colonel Henry L. Peck, who was commanding the proceedings, gave a silent signal on each occasion, sending the men to their deaths. Agee was hanged first and, as he marched to the gallows, he repeated a plea for mercy. Smith was next and, when he stood on the trapdoor, he asked to shake hands with Lieutenant Colonel Henry L. Peck, who said, 'Good luck, son.' Smith replied, 'See you all somewhere.' Watson was last and, as he stood on the trapdoor, he said to the chaplain, 'All I want you to do is pray for me.' The whole grim process took a total of 2 hours to complete, the crowd watching the entire time. Their bodies were initially buried at the American Military Cemetery in Marigny, France, but their remains were secretly exhumed by the Graves Registration Service in 1949 and moved to the Oise-Aisne American Cemetery in Plot 'E'. Agee is in Row 1, Grave 14, Smith is in Row 3, Grave 67 and Watson is in Row 3, Grave 55.

Amongst the numerous Board of Review documents, you will find similar stories to that of Alexina Vingtier, some with very different outcomes, but with all of the victims being subjected to similar acts by men of the Allied Forces. Remember her.

Monday, 18 September 1944, France

Victim	Raymonde Dehu, French civilian
	Age: 17
	Raped
Assailants	Sergeant Johnnie E. Hudson (black)
	Age: 21
	Service No.: 34741799
	T/5 Leo Valentine Sr (black)
	Age: 20
	Service No.: 32954278
	Unit: 396th Quartermaster Truck Company
	T/5 Oscar Neil Newman (white)
	Age: 26
	Service No.: 35226382
	Unit: Headquarters Company, 712th Railway Operating Battalion

During the Second World War, the segregation embedded in US civilian life spilled over into the military. Most African Americans were assigned to non-combat units and performed service duties, such as supply, maintenance and transportation. Many drove for the famous 'Red Ball Express', which carried much-needed supplies to the advancing First and Third Armies through France and Germany. Although black and white troops rarely mixed, there were occasions when this did happen, sometimes with deadly consequences.

On 18 September 1944, 17-year-old Raymonde Dehu was driven along this road and raped by Sergeant Johnnie E. Hudson, T/5 Leo Valentine Sr and T/5 Oscar Neil Newman after she had been kidnapped in the village of Sézanne, France.

Sergeant Johnnie E. Hudson and T/5 Leo Valentine Sr were black soldiers serving with the 396th Quartermaster Truck Company, operating near Sézanne, France. On 18 September 1944, Sergeant Hudson requested the use of a jeep to drive into town. This was granted and Hudson headed off, with Valentine in the passenger seat. Although he had not given a reason for wanting to use the vehicle, it soon became obvious as both men headed to the nearest bar. As they drank, they met up with a white soldier, T/5 Oscar Neil Newman, a 6ft, blue-eyed, brown-haired Lutheran from Macron, Ohio, who was serving with the Headquarters Company, 712th Railway Operating Battalion. As the trio drank, there was talk of going to Châlons and of taking a bottle of champagne back to camp for the officers. The three soldiers then drove the jeep from Sézanne 17 miles north to Fromentières. Here, at about 6.00 p.m., Newman and Valentine entered the shop of Madeleine Pionnier where they asked her daughter Renée for liquor and sex. They were refused both and left. They then drove to the shop of Germaine Dehu and her 17-year-old daughter, Raymonde. Newman went in and asked about 'butter and cheese', but was told they had none. Newman pointed to the jeep and repeated the word 'butter', and Germaine, believing he meant he had butter to sell, followed him outside, with her daughter close behind. When they got to the vehicle, Valentine was in the driver's seat and Hudson was lying down on the back seat. Newman suddenly seized Raymonde, put her in the front seat next to Valentine and jumped in to block her escape. Germaine grabbed at her daughter, but Newman broke her grip. The jeep was then driven through the village at a rapid rate eastward toward the village of Champaubert. When they reached the village of Étoges, they turned off and headed for Beaunay. All the time, Raymonde was struggling and calling for help, but Newman pushed her into the back seat where Hudson held her tightly. Whilst in the jeep, Newman removed her underwear, exposing her 'hygienic bandage' as she was menstruating. When they reached Beaunay, they stopped in a field, and Newman and Valentine dragged Raymonde from the jeep and threw her to the ground. She still had on her outer garments and continued to struggle, but Valentine twice placed the barrel of his rifle against her forehead. Without undressing Raymonde, Newman then raped the 17-year-old, and when he had finished, Valentine took his place with the girl. After Valentine had finished, Raymonde escaped and found a French cyclist from whom she asked protection. He took her on his bicycle, but the soldiers followed in the jeep and when they overtook the pair, Valentine threatened the cyclist with a rifle and chased him off. They then put Raymonde in the jeep and drove onto a side road, halted and this time Raymonde was stripped naked and her clothing chucked out of the vehicle except for her blouse. She was thrown to the ground and Newman raped her again, and then Valentine followed for a second time. Although Hudson then laid on top of her, he did not have sex with the girl, which may have saved his life. She broke away from the soldier, and he made no effort to continue. Raymonde was then put back in the jeep and allowed to put on her blouse, but she had no other clothing, so Hudson put his field jacket on her. By then it was 10.30 p.m. and she was driven into Beaunay, where Hudson reclaimed his jacket and set her free. They started for the town of Châlons-en-Champagne but were stopped by the MP at a road check, where they were arrested. Each man later gave an unsworn statement confessing to rape. Raymonde was examined by Dr Henri Provendier in Montmort-Lucy, at midnight. He said, 'She reminded me of a person I have already seen that had been questioned by the Gestapo.' Raymonde had many bruises and scratches, but the doctor had no instruments with which to examine her private parts. On 19 September, she was examined by First Lieutenant N.M. Hornstein, at the 28th US Field Hospital. She had numerous cuts, superficial abrasions, bruising and damage to her genitals.

All three men were brought before a GCM in Reims, on 3 October 1944, where they pleaded not guilty to the crime. Leo Valentine Sr was a married man from Gastonia, North Carolina, whose wife was expecting their third child when he was brought before the court. Captain Donald H. Martin, Commanding Officer of the 396th Quartermaster Truck Company, testified that the characters of Hudson and Valentine had been excellent. All were found guilty of rape, but only Newman and Valentine were sentenced to death. Hudson, who had not had sex with Raymonde, had handed her a small Catholic medal, which she put around her neck to protect herself, and given her his field jacket at the end of the ordeal, perhaps realising the consequences of their actions. Following approval and review, the sentence was confirmed on 5 November 1944, by General Dwight D. Eisenhower. On 24 November 1944, Newman and Valentine were transported to the village of Beaunay, where they had carried out the brutal rape. Here a temporary gallows had been erected by engineers inside a barn on the edge of the village. A group of thirty-seven officials, witnesses and spectators gathered and watched as each man was led up the steps, where Master Sergeant John Clarence Woods placed hoods over their heads and secured ropes around their necks. Lieutenant Colonel Henry L. Peck, who was commanding the proceedings, gave a silent signal on each occasion, sending the men to their deaths. Valentine was hanged first, his last words being, 'See my wife and children are taken care of.' Newman was next, saying, 'I am awful sorry for everything I did. If I wasn't drunk, I would not have done it. God bless you all boys. God bless the Army.' The whole grim process took less than an hour to complete, the crowd watching the entire time. Their bodies were initially buried at the American Military Cemetery in Solers, France, but their remains were secretly exhumed in 1949 and moved to the Oise-Aisne American Cemetery in Plot 'E'. Newman is in Row 4, Grave 80 and Valentine is in Row 2, Grave 41. Sergeant Johnnie E. Hudson was sentenced to serve a term of life at hard labour at the US Penitentiary in Lewisburg, Pennsylvania, but was released on remission in 1958.

Although the parents of Raymonde Dehu attended the executions, the 17-year-old victim stayed away. It is hard to imagine how those terrifying hours affected the rest of her life, but there is no doubt they did. Remember her.

Wednesday, 20 September 1944, France
Victim   PFC William D. Adams (black)
              Age: 30
              Service No: 34004663
              Murdered
Assailant   Private James W. Twiggs (black)
              Age: 25
              Service No.: 38265086
              Unit: Company 'F', 1323rd Engineer General Service
                    Regiment

The phrase 'playing the dozens' is a very derogatory expression used by US soldiers when talking about parents, especially a mother. But it is exactly this turn of phrase that transformed a discussion into an ugly confrontation, which concluded with the death of one of the participants. On 20 September 1944, Company 'F', 1323rd Engineer General Service Regiment was bivouacked in the village of Bellefontaine, France. Amongst the troops was 22-year-old Private James W. Twiggs, who had been inducted into the army in Lafayette, Louisiana, in 1942. He was arguing with Private William D. Adams about how an illegitimate child bore the name of its father, but Adams insisted that the child took the name of its mother. A simple discussion soon got out of control and Adams called Twiggs, who had been in prison for theft, a thief. Twiggs then said, 'When I was in there your mammy was in there.' This comment incensed Adams, who said, 'I don't play the dozens' and 'don't allow talk about my mother, who died in my arms'. Adams demanded the comment be taken back but Twiggs refused, saying, 'Unless you say I didn't steal, I mean it.' The men then separated.

Adams returned 10 minutes later with a carbine, but found Twiggs was not in his tent, so he put the carbine by his side and when Twiggs returned, he pointed it at him. T/5 Lawrence L. Grant jumped between the two men, and Adams said, 'Get back, anybody between this is dead.' Adams then asked Twiggs if he would retract his remark, to which Twiggs responded, 'I knew you had a gun. I saw you when I come from the motor pool. Give me the same chance as you've got, and we'll shoot it out.' There was a short stand-off and Adams walked away toward the orderly room saying, 'If I'd been in civilian life I'd have blowed his head off; I had been putting up twenty and thirty days for AWOL but I'd put up twenty years for him talking about my mother.' To this point the entire argument had taken 45 minutes. At 5.00 p.m., Twiggs went to the supply room where he collected his rifle, under the pretence that he was going to clean it, and returned to his tent. There was a standing order that each soldier was to clean his weapon once a week and it would be inspected on a weekly basis, but most soldiers cleaned their weapons once a month before the inspection and there was no inspection scheduled for that week. A short while later, Adams was walking through the Company 'F' area from the water point carrying a 5-gallon can of water in one hand and a bucket of water in the other. A shot rang out and the unarmed soldier collapsed to the ground. After the shot was fired, Private John H. Neal saw Twiggs carrying his M-1 rifle. He asked Twiggs, 'Who shot Adams?' and Twiggs replied, 'I did.' Twiggs then continued toward the supply tent. First Lieutenant Vinson K. Robinson heard the shot and rushed to Adams, who was still breathing when placed in a jeep. He was taken to the dispensary where he was later pronounced dead.

Twiggs appeared before a GCM at Omaha Beach Section, France, on 25 October 1944, charged with murder. Born on 4 January 1920 in Topeka, Kansas, he had been inducted into the US Army on 3 December 1942 at Camp Wolters, Texas. His service record, although not the best, was no worse than many of his contemporaries and he was found guilty of the crime and sentenced to death. Major General Clay approved the sentence and General Dwight D. Eisenhower signed the order of execution on 16 December 1944. On 22 January 1945, Twiggs stood before temporary gallows, located in a small ravine at the Loire DTC. A small group of officials, witnesses and spectators watched as Lieutenant Colonel Henry L. Peck led him to the steps of the scaffold. After guards escorted him up the flight of thirteen steps, Master Sergeant John Clarence Woods placed a hood over his head and secured a rope around his neck. Lieutenant Colonel Peck then gave a silent signal and, at 11.02 a.m., the trapdoor sprang open, sending the soldier to his death. His body was then transported to the US Military Cemetery at Marigny for burial. In 1949, his remains were removed from this location and secretly re-buried in the Oise-Aisne American Cemetery in Plot 'E', Row 4, Grave 88.

PFC William D. Adams rests with the honoured dead at the Normandy American Cemetery, Colleville-sur-Mer, France in Plot J, Row 13, Grave 24. Remember him.

Tuesday, 21 September 1944, France

Victims	Lucienne Barry, French civilian (white)
	Age: 40
	Raped
	Germaine Pivel, French civilian (white)
	Age: 18
	Raped
	Christiane Pivel, French civilian (white)
	Age: 14
	Raped
	Mireille Weber, French civilian (white)
	Age: 14
	Raped
Assailants	Private John David Cooper (black)
	Age: 22
	Service No.: 34562464
	Private J.P. Wilson (black)
	Age: 27
	Service No.: 32484756
	Unit: 3966th Quartermaster Truck Company

The threat of isolated German soldiers who, possibly armed, might be hiding in barns, lofts and outbuildings was very real as the Allied forces progressed across France. However, the excuse of, 'looking for Germans' was one that was repeated on numerous occasions in order to allow soldiers to gain access to premises, where they would then proceed to terrorise the occupants. Theft, rape and murder were not uncommon and, on occasions, the perpetrators, if caught, would face the ultimate penalty. It was under the pretence of searching for Germans that two black soldiers, Private John David Cooper and Private J.P. Wilson, committed a series of crimes in September 1944.

Lucienne Barry, Maurice Paquin, Paul Weber and his daughter, Mireille, one of his eleven children, were living on an isolated farm in Ferme de Marville, France. At about 2.00 a.m. on 21 September 1944, the two soldiers, each armed with a rifle, fired two shots outside the farmhouse, then knocked on the door. They appeared at Weber's window with a flashlight and said they were searching for Germans.

Weber, believing they were genuine, lit a candle and opened the door. He did not think it strange as Germans had previously searched the premises. One of the soldiers immediately extinguished the candle and shone the flashlight in Weber's eyes. They made him follow them and looked in all the rooms of the house, including that occupied by Madame Barry and Mireille. They also searched the stable, continually keeping their rifles pointed at the Frenchman. The soldiers told Weber, Paquin and four other male occupants of the house that they were going to take them to see 'their Captain at the camp'. The six men went out into the courtyard and one of the soldiers forced them into the basement at gunpoint. They were told, 'the first one of you that goes out will be shot', then the door of the basement was bolted from the outside. One of the soldiers fired a shot and then they left. Some 40 minutes later, a boy released the men and Mireille told her father how she and Lucienne had been raped at knifepoint.

The following night, the two soldiers entered the village of Lérouville. Firstly, they went to the home of Jean Frey, where they knocked on the door, but he would not let them in. They broke a window and entered the home, pretending they were looking for German paratroopers. After searching the house, Wilson claimed he was 'Captain Gainer', and took notes of who was in the house, which led Frey to believe the search may be genuine. Finding nothing to their liking, the soldiers carried along the street to the home of Henriette and Sylvain Boidin, where they repeated their actions. They then moved on to the house of Gustave Pivel, who lived there with his wife and two daughters, Germaine and Christiane. Here, they banged on the front door and when Gustave did not open it, they fired shots through the kitchen window. Upon opening the door, the soldiers claimed they were looking for Germans. Gustave Pivel was ordered out of the house, leaving his wife and children alone. The soldiers returned, grabbing the teenagers by their arms and stating that their captain wanted them for 'information'. The girls were marched to a nearby quarry, where Wilson raped Germaine. Christiane tried to run away but Cooper caught her and then raped her. Afterwards he made her sit with him on a nearby bridge, holding onto her skirt, until her sister returned, after which they were both released.

The rapes were reported to the authorities and identification parades were organised at units close to the homes that had been invaded. Cooper was identified at one of these parades by one witness and by seven witnesses at a subsequent parade. One female witness also picked out Wilson but wouldn't point at him because he had shaved off a little growth of hair below his lower lip. It was established that when Wilson was taken into custody on 26 September he had a growth of hair below his lower lip but the next day he had shaved it off. Captain Walter G. Cederberg, commanding the company, said the two soldiers were truck drivers. He had never ordered either of them, or any member of his command, to search any houses in France or to arrest, place in custody or restrain any French civilian. Both men were brought before a GCM in Nancy, on 25 October 1944, where they pleaded not guilty to the crime. Private John David Cooper, born on 11 June 1912 in Dover, Georgia, was a former coal-truck driver who had been inducted into the US Army on 26 December 1942 at Fort Benning, Georgia. Private J.P. Wilson was born on 24 January 1918 in Columbus, Mississippi, and had also been inducted into the US Army on 26 December 1942, at Fort Dix, New Jersey. Captain Walter G. Cederberg and Agent William P. Graham, of the Criminal Investigation Department, had discovered a duffle bag in the tent where Wilson slept which contained several articles of clothing with the name 'J.P. Wilson' marked on the collar. They also found a field jacket, an unmarked shirt featuring the stripes of a staff sergeant, a driver's medal with one bar, an expert medal with four bars, a brass whistle and chain, and a small pocket diary, with Wilson's name on one page and Cederberg testified that it contained some of Wilson's writing. Both men were found guilty of the charges against them and were sentenced to death. The sentences were approved on 15 November 1944 by Lieutenant General George S. Patton and General Dwight D. Eisenhower signed the order confirming the death penalties on 14 December 1944. Before a date could be set for the executions, J.P. Wilson escaped from custody, but the wheels of justice continued to turn. On 9 January 1945, Private John David Cooper was taken to the quarry at Lérouville, where he had committed his crimes, and, under the supervision of Lieutenant Colonel Henry L. Peck, was hanged by Master Sergeant John Clarence Woods in front of a crowd of seventy-one officials, witnesses and spectators. Eventually, Private J.P. Wilson was apprehended, and he too was returned to the village that was the scene of his crimes and, on 2 February 1945, he stood on the same temporary gallows as Cooper and suffered the same fate. Two of his victims were at the execution. Their bodies were initially buried at the American Military Cemetery in Limay, Meurthe-et-Moselle, France, but their remains were secretly exhumed in 1949 and moved to the Oise-Aisne American Cemetery in Plot 'E'. Cooper is in Row 4, Grave 81 and Wilson is in Row 1, Grave 9.

Sunday, 24 September 1944, France

Victims	Albert Lebocey, French civilian (white)
	Age: 45
	Murdered
	Germaine Lebocey, French civilian (white)
	Age: 44
	Raped
Assailant	Private Olin W. Williams (black)
	Age: 23
	Service No.: 34649494
	Unit: 4194th Quartermaster Service Company

Albert Lebocey and his wife, Germaine de Saint-Nicolas, lived with their young daughter in Le Chêne Daniel, Chérencé-le-Héron, a small commune in Normandy. On the evening of 23 September 1944, three black soldiers, Private Odell Austin, Private Chester Coet and Private Olin W. Williams, arrived at the house and demanded cider. The apple juice they had on the table was not drinkable, so the soldiers drank some cognac they had brought with them, along with coffee served by the Leboceys. At 9.00 p.m., Germaine took her daughter upstairs to put her to bed and heard footsteps on the stairs behind her. She encountered Williams halfway up and as she descended, he tried to grab her, but she avoided his grasp. She told the soldiers she was disappointed with them and two left, leaving Williams behind. She then made Williams leave and retired to the second-floor bedroom with her husband. At 3.00 a.m., Williams returned, but now he was armed with a carbine, and knocked on the door. Germaine opened the second-floor window and threw the contents of a chamber pot at him. Angry at her actions, Williams broke down the door and entered. Albert got up to protect her from the angry soldier and, as he reached the foot of the stairs, Williams fired a shot at him. Albert hollered, 'Swine', and with that, Williams fired again. Albert fell to the floor, dying almost immediately. After Williams had shot her husband, he threw Germaine to the floor and grabbed her by the throat. She tried to pull away, and when she screamed, he put his other hand over her mouth. He pulled open her thighs as she continued screaming, struck her in the face, then raped her. In 10 minutes the ordeal was over, at which point Germaine and her daughter escaped from the house. She first went to her mother's home, and then continued to the camp where she saw a group of soldiers and begged for help.

Germaine recognised her attacker at two identification parades on 24 September, one in the work area and the other in the bivouac area. At the first identification, she pointed to him and said, 'There he is. It is you who have killed my husband.' An investigation then got underway but did not conclude until 10 October, by which time the unit was serving in Belgium. Williams was eventually arrested and appeared before a GCM on 15 December 1944, where he pleaded not guilty to the crime of murder and rape. The case appeared to be an open and shut one, with the court finding him guilty of the crimes and sentencing him to death. Some delays occurred in reviewing the case and General Dwight D. Eisenhower did not sign the confirmation order until 4 March 1945.

Five days later, on 9 March, Williams was driven to a field surrounded by hedges in Le Chêne Daniel, France, the scene of his crimes, where army engineers had erected a temporary gallows. At 10.00 a.m., in front of a group of officials and witnesses, including Albert Lebocey's brother, Williams was asked if he had any last statement to make. He remained silent. Master Sergeant John Clarence Woods placed a hood over the prisoner's head, tightened the noose around his neck and at 10.05 a.m. the trap was sprung; 14 minutes later he was pronounced dead. His body was buried in the American Military Cemetery at Marigny, France, but his remains were secretly exhumed in 1949 and transported to the Oise-Aisne American Cemetery, where they are buried in Plot 'E', Row 1, Grave 20.

Albert Lebocey is buried in Le Chêne Daniel, Chérencé-le-Héron. Remember him.

Sunday, 24 September 1944, France
Victim	Lucie Hualle, French civilian (white)
	Age: 57
	Raped
Assailants	Corporal Arthur J. Farrell (white)
	Age: 38
	Service No.: 32559163
	Corporal Wilford Teton (American Indian)
	Age: 23
	Service No.: 39315061
	Unit: 'C' Troop, 17th Cavalry Reconnaissance Squadron

Amongst the US forces involved in the breakout from the Normandy bocage into the Brittany countryside was the 17th Cavalry Reconnaissance Squadron, which landed at Utah Beach on 15 July 1944 and entered Brittany with Task Force 'A' on 3 August. Two of the men serving with 'C' Troop were Corporal Arthur J. Farrell, a 38-year-old white man from New Jersey, and Corporal Wilfred Teton, a 23-year-old Shoshone Indian from Marion County, Oregon. On the evening of 24 September 1944, their unit was in the vicinity of Au Fayel, Brittany. Farrell and Teton, who had both been drinking, knocked at the home of Andre and Denise Descormiers. When the door was opened, they entered the house and Farrell immediately approached a bed where Andre's mother was sleeping and pulled back the covers. He then quickly covered her up again, perhaps having expected to find a younger woman. Teton, who had sat himself at a table in the house, then escorted Andre Descormiers to the nearby home of 57-year-old Lucie Hualle. Descormiers informed Lucie that an American soldier wished to speak to her, but she refused to get out of bed and sent the pair away.

The Frenchman returned to his home followed by Teton, and asked the Americans to leave, but they refused to go. Teton proceeded to handle a revolver he was carrying, and Denise became frightened by his demeanour, so she left the house and fetched their neighbour, Hillion Adrieu. Teton then placed some bullets in his revolver, pointed the weapon at Adrieu's chest, led him outside and told him to 'go away and go to bed'. By about 9.00 p.m., Denise felt that Teton's behaviour had deteriorated further, so she attempted to fetch Adrieu again. This time, Teton followed her outside into the courtyard, struck her with his fist and knocked her down. She screamed and when Andre tried to help her, Farrell grabbed him and pushed him into a piece of furniture. Andre took Farrell by the arm, flung him outside the house and then went toward Teton, who fled. The couple locked their door, believing that the incident had ended. On hearing the shouts of Denise, Lucie Hualle had become frightened and did not want to stay in her home alone. She decided to make her way to the nearby village but having gone just 15m from her door, she was grabbed by Farrell, who threw her to the ground. The burly soldier then commenced a 60-minute sexual assault upon Lucie, throughout which Teton, on his knees, held the revolver against her and forced her to toy with his private parts, although he did not rape her. Hillion Adrieu could hear what was happening but, afraid that he may be shot by Teton, he did not leave his house. Eventually, Andre, who was also fearful of being shot, managed to contact the US forces.

First Lieutenant Maurice C. Reeves, 1391st Engineer Forestry Battalion, drove to the scene with an interpreter. He saw Farrell stagger around a building about 75yd away from the home of Lucie Hualle holding a Mauser pistol, which he pointed at Reeves. He managed to bring Farrell under control, gained possession of the pistol and took him to the French civilians, where Lucie Hualle, whose face and clothing were covered in blood from a scalp wound, identified him. Teton, however, had escaped, but not for long, and was soon arrested. A GCM took place at Rennes on 16 October 1944, when the two men pleaded not guilty to the charges against them. Following a gruelling week-long trial, Teton was sentenced to life imprisonment with hard labour, whilst Farrell was sentenced to death. After the court findings had been reviewed and the sentence approved, General Dwight D. Eisenhower signed the confirmation order on 19 November 1944. The plot twisted at this point when Farrell asked to speak to Major Harry M. Campbell, the Commanding Officer of the Brittany Base Guardhouse. He claimed that it was not him who had raped Lucie, it was Teton and, if an agreement was reached not to hang the Indian, he would confess to the crime. Teton was interviewed and claimed he had committed the rape, not Farrell. This instigated a further, in-depth investigation, whereby it was found that Farrell was doing all he could to avoid being hanged, and Teton was lying. The sentences remained unchanged. On 19 January 1945, in bitterly freezing winter conditions, Farrell arrived at the village of Saint-Sulpice-des-Landes where US engineers had constructed a gallows in the courtyard of the village school. He was escorted to the steps by two guards who tied his hands behind him, and then Lieutenant Colonel Henry L. Peck read out the GCM order for his execution. Farrell was then marched up the steps, his ankles bound and placed on the trapdoor of the gallows. Peck then gave a signal to Master Sergeant John Clarence Woods, who sprang the trapdoor. It would be 13 long minutes before the three US medical officers would confirm that Farrell was dead. His body was then transported to the US Military Cemetery at Marigny, where it was buried on 22 January 1945. As with many of the other executed US soldiers, his body was removed from the cemetery in 1949 and re-buried in Plot 'E' at the Oise-Aisne American Cemetery, Row 1, Grave 21.

Wilford Teton remained in prison until his release in 1955 and passed away on 10 December 2015 at the age of 94 and is buried in the Riverton Crest Cemetery, Seattle, King County, Washington. Lucie Hualle, born in 1887, had seen how the tragedy of the First World War had impacted upon her community and watched as Nazi tyranny enveloped her country twenty years later. Her dreams of liberation were then smashed by the very people it had been entrusted to. Remember her.

THE PLOT OF SHAME

Monday, 25 September 1944, Northern Ireland
Victim   Patricia Wylie, Irish civilian (white)
                Age: 7½
                Raped and murdered
Assailant   Private William Harrison Jr (white)
                Age: 22
                Service No.: 15089828
                Unit: No. 2 Combat Crew Replacement Centre, United States Army Air Force

There were touching scenes on 27 September 1944 in the Mullinahoe Cemetery, Ardboe, Northern Ireland, when the burial of Patricia Wylie, the daughter of Patrick and Mary Wylie, took place. The white, flower-bedecked coffin belied the circumstances of her death at the hands of a US serviceman who was stationed at nearby USAAF Station 238, formerly RAF Cluntoe. The man, 22-year-old Private William Harrison Jr, was a soldier with serious mental issues, who was serving at No. 2 Combat Crew Replacement Centre, which trained the men who would fly the Boeing B-17 'Flying Fortress' and Consolidated B-24 'Liberators' of the heavy bomber groups. The United States Army Air Force had over 3,500 troops on the base, tripling the population of Ardboe, and the men had plenty of money which they pumped

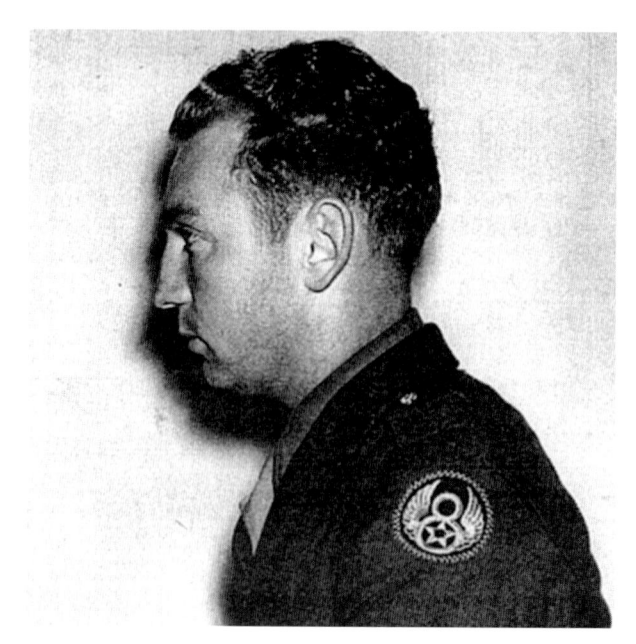

Private William Harrison Jr who befriended and then raped and murdered 7½-year-old Patricia Wylie near Belfast, Northern Ireland, on 25 September 1944.

into the local economy, making them extremely popular with the local population, particularly bar keepers.

On 25 September 1944, Harrison called at the Wylie home, as he had become friendly with the family in June 1944 when Patrick Wylie had bought him a cup of tea. Harrison had been at the home for about 30 minutes when he asked Mrs Wylie to let her little daughter go with him, on the pretence of buying some sweets and mineral drinks. At first, she felt Harrison should wait until Patrick came home before deciding what to do, but, eventually, she agreed to let her daughter go and both walked out hand in hand. It was the last time she would see her daughter alive. On the pretext of taking a shortcut, Harrison took the girl into a nearby field where he sexually assaulted her and then choked her to death, leaving her dead, half-naked body near a haystack. When she failed to return home, the Wylies became concerned and called the police and MP. A search was soon underway, during which Patrick Wylie saw Harrison in the doorway of Dormans pub. When he asked where his daughter was, Harrison said he had left her by a mobile shop, and that she was holding lemonade and lollipops when he last saw her. Harrison then continued with his drinking and finally caught a taxi back to the base where he made some attempt to sleep.

In the meantime, Patricia's half-nude, strangled body was found in a field a short distance from her home by four civilians, Michael Dorman, Peter Dorman, Bernard Hagan and Daniel Montague. She was lying near several haystacks in a field a short distance from a rough cart track. Peter Dorman said the four men had been searching for about half an hour in the darkness and after they entered a field where there were four ricks of hay he spotted a basket. He thought the girl must have been somewhere nearby, then he saw a small amount of hay tossed in a line near one of the stacks. One of the others began to pull at the haystack and he saw the girl, lying face downwards, covered with blood, her left eye swollen and bruises on each side of her throat. District Inspector Kennedy, a fingerprints expert, and other members of the Belfast police force, along with US MPs, began exhaustive enquiries to find the killer, beginning with the last man who saw her alive, Private William Harrison. When he was interviewed by MPs, they noticed abrasions on his hands, which he said was the result of having a fight with another soldier. Eventually, he admitted choking the girl, but was uncertain about having sex with her. This was enough for the investigators, and he was immediately arrested.

In a lengthy GCM, which commenced on 6 November 1944 but did not conclude until 6 December, it was established that Harrison was a disturbed young man. He was born in Ironton, Ohio, on 22 July 1922. An only child, whose father had lost both legs in a motorcycle accident, he was a sickly individual who, after he graduated from high school, became a motor mechanic. He enlisted in the Army Air Corps on 4 February 1942 and had a poor disciplinary record and, more alarmingly, he exhibited an unstable mental condition. On 24 April 1943, whilst assigned to the 93rd Bomb Group, doctors at the 2nd Evacuation Hospital diagnosed Harrison with 'constitutional psychopathic state, inadequate personality'. A medical board, however, found that although he was a flawed individual, who had resorted to the use of alcohol, he had no definite mental disease and recommended that he return to duty. In June 1944, Harrison attempted suicide, and whilst at the 79th General Hospital a similar diagnosis was made. This was all too late for Patricia Wylie, she was dead at the age of 7½.

Significant efforts were made to defend Harrison, but the court found him guilty and he was sentenced to death. Following approval and review, the sentence was confirmed on 2 January 1945 by General Dwight D. Eisenhower. But now clemency was being sought, and appeals from various parties, including Congressman Edward McCowen of Ohio, enquired if the sentence could be commuted to life imprisonment. The case even reached the heady heights of the White House, where President Roosevelt was asked to intervene. Roosevelt wisely stated that he would not even consider reviewing the case. At 2.00 a.m. on 7 April 1945, Harrison was positioned on the trapdoor of the execution chamber at Shepton Mallet Prison by two guards. As several officials and witnesses looked on, Thomas Pierrepoint, assisted by Herbert Morris, quickly placed a white hood over his head and adjusted the rope around his neck. A silent signal from the officer in charge of the proceedings, Major Philip J. Flynn, and Harrison fell to his death. His body was first buried in Brookwood American Military Cemetery, Surrey, where he was given a small provisional wooden cross. In 1948, the army transferred the remains to the American Military Cemetery at Cambridge. A year later his remains were secretly removed and reinterred in Plot 'E' at the Oise-Aisne American Cemetery, France, and are in Row 3, Grave 62.

Sadly, there is little else that can be written about Patricia Wylie, a child needlessly murdered by a US soldier. The Public Records Office of Northern Ireland record her effects as just £1. Remember her.

Monday, 9 October 1944, France
Victim   Victor Bellery, French civilian (white)
                  Age: 42
                  Murdered
Assailant   Private Matthew Clay Jr (black)
                  Age: 24
                  Service No.: 38490561
                  Unit: 3236th Quartermaster Service Company

Incidents often occur during which, in a few brief moments, lives are changed forever. Such is the case of Victor Bellery, a fit and healthy 42-year-old baker who in autumn 1944 was living with his 37-year-old wife, Augustine, and their two children, aged 6 and 8, in a one-room bakery in the village of Fontenay-sur-Mer, France, which is just 2 miles from Utah Beach, at the westernmost of the D-Day landing beaches. A former airstrip, known as Advance Landing Ground 'A-7', was close by and was being used for the storage of supplies by the troops of the US Transport Corps and as a French refugee camp. On the night of 9 October 1944, the family were asleep when the door of the bakery was suddenly kicked in by a drunken black soldier, Private Matthew Clay, who demanded cider, but it was refused. Victor appears to have attempted to get out of bed, or was dragged out, and Clay forced him to the front door where he stabbed him

The village cemetery in Fontenay-sur-Mer, France, close to Utah Beach. This is the last resting place of local baker Victor Bellery, who was murdered by Private Matthew Clay Jr on 9 October 1944.

repeatedly in the back and neck with his bayonet. Terrified, Augustine tried to defend her husband by pulling him free of Clay's grasp, but she was stabbed three times on the wrist and shoulder by the assailant, who then ran away as quickly as he had arrived. Victor Bellery died that night from his injuries, leaving a widow and two fatherless children.

At 10.45 p.m., Lieutenant S. Aber, of 104th Division, and T/5 Peter Almoslino were at the air strip in front of the French refugee camp when they were informed that someone had been murdered and another injured. At the same time, they heard footsteps and called, 'Halt!' A figure 30yd away stopped and shone a flashlight. Aber ordered the person to advance and, as he came nearer, ordered him to drop the flashlight, as well as something he was carrying in his other hand. Aber identified Clay, who spoke incoherently and appeared drunk. Aber asked what he was doing, and Clay replied he was looking 'for the criminal'. Almoslino picked up the flashlight and a bloody bayonet and turned them over to the MP, along with Clay. Agents Robert E. Fuller and Robert A. Shultz, of the 17th Criminal Investigation Section based in Cherbourg, went to the Normandy Base Stockade on 13 October to interview Clay. The soldier made a statement, but used the name John Louis when signing it, and claimed that he had been attacked by the Bellerys and was merely defending himself. He was drunk and had requested some cider when they came at him with a mallet, and he feared for his life.

On 20 January 1945, Private Matthew Clay Jr appeared before a GCM convened at Cherbourg, where he pleaded not guilty to the crimes. Born on 26 July 1920, at Avery Island, Iberia Parish, Louisiana, he was inducted into the US Army in Lafayette, Louisiana, on 11 December 1943. He was the sole defence witness, and told much the same story, how he was only looking for a drink and had been attacked by the Bellerys, claiming that they hit him with the mallet, which he then later denied. The court quickly found him guilty of murder and assault with a deadly weapon and sentenced him to death. General Dwight D. Eisenhower confirmed the death sentence on 29 March 1945.

On 4 June 1945, with the war in Europe now over, the sun shone upon Fontenay-sur-Mer, where Victor Bellery had been so cruelly murdered. In a small orchard about half a mile outside the village, US Army engineers had constructed temporary gallows. At 11.00 a.m., Private Matthew Clay Jr dismounted from a personnel carrier and, led by Lieutenant Colonel Henry L. Peck, was escorted to the steps of the gallows, where the GCM order for his execution was read out. Clay, with his arms around his head, cried and said, 'Lord, have mercy on me.' The guards had to force his arms behind his back and to bind his wrists. Master Sergeant John Clarence Woods placed a hood over Clay's head and secured a rope around his neck. Lieutenant Colonel Peck then gave a silent signal and the trapdoor sprang open, sending the soldier to his death. His body was then transported to the US Military Cemetery at Marigny, where it was buried on 22 January 1945. As with many of the other executed US soldiers, his body was removed from the cemetery secretly in 1949 and re-buried in Plot 'E' at the Oise-Aisne American Cemetery, France, in Row 1, Grave 3.

Should you visit the village of Fontenay-sur-Mer, you will find the grave of Victor Bellery in the local cemetery. Remember him.

Tuesday, 10 October 1944, Italy

Victim   Eolo Ferretti, Italian civilian (white)
                 Age: 44
                 Murdered
Assailant   Private Werner E. Schmiedel (white)
                 Age: 26
                 Service No.: 7041115
                 Unit: 403rd Replacement Company, 18th Replacement Battalion

(With grateful thanks to David Venditta and Joseph LoPinto for their assistance with this story)

On 4 June 1944, Rome was liberated from Nazi occupation and would quickly become a magnet for deserters eager to escape the dangers of the front line. Some of these individuals would form criminal gangs which travelled the city and surrounding countryside, terrorising Allied soldiers and Italian citizens in a spree of violence, robbery and murder. Just a few blocks from the Colosseum is Via Principe Amedeo, and at No. 223 was located a small wine shop owned by Antonio Ferretti, his son, Eolo, and his daughter-in-law, Maria. At about 8.30 p.m. on 9 October 1944, they were in their shop when two MPs walked in, carrying pistols. They pointed at the padlocked cash drawer behind the counter, pulled the handle and, after remarking that some glasses were dirty, they left the shop empty handed. The two soldiers were Private Werner Schmiedel, alias Robert Lane, and Private James W. Adams, who, along with Private Anthony Tavolieri, Private Carl F. Green and Private Delmar Joseph McFarlane, a Canadian, formed part of the infamous 'Lane Gang', one of the most violent group of deserters operating in the Italian capital.

The following evening, 10 October, the two men returned to the shop, holding pistols in the air. Antonio, Eolo and Maria were inside, along with Libero Galieti, Alfredo Venanzoni, Pasquale Romano, Camillo Bocchini and Pietro Bonza. They were told to put their hands in the air and form a line in front of an ice chest in the shop. Schmiedel ordered everyone to throw their wallets on the table. When one of the men took out his wallet, a large amount of money could be seen, and Adams snatched the wallet from the man's hand. When Antonio Ferretti saw this, he said to Schmiedel, 'Now, look here Sergeant, you don't want documents; its money you are after.' Schmiedel went over to Antonio and told him to produce his pocketbook. Antonio replied, 'What am I going to give you? I have no money or documents.' Schmiedel, who was holding a pair of Military Police gloves, slapped Antonio on the left side of his face. At that moment Pasquale Romano turned his head and Schmiedel jumped into the middle of the room and fired a shot. The bullet glanced off the side of Pasquale Romano's head, hit the ice chest, then ricocheted into Eolo Ferretti's abdomen, causing his spleen to rupture, entering his left kidney and triggering a significant internal haemorrhage. The two men made their escape and Eolo was taken to the St Giovanni (St John's) Hospital, where he died from his injuries. Schmiedel was now a wanted murderer.

Werner Schmiedel, born in Germany in 1923, had been brought to the United States by his parents where they lived in Weisenberg, Lehigh, Pennsylvania. He enlisted in the US Army on 18 June 1940, but spent much of his time being AWOL, for which he faced several courts martial. He was a perpetual guardhouse escapee, breaking out on numerous occasions and, eventually, on 19 August 1944, a GCM sentenced him to twenty years, but Brigadier General Francis H. Oxx reduced the period of confinement to ten years. A surprising outcome, given that in the same week, Private Eddie Slovik would desert his unit, for which he would be executed. In thanks to Oxx, Schmiedel escaped confinement on 2 September 1944 and began his last crime wave. The deserter made his way through war-torn Italy to Sparanise, 20 miles north-west of Naples. On 7 September, he and his compatriots robbed an Italian man of 150,000 lire. The gang moved to Formia, where they then robbed two MPs of their pistols and brassards on 17 September 1944. Later that day, the trio and two other gang members robbed Polish Lieutenant General Wladyslaw Anders' driver near Capua. Eventually, they arrived in Rome, where they continued to operate, in Chicago-gangster style, leading to the death of Eolo Ferretti and Schmiedel's final capture.

Agents serving with the US Army's Criminal Investigations Division in Rome were hot on the tail of Schmiedel, including Technical Sergeant John LoPinto of Ithaca, New York. After authorities identified Schmiedel's

Left: Private Werner E. Schmiedel. *Right*: Technical Sergeant John LoPinto. (*Photo: Courtesy of Joseph LoPinto and David Venditta*)

girlfriend, a prostitute named Fausta Piva, John LoPinto and several other agents found her in a dance hall. LoPinto asked her to dance, and as they took a few turns, one of his associates went through her purse. He snatched a photo of Schmiedel, hurried off to CID headquarters and had it copied, and then put it back in her purse within the hour, before she knew it was missing. Copies of the pilfered picture were distributed throughout Rome, Naples and the surrounding areas, and on the morning of 3 November 1944, Agent Eugene F. Land, Criminal Investigations Division, was looking for a man they knew to be named Roberto Lane. By pure chance, Schmiedel passed him on the street, and looking at the photograph he recognized the deserter. Land followed him into an establishment known as Rocky's Bar where he ordered

Guns, ammunition and equipment used by the 'Lane Gang' during their short reign of terror. (*Photo: Courtesy of Joseph LoPinto and David Venditta*)

Schmiedel to put up his hands, then searched his jacket and found a loaded .38 calibre Smith and Wesson revolver. Land arrested him.

This, however, was not the end of the story. At about 1.40 a.m. on Christmas Eve 1944, eight prisoners escaped from the Central Military Police Jail in Piazza Collegio Romano. Amongst them were Schmiedel and two other gang members, Delmar McFarlane and Carl Green. Within hours, MPs seized Green and two others and locked them up. Two days later, on 26 December 1944, John LoPinto received confidential information to the effect that Schmiedel and McFarlane were hiding in an apartment at 13 Via Carla Alberto. LoPinto, Monahan and Manfredi of the CID and Sergeant Eric Swetnam of the British Special Investigation Branch hatched a plan to seize the two fugitives. Eight MPs and five Italian police were called to cover the exits of the apartment building. The five civilian police, in plain clothes, were placed around the front entrance of the building with orders to let no one leave. When it was ascertained that the fugitives were still in the apartment, LoPinto and the other agents entered the building and proceeded up the stairs. Schmiedel and McFarlane were ordered to come out. They did not respond, so the agents went into the apartment, followed by some MPs. Schmiedel and McFarlane were concealed in a standalone closet, a wardrobe. Again, they were ordered to come out and didn't respond. Manfredi and Swetnam pushed over the closet and, as it was falling over, Schmiedel and McFarlane jumped out of it in the face of drawn guns. They were dressed in civilian clothes and had recently bleached their hair. As evidence, bottles of hair-bleaching chemicals were found on a stand near the closet. The two thugs were returned to the Central MP Jail, without a shot being fired, bringing the swaggering malcontent to justice.

Schmiedel appeared before his final GCM on 25 March 1945, where he was convicted of his crimes and sentenced to death. This time there was no clemency from Brigadier General Francis H. Oxx, who approved the sentence. General Joseph McNarney confirmed the death sentence on 21 April 1945. With the war in Europe over, Private Werner E. Schmiedel, who had never fired a shot on the front line, was hanged on 11 June 1945 at Aversa, Italy. The army initially buried Schmiedel at the US Military Cemetery at Naples, but he was amongst those who were secretly exhumed in 1949 and transported to the Oise-Aisne American Cemetery. His remains are buried there in Plot 'E', Row 3, Grave 53.

Amongst the crowd of onlookers that day who watched Schmiedel hang was Technical Sergeant John LoPinto. I thank him for his service, I thank Joe LoPinto for sharing his father's story and David Venditta for his help in telling it. Sadly, John LoPinto passed away in 1988 at the age of 80. Remember him.

Wednesday, 11 October 1944, France
Victim   Auguste Lefèbvre, French civilian (white)
                Age: 52
                Murdered
Assailants   Private James L. Jones (black)
                Age: 32
                Service No.: 34221343
                Private Milbert Bailey (black)
                Age: 30
                Service No.: 32794118
                Unit: 434th Port Company, 501st Port Battalion

Auguste Lefèbvre was a true hero. At the outbreak of the First World War, he served with the French Army and fought at Guise (Aisne) where he was wounded in the leg by shrapnel. He returned to a combat unit in 1915 and in 1918 was seriously injured by a bullet that passed through his neck. He would be decorated with the Croix de Guerre 1914–18 with bronze oak leaf, in recognition of his bravery. Auguste moved to La Pernelle, on the

The plaque installed in the village of La Pernelle, in memory of Auguste Lefèbvre, a brave French soldier of the First World War who was stabbed to death by a US soldier in a struggle at his home on 11 October 1944.

Cotentin Peninsula, in 1920, where he worked as an agricultural labourer. Here he settled into married life and fathered four children. By autumn 1944, he was a fit and healthy 52-year-old living a happier life as he and his family had been released from the grip of Nazi tyranny.

At about 8.00 p.m. on 11 October 1944, Auguste Lefèbvre was having a meal with his employer, who lived a short distance away. His wife was at home with their son, Eugene, and their 19-year-old daughter, Marguerite. Three black soldiers came to the house and asked for cognac, which the boy refused. About 10 minutes later they returned, knocked on the door and said, 'Police.' The door was locked so the soldiers prowled around the house and broke a windowpane. Madame Lefèbvre noticed that they were wearing white masks. They called for help and Marguerite escaped from the house, followed by her mother. As they were running down the road one of the soldiers threw Madame Lefèbvre to the ground. She got up and ran towards the house of a neighbour, crying for help. As she approached her neighbour's gate, one of the soldiers struck her on the head. The neighbour and his wife, on hearing her cries, came out of their house and the soldier then ran away. Meanwhile, Auguste and his employer had heard the cries for help coming from his house and made his way back home. A few minutes later Madame Lefèbvre and her neighbours also returned to the house. On their arrival they found Auguste clasping his stomach with his hands. He said he had been stabbed with a knife and was bleeding profusely. There was a wound about 5cm long on the right side of his abdomen. He did not say how he had received it except to remark, 'Dirty beasts.' An attempt was made to apply bandages and find a doctor. His face changed colour, his speech failed and in 15 minutes he was dead.

Marguerite, having left the house at the same time as her mother, ran towards the home of her father's employer, which was about 25m away. A black soldier caught her at this point, threw her to the ground and slapped her face. Another soldier was present, together they both struck her and wrapped her head in a raincoat. They took her to a nearby field where the soldiers tore off her clothes and raped her, all three taking it in turns to abuse her. This terrifying incident carried on for about 2 hours, after which the soldiers carried to another field about 2km away and raped her again. In all she was raped by each of the soldiers some three times. Eventually, at 1.30 a.m. she escaped and, exhausted, struck and bitten on the face, she made it back to her home. Marguerite was still in hospital when the assailants were tried for her father's murder. Court records relating to his case do not seem to have survived in full. What is known is that investigators from the Criminal Investigation Division apprehended three members of the 434th Port Company who were stationed near the village. These were Private Milbert Bailey, Private James L. Jones and Private John Williams. Each one was interviewed and gave statements that placed them at the location at the time the attacks took place. Some physical evidence existed that pointed to the trio being the culprits and they admitted that they were drunk and had seen Marguerite at the house where they had been refused cognac. Deciding to go back to 'get some pussy', Bailey placed a handkerchief over his face, whilst Jones and Williams wore makeshift masks made from the sleeves of Williams' undershirt. Jones was carrying a knife and it was, most likely, him who stabbed Auguste Lefèbvre, as the others were busy with Madame and Marguerite Lefèbvre. The three men were found guilty of rape and murder and sentenced to death by hanging.

On 19 April 1945, all three men found themselves back in the village of La Pernelle. There, in a small field overlooking the Atlantic Ocean, US Army engineers had constructed a temporary gallows. The executions began at 10.08 a.m., beginning with Private Milbert Bailey, who was born on 6 September 1914 at Head of Island, Livingston Parish, Louisiana, and enlisted on 20 September 1941 at Camp Livingston, Louisiana. His execution was followed by that of Private James L. Jones, who was born on 12 December 1912 in Reform, Pickens County, Alabama, and was inducted into the US Army on 6 May 1942 at Fort Benning, Georgia. The last to be hanged was Private John Williams, a divorced man with a child who was born on 8 March 1917 in Orlando, Orange County, Florida, and inducted into the army on 6 February 1943 in New York. Each man was led to the gallows by Lieutenant Colonel Henry L. Peck, at which point Master Sergeant John Clarence Woods placed a hood over their heads and secured a rope around their necks. Lieutenant Colonel Peck then gave a silent signal and the trapdoor sprang open, sending each soldier to his death. Their bodies were then transported to the US Military Cemetery at Marigny for burial. In 1949, they were removed from this location and secretly re-buried in Plot 'E' in the Oise-Aisne American Cemetery, Bailey in Row 4, Grave 90, Jones in Row 4, Grave 84 and Williams in Row 4, Grave 94.

As for Auguste Lefèbvre, he is buried in the local churchyard, his name is mentioned on the La Pernelle war memorial and, in March 2020, a plaque commemorating him was affixed to the wall of the local church. Remember him.

Friday, 13 October 1944, France
Victim   Berthe Robert, French civilian (white)
                   Murdered

THE PLOT OF SHAME

Assailant   PFC Haze Heard (black)
                 Age: 22
                 Service No.: 34562354
                 Unit: 3105th Quartermaster Service Company

In autumn 1944, Berthe Robert lived in the small Calvados village of Mesnil-Clinchamps with her husband, Eugène, and her two children, Alfred, aged 21, and Yvonne, aged 18. Also living in the house was a farm labourer, Jules Guilloche. On 13 October 1944, the 3105th Quartermaster Service Company, an African American unit, was bivouacked outside the village. At about 8.00 p.m., a black soldier armed with a rifle entered the house and asked for cider and Alfred gave him a glass, which he drank, after pouring some brandy into it from a bottle he had brought along with him. The soldier became drunk, but not so drunk that he didn't know what he was doing. He remained in the house for about an hour, during which time he purchased two eggs. He left the house at about 9.00 p.m. saying, 'Good night', but returned about 15 minutes later and, after being let in, asked for 'Mademoiselle'. He was told to leave by Eugene Robert, as it was time to go to bed. The soldier went out of the front door and Eugene locked it behind him. Almost immediately, there were two shots fired through the window, both of which struck Berthe Robert in the head, killing her instantly. A moment later, two more shots were fired through the door, but these did not strike any of the people in the house. After determining that his wife was dead, Eugene Robert left by way of the rear door of his home to seek help from officers whom he knew to be about 300m away. The soldier then appeared, entered the house through the rear door and pointed his rifle at those remaining in the room. Alfred Robert took the soldier by the arm and pointed to his deceased mother, showing him the result of his act, whereupon the soldier manipulated the bolt of his rifle, and made ready to fire again at the dead body. He then approached Yvonne, saying, 'Mademoiselle, zig-zig?' Yvonne, in anger, bravely took his gun away from him and threw it out the door. Alfred, Yvonne and Jules Guilloche then grappled with the soldier, subdued him and took him outside where they tied him to an apple tree. Eugene Robert returned, accompanied by Major Mead Hartwell and Captain Joseph Bronstein, the Commanding Officer of 3105th Quartermaster Service Company. They found the body of Berthe Robert inside the house, slumped in a chair in a pool of blood, and a black soldier lying on the ground tied to a tree outside. He was begging for mercy; he had been kicked and beaten and his face was cut and swollen. One of the Frenchmen was restrained from kicking him any further. Captain Bronstein asked the soldier his name. He claimed he couldn't remember but as the captain turned to leave, the soldier said he was PFC Haze Heard of the 3105th Quartermaster Service Company. Yvonne recovered the weapon, a .30 calibre 1903 rifle, and handed it to Major Hartwell. The fate of the soldier was sealed.

PFC Haze Heard appeared at a GCM on 25 January 1945 in Granville. It was a straightforward event, and the soldier, who was born in Toccoa, Stephens County, Georgia, on 7 June 1922, was sentenced to death. The sentence was approved by Brigadier General Henry S. Aurand and confirmed by General Dwight D. Eisenhower on 18 March 1945. On 21 May 1945, Heard was transported back to the village of Mesnil-Clinchamps, where, in an orchard owned by Eugene Robert, army engineers had constructed a temporary gallows. At 11.00 a.m., Haze dismounted from a personnel carrier and led by Lieutenant Colonel Henry L. Peck was escorted to the steps of the gallows, where the GCM order for his execution was read out. His guards bound his wrists and ankles, then Master Sergeant John Clarence Woods placed a hood over his head and secured a rope around his neck. Lieutenant Colonel Peck then gave a silent signal and the trapdoor sprang open, sending the soldier to his death. His body was transported to the US Military Cemetery at Marigny, where it was buried. As with many of the other executed US soldiers, his body was removed from the cemetery secretly in 1949 and re-buried in Plot 'E' of the Oise-Aisne American Cemetery in Row 2, Grave 38.

Author Colonel French L. MacLean contacted the Robert family during his research for the book *The Fifth Field* and established that amongst the spectators that day were all those who were present at the time Berthe Robert was murdered. Remember her.

Tuesday, 24 October 1944, Belgium
Victim   Henriette Tillieu Ep Deremince, Belgian civilian (white)
                    Age: 51
                    Raped
Assailants   Private Mervin Holden (black)
                    Age: 24
                    Service No.: 38226564
                    Private Elwood J. Spencer (black)
                    Age: 20
                    Service No.: 33739343
                    Unit: 646th Quartermaster Truck Company

In autumn 1944, as the Allied armies advanced towards the Rhine and V-1 rockets began to fall upon the Belgian cities of Brussels and Antwerp, Emile Deremince, an accountant, was living at Rue Lucien Nameche, Namur, Belgium, with his 51-year-old wife, Henriette Tillieu Ep Deremince, and their only son. There was still uncertainty in the air, despite the Allied advance, and any unsolicited knock at the door elicited a feeling of fear and trepidation. At 11.00 p.m. on 24 October 1944, the front doorbell rang at the Deremince home. When Emile asked who it was, a voice shouted, 'Police!' Emile then asked, 'But why?' and got the same response. Someone then struck the door, Emile opened it and two black soldiers walked in, one with his right hand in his pocket, as though he had a weapon. The other soldier, described as larger and darker, followed with a knife in his hand. Emile asked what they wanted, but they just pushed him aside. The invaders were Private Mervin Holden and Private Elwood J. Spencer, who then searched each room of the house, forcing the family to go with them. By the time they had reached the attic, both men were holding a knife, which they used to herd the family up the stairs. Then each man in turn urinated in the attic as the other held the hostages. Spencer tried to push Emile into one room of the attic and motioned for Holden to take Henriette into another room. As Holden pushed her, she screamed, 'No, no! I don't want to' and returned to the landing. Spencer shook the terrified woman and seized her by the neck. When Emile tried to go to her rescue, Holden put his knife in his belt, grabbed Emile by the throat, shook him and pushed him against the wall. Emile used both hands to try to pull Holden's hand free, so Holden released his grip and stepped back.

Helpless, Emile believed that these men intended to kill the family. Henriette put her hand on Spencer's face and said, 'You are not bad, you are good', telling him that US soldiers had come to their house previously. She attempted to run down the stairs, but Spencer caught her on the landing of the second floor and hit her. He grabbed her by the hand and shook her so hard that a stone in her ring fell out, and she screamed. Spencer held Henriette in a corner of the wall on the landing, placed his knife against her throat, put his hand under her dress and tried to raise it. Emile, who was still on the third-floor landing, yelled at Holden, 'For God's sake, don't let him do it.' Henriette yelled back, 'There's nothing I can do. He has his knife against me.' Taking Henriette by knifepoint, Spencer pushed her into a room, where he raped her, whilst Holden continued to hold Emile captive on the third-floor landing. After Spencer finished, he took Henriette out of the room and when they reached the lower landing, she said, 'Now go to bed,

1944: THE YEAR ENDS

now leave us alone.' Instead, Spencer motioned to Holden to take the woman into the bedroom, which he did, then pushed Henriette onto the bed and raped her. The soldiers then escorted the Dereminces down the stairs and left the house.

The couple reported the incident to the US authorities the following day. A medical inspection was arranged but, because Henriette was an aging woman, who had borne a child and had taken 'hygienic precautions' after the assault, the Medical Officer was unable to tell if she had, in fact, been raped. Despite this, an identification parade was arranged, using men from nearby units and it was here that Emile and Henriette recognised the two assailants. On 26 October, Agent Obed T. Kilgore, of the Criminal Investigation Division, took a statement from each man. Spencer claimed that they had sex at the Deremince home, but that it was consensual. If both men had maintained this, it would have been difficult to prove otherwise. However, Spencer gave the game away by stating that Holden had a knife, which he held in front of the husband. Holden, in his statement, claimed that Spencer had pushed Henriette against the wall and she had told him, 'No.'

Private Mervin Holden, born in Robeline, Natchitoches Parish, Louisiana, on 1 October 1920, was inducted into the army in Shreveport, Louisiana, on 24 September 1942. Private Elwood J. Spencer, born in Gastonia, Gaston County, North Carolina, on 4 December 1924, was inducted into the army in Fort Myer, Virginia, on 6 April 1943. Both men appeared before a GCM at Maastricht, Holland, on 14 November 1944. Each man continued to claim that the sex was consensual, but the court did not believe this, and they were both sentenced to death by hanging. The sentences were approved by Lieutenant General William H. Simpson and confirmed by General Dwight D. Eisenhower on 23 December 1944.

On 30 January 1944, the two soldiers were transported to Namur, where they had committed their crimes. Here, in the courtyard of the Fort d'Orange, the Citadel of Namur, US Army engineers had constructed a temporary gallows. The executions were scheduled to start at 11.00 a.m., starting with Private Mervin Holden, who sang a religious song, even as he fell through the trapdoor. This was swiftly followed by Private Elwood J. Spencer, who asked if he could 'see the rope' before he died. This request was denied. Each man was led to the gallows by Lieutenant Colonel Henry L. Peck, at which point Master Sergeant John Clarence Woods placed a hood over their heads and secured a rope around their necks. Lieutenant Colonel Peck then gave a silent signal and the trapdoor sprang open, sending each soldier to his death. Their bodies were then transported to the US Military Cemetery at Andilly for burial. In 1949, they were removed from this location and secretly re-buried in Plot 'E' of the Oise-Aisne American Cemetery. Holden in Row 1, Grave 8 and Spencer in Row 2, Grave 33.

Saturday, 28 October 1944, Belgium
Victim   Private Randolph Jackson Jr (black)
                  Age: 19
                  Service No.: 35646330
                  Murdered
Assailant   Private Benjamin F. Hopper (black)
                  Age: 24
                  Service No.: 32720571
                  Unit: 3170th Quartermaster Service Company

On some occasions, trial documents are particularly short and devoid of information. Such is the case of Private Randolph Jackson Jr, of Logan County, West Virginia, who joined the US Army on 1 January 1943 at Huntington, West Virginia. Like many African Americans, he did not get the opportunity to serve on the front line, instead he was assigned to a role in the support functions. He would almost certainly have survived the war if it were not for a stupid, petty argument.

On 27 October 1944, Private Jackson was working in the railroad station at Herbesthal, Welkenraedt, Belgium, on the outskirts of Liège. He and his comrade, Private James W. Rogers, decided to have a beer in a local cafe once they were off duty. Just after midnight, the two soldiers prepared to return to their camp, and as they did so, they passed by the Mason des Huiets

The last resting place of Private Randolph Jackson Jr in Arlington Military Cemetery, Virginia. He was murdered by Private Benjamin F. Hopper in a 'playful argument' on 28 October 1944.

Heures Café, where they could hear English being spoken, so decided to go inside. Sitting at a table were three US soldiers, two of whom were from their own unit, along with a Mexican soldier. Rogers began to sing songs in Spanish with the Mexican, whilst the others chatted. The cafe owner, desperate to close, was attempting to usher the soldiers out of the door. Finally, they started to gather their equipment in readiness to leave, at which point Jackson was involved in what was described as a 'playful argument' with Private Benjamin F. Hopper. Suddenly, Hopper said that if he had a gun he would shoot Jackson, and things quickly turned violent. Jackson said, 'Oh, you wouldn't do that. I will give you my gun and even put one in the chamber.' He did this and handed the gun to Hopper. It seems that nobody took the threat seriously, until Hopper took hold of the rifle, stood back and fired. He then continued to fire the weapon, slowly moving closer to Jackson until he was stood over the body and the ammunition had been expended. There was total silence in the cafe and Jackson was dead. Rogers went to the door and called to Hopper, 'Don't go away and leave the boy. Help me take him to a hospital.' Hopper answered, 'You didn't see nothing' and ran away.

The case was straightforward, and MPs arrested the killer on the same day. His GCM was convened at 10.00 a.m. on 23 November 1944 at Soumagne, Belgium, the location of the First Army Headquarters. Private Benjamin Hopper pleaded not guilty to the charge of murder and elected not to testify. His defence presented no evidence on his behalf. Hopper told an army psychiatrist that during the argument, Private Jackson pointed his rifle at him and threatened, 'Goddamn it, I'll shoot you', but this was never confirmed. The jury found him guilty and sentenced him to death by hanging. The JAG was concerned that there were issues concerning premeditation, and recommended that the sentence be commuted to life imprisonment, which the commander of the First Army, Lieutenant General Courtney H. Hodges, supported. For his part, Hopper felt he had not had a fair trial as his defence counsellor said he would do all the talking, but instead, simply said 'not guilty'. However, Brigadier General Edward C. Betts recommended no clemency and General Dwight D. Eisenhower signed the order of execution on 12 February 1945.

Hopper had, by now, been transferred to the Loire DTC at Le Mans, France. Here, on 11 April 1945, Hopper, born in Hickory, Catawba County, North Carolina on 20 August 1920, was escorted to a temporary gallows, located in a small ravine. A crowd of forty-six officials, witnesses and spectators, including eight general prisoners, four white and four black, watched as Lieutenant Colonel Henry L. Peck led him to the steps of the scaffold. After guards ushered him up the flight of steps, Master Sergeant John Clarence Woods placed a hood over his head and secured a rope around his neck. Lieutenant Colonel Peck then gave a silent signal and the trapdoor sprang open, sending the soldier to his death. His body was then transported to the US Military Cemetery at Marigny for burial. In 1949, his remains were removed from this location and secretly re-buried in the Oise-Aisne American Cemetery in Plot 'E', Row 1, Grave 7.

Under the Return of the Dead Program, the body of Private Randolph Jackson Jr was returned to the United States where it is buried in Arlington Military Cemetery, Virginia, in Plot 12, Grave 3140. Remember him.

Sunday, 12 November 1944, France
Victim   Corporal Laurence Broussard (black)
                   Age: 24
                   Service No.: 37053033
Assailant   Private Tom E. Gordon (black)
                   Age: 30
                   Service No.: 34091950
                   Unit: 3251st Quartermaster Service Company

The mixture of alcohol, testosterone and live fire arms is a deadly one, particularly when soldiers are in the confines of their barracks, and the case of Corporal Laurence Broussard is testament to this. Corporal Broussard was serving with the 3251st Quartermaster Service Company, stationed in the French port city of Marseille, and would become the victim of yet another straightforward case of drink-fuelled murder. At 1.30 a.m. on 12 November 1944, Corporal Broussard was in his bunk when Private Tom Gordon returned from a drinking session. Gordon was being loud and annoying the sleeping soldiers. First Sergeant Otto McQueen told him to 'shut up' or he would lock him up in the stockade, to which Gordon responded that he 'didn't give a damn'. McQueen sent for the Corporal of the Guard, but he could not be found. Gordon, who was by now crying, said, 'I wish I had a pistol; I'd kill all of these rotten mother fuckers.' He was then heard to say, 'I'm going to kill the first son of a bitch that raises hell with me, and I bet it will be Broussard.' Gordon continued to wander around the small barrack room, looking at the lockers and, suddenly, shots rang out. Confusion now reigned in the barrack room. Broussard hollered, 'Come over and do something for me I'm shot.' Then another shot was fired and Corporal Willie J. Best, shouted, 'I'm shot too.' He had been lying in the upper bunk when he heard two shots. He jumped out of bed, got behind a post and saw Gordon coming towards him holding a rifle. Gordon had taken aim and fired, the bullet striking him in the thigh. PFC John D. Brown was sleeping in his bunk and heard a shot, which glanced off the bottom of his bed and struck him in the buttocks. Private James Johnson tried to wrestle the weapon from Gordon but was unable to do so. Gordon, who did not appear to be so drunk that he didn't know what he was doing, then made his escape. Corporal Laurence Broussard was found, bleeding, in a serious condition, lying at the side of his bunk. He was taken to the station hospital at 3.00 a.m. where medics discovered a gunshot wound had perforated his abdomen. On 18 November Broussard died from his injuries.

Gordon was eventually arrested and returned to military control. Major Alfred O. Ludwig, psychiatric consultant for the Seventh Army, found that the soldier, born in Greenville, South Carolina on 7 March 1915, had a mental age of about 9 years. He thought, however, that Gordon would be able to determine right from wrong and would know it was wrong to shoot and kill another man. His GCM was convened at Luneville, France, on 13 February 1945. He pleaded not guilty to the charges of murder and being AWOL and chose to make an unsworn statement at the trial. He claimed that he went out drinking and couldn't remember anything until 13 November, when MPs told him he had shot someone. The jury did not accept this explanation, found him guilty of all charges and sentenced him to death by hanging. Lieutenant General Alexander M. Patch approved the sentence and General Dwight D. Eisenhower signed the order of execution on 6 May 1945, just as hostilities were ending in Europe, but Tom Gordon would never see the shores of the United States again.

On the morning of 10 July 1945, as light rain fell across the city of Le Mans, Private Tom E. Gordon who had, by now, been transferred to the Loire DTC, stood before the temporary gallows that many others had perished upon. A crowd of twenty-one officials, witnesses and spectators watched as Lieutenant Colonel Henry L. Peck led him to the steps of the scaffold. After guards escorted him up the flight of steps, Master Sergeant John Clarence Woods placed a hood over his head and secured a rope around his neck. Lieutenant Colonel Peck then gave a silent signal and the trapdoor sprang open, sending the soldier to his death. His body was then transported to the US Military Cemetery at Marigny for burial. In 1949, his remains were removed from this location and secretly re-buried in the Oise-Aisne American Cemetery in Plot 'E', Row 1, Grave 10.

The body of Corporal Laurence Broussard was returned to the United States where he is buried in the Johnson Memorial Park Cemetery, Groves, Jefferson County, Texas. Remember him.

Saturday, 18 November 1944, France
Victim   Corporal Tommie Lee Garrett (black)
                Age: 20
                Service No.: 34745711
Assailant   Private George Green Jr (black)
                Age: 20
                Service No.: 38476751
                Unit: 998th Quartermaster Salvage Collecting Company

Champigneulles is a commune on the outskirts of the city of Nancy, France. It was here, a long way from the combat zone, that the life of Corporal Tommie Lee Garrett, who was serving in 998th Quartermaster Salvage Collecting Company, would come to an end over nothing more than a simple grudge. At about 8.30 a.m. on the morning of 18 November 1944, Garrett was working in a warehouse, sorting OD trousers for salvage with a group of other soldiers from his unit. He was sitting on a bench classifying the pieces of kit when, suddenly, a shot rang out and Garrett fell down

The grave of Corporal Tommie Lee Garrett in Lorraine American Cemetery, Saint-Avold, France.

dead into the pile of clothing. T/5 Lawrence R. Jenkins saw a soldier, Private George Green Jr, holding his rifle at port arms. Sergeant Albert Reynolds took the gun from Green and asked why he had taken a shot at Garrett. Green replied, 'That man drew a knife on me.' The incident he was referring to had happened about an hour or so earlier. The men were cleaning the squad room when Garrett asked Green if he had spilled urine from a container on the floor. When Green answered, 'Yes, but you don't have to talk so big about it', Garrett grabbed him by the collar and told him he would have to clean it up. A witness to this said that Garrett was carrying an open knife in his hand at the time, although he did not appear to be angry about the matter. Private Thomas Essex overheard Green say 'that there was someone he was going to get'. When Essex asked who he was referring to, Green replied that it was none of his business.

Green was arrested by the MP and appeared before a GCM on 9 December 1944, which was held in Nancy. He pleaded not guilty and elected not to take to the witness stand. Regarded as a good and efficient soldier by his platoon sergeant, Green, born in Stephens, Ouachita County, Arkansas, was not a known troublemaker and did not have a poor relationship with Garrett. He had joined the US Army on 19 April 1943 and had been assigned to his company on 8 January 1944. His former employer at the Red River Ordnance Plant, Texas, stated that Green 'made a good employee with the war plant while employed with them' and 'never was intoxicated or arrested and that his reputation was good'. Witnesses to the incident involving the urine stated that Garrett was carrying a knife, as he always did for his job, but did not threaten Green with it. The court unanimously found him guilty of the crime and sentenced him to death by hanging. General Dwight D. Eisenhower signed the order of execution on 25 February 1945. Despite written pleas for clemency from both Green and his wife, the execution was set for 15 May 1945.

On the morning of the execution, the sun shone over the city of Le Mans. Private George Green Jr stood before the temporary gallows at the Loire DTC. A crowd of fifty officials, witnesses and spectators watched as Lieutenant Colonel Henry L. Peck led him to the scaffold. After guards escorted him up the flight of thirteen steps, Master Sergeant John Clarence Woods placed a hood over his head and secured a rope around his neck. Lieutenant Colonel Peck then gave a silent signal and the trapdoor sprang open, sending the soldier to his death. His body was then transported to the US Military Cemetery at Marigny for burial. In 1949, his remains were removed from this location and secretly re-buried in the Oise-Aisne American Cemetery in Plot 'E', Row 2, Grave 36.

Corporal Tommie Lee Garrett, born on 7 June 1924, in Opelika, Alabama, never returned home to the United States. Instead, he lays buried with the honoured dead at Lorraine American Cemetery, Saint-Avold, France in Plot B, Row 18, Grave 48. Remember him.

27 November 1944, Italy
Victim   Carla Sabatini, Italian civilian (white)
                  Age: 14
                  Raped
Assailant   Private Lee A. Burns (black)
                  Age: 31
                  Service No.: 38520648
                  Unit: 792nd Ordnance (Light Maintenance) Company

Amongst the cases featured in this book are those over which a question mark hangs. This is one such case. The act was one of violent terror in which a young Italian teenager was brutally raped in front of her family by a soldier of the liberating US Army. But was this the man they hanged?

In winter 1944, Fedora Sabatini and her daughter, Carla, a 14-year-old student, lived in the home of Fedora's father, 87-year-old Lorenzo Rinaldo, in the small commune of Maggiano, Italy, some 10 miles from the city of Pisa. The house was about two blocks from the camp of 792nd Ordnance (Light Maintenance) Company, serving with the 92nd Infantry Division, an African American unit. One of the men in the company was Private Lee A. Burns, born in Homer, Claiborne Parish, Louisiana, on 9 November 1913. He knew both the girl and her mother and had been to their home previously. At 10.00 p.m. on 27 November 1944, Captain Cecil B. Morris and Corporal Dewey Lewis, both of the 792nd, arrived at the Sabatini home. Here, they found Private Aldene Worthey and Private Burns and ordered them to return to the camp with them, and that they were to remain there. At 11.45 p.m., Fedora Sabatini claimed that four black soldiers arrived at the house, said they were MPs and when Lorenzo Rinaldo opened the door they entered, searched the entire house and left. About half an hour later one of them returned, alone. Armed with a rifle, the soldier looked in all the rooms then entered the bedroom occupied by the two women and told them to get out of bed. After Carla put a coat on over her nightdress, he pointed his weapon and forced all three members of the household downstairs to the kitchen. Carla ran to the door and attempted to leave, but the soldier forced her to return. The soldier approached Carla and said

'*Figi figi*', and indicated to her that she had to let him do as he wished otherwise he would shoot the other two. Carla ran to her mother who held her tightly, but the soldier dragged her away, put her near a table and unbuttoned his trousers. The old man begged him to release the girl, but the soldier fired a shot into the kitchen floor. Fedora screamed for help but the assailant hit her several times on the head when she attempted to rescue Carla. When Fedora kneeled at his feet and asked him to, 'Take me, but leave the child alone, as she is too young', he repeatedly hit her on the head. Then he forced all three people to go upstairs. The two women entered the bedroom and Carla ran to the window, opened it and called for help but the soldier caught her by the hair, closed the window, dragged her to the bed and pinned her against it. Here, in front of her mother and grandfather, he carried out a vicious and brutal rape. The whole incident lasted some 90 minutes, after which the attacker left the house. The following day, Fedora went to the orderly room of the 792nd where, through an interpreter, she stated her daughter had been raped. She had with her a piece of paper with Burns name written on it. Burns and Worthy were called into the office and Fedora identified Burns as the attacker. Three days later, on 30 November, Fedora returned and spoke to Captain Morris, again via an interpreter. Morris called Burns and three other men into his office. He pointed at the first three and asked Fedora if any of these were the assailant, she stated they were not. When he pointed at Burns, she said, 'He is the one.' On 4 December, a week after the event, Carla was examined by Captain Willard G. French at the 170th Evacuation Hospital. He indicated that the girl had no bruises or scratches on her body, but that something had been inserted into her genitals within the past few days, although he could not say what. There was no evidence of spermatozoa found on the girl's body.

Private Lee A. Burns appeared before a GCM on 19 January 1945, where he pleaded not guilty. Burns opted not to take to the witness stand, but this may have been on the advice of his defence counsel. It was evident from the timeline provided by both Fedora and his comrades that Burns appeared to be in two places at the same time. How could he be at the Sabatini home at 10.45 p.m. when Corporal Lewis had seen him in his quarters at 10.40 p.m.? The defence chose not to raise this valid point. Despite this, in a trial that lasted just 2 hours and 40 minutes, Burns was found guilty of the crime and sentenced to death by hanging. The sentence was approved by Brigadier General Adam Richmond and the order of execution was signed by Lieutenant General Joseph T. McNarney on 19 February 1945.

THE PLOT OF SHAME

On the afternoon of 27 March 1945, Major W.G. Neiswender, Commanding Officer of the PBS Garrison Stockade No. 1 at Aversa, Italy, presided over the execution of Private Lee A. Burns. Three US Army officers opened the trapdoor, sending the soldier to his death. His body was then transported to the US Military Cemetery at Naples for burial. In 1949, his remains were removed from this location and secretly re-buried in the Oise-Aisne American Cemetery in Plot 'E', Row 4, Grave 74.

3 December 1944, England

Victim	Joyce Broome, British civilian (white)
	Age: 26
	Raped
Assailants	Private Cubia Jones (black)
	Age: 25
	Service No.: 34563790
	Corporal Robert L. Pearson (black)
	Age: 21
	Service No.: 38326741
	Unit: Company 'A', 1698th Engineer Combat Battalion

Joyce Broom was a 26-year-old married woman, living in Bonfire Close, Chard, Somerset. A machinist in a textile factory, she was in her ninth month of pregnancy when on the evening of 3 December 1944 she left her home to go to the cinema, but never made it there. Soon after leaving her house, Joyce became aware that she was being followed. She turned and saw two black soldiers who had come up very close to her. One of them said, 'Hello!', to which she replied, 'Hello, I don't know you and you don't know me.' As she began to walk away, the two men grabbed hold of her wrists and restrained her. She pleaded with them to leave her alone, telling them that she was not only married but also heavily pregnant. It made no difference to the men, who then began to drag her off. One of them slapped a hand over her mouth to prevent her from crying out. A scuffle developed as Joyce tried to escape, resulting in all three of them falling to the ground. The two men then dragged the expectant mother to a gate leading to an orchard, and then into a field. Once they felt that they were far enough from the road, Joyce was thrown onto her back, and it was obvious to her that they intended to rape her. She begged them to stop and leave her alone, to which, surprisingly, one of the men told her that they loved her. She was then raped by one of the men, whilst the other restrained her and prevented her from struggling. After the first man had finished, they changed places and the one now holding her down brandished a knife in front of her face. After the second man had raped her, he stood up and, at that moment, Joyce managed to snatch the knife. The men, having accomplished their purpose told her, 'Don't say anything about this to anyone or we will kill you.' Joyce, distraught, reached the road, where she encountered a neighbour, Frederick Bandy, who described her as pale, tearful and agitated. She told him what had happened and he quickly saw her safely to her home, then fetched Sergeant Arthur Doughty from Chard Police Station. He arrived with Dr Albert Glanville, who examined Joyce, finding she had a bruised lip and a swollen nose, consistent with having had a hand clamped over her mouth.

The US military authorities went to the nearest African American unit based at Chard, the 1698th Engineer Combat Battalion, where they carried out a clothing check. As a result, they found a soldier from Company 'A', Corporal Robert Pearson, had fresh, wet mud on his trousers. The following morning, another soldier, Private Cubia Jones, was also found to have muddy trousers. No one else in their unit had clothes that were in the same condition. On 4 December, the day after the attack, James E. Connor of the 32nd Military Police Criminal Investigation Section interviewed both soldiers in front of their Adjutant, First Lieutenant Albert C. Riggs. They were asked to explain how they managed to get their trousers in such a mess. The two men admitted to meeting Joyce Broom, but claimed she had consented to having sex with them and went as far as saying that she had enjoyed it. Pearson denied having a knife or even seeing one, but Jones admitted he owned a knife, but had misplaced it. Military justice, on this occasion, was swift and both men were brought before a GCM held at Chard in December 1944, where they pleaded not guilty to the crime. Both men declined to take to the witness stand. For her part, Joyce was unable to confirm that the men who stood in court were the two who raped her. She maintained that she was an unwilling participant. There was very little for the court to consider, and the two soldiers were found guilty and sentenced to death by hanging.

Major General Milburn approved the sentences, with General Dwight D. Eisenhower signing the confirming orders on 12 February 1945. A Board of Review examined the court proceedings and determined that the GCM had been conducted appropriately and in accordance with US military law. At 1.00 a.m. on 8 January 1945, in what would be a rare double execution, Major Herbert R. Laslett, the Commanding Officer of 2912th DTC, stood before a group of officials and witnesses in the cramped execution room at Shepton Mallet Prison as both men were led onto the gallows together. Thomas Pierrepoint and Herbert Morris prepared both men as quickly as the could for execution. A silent signal was given by Major Laslett and both men dropped through the trapdoors. They were pronounced dead 17 minutes later.

Their bodies were initially buried in Brookwood American Military Cemetery, Surrey. In 1948 they were reburied in the American Military Cemetery in Cambridge and, a year later, they were removed from the ground for a second time and secretly transported to the Oise-Aisne American Cemetery where they were buried in Plot 'E'. Private Cubia Jones, of Thompson, Georgia, is buried in Row 1, Grave 15. Corporal Robert L. Pearson, of Mayflower, Arkansas, is buried in Row 1, Grave 22.

3 December 1944, England
Victim   Sir Eric Tiechman, British civilian (white)
                Age: 60
                Murdered
Assailant   Private George Edward Smith (white)
                Age: 28
                Service No.: 33288266
                Unit: 784th Bombardment Squadron, 466th
                    Bombardment Group (H)

On the day that Joyce Broom was raped in Somerset, US MPs were also busy with a second case, this time a murder in the county of Norfolk. Sir Eric Teichman, born on 16 January 1884, was the son of Emil Teichmann and Mary Lydia Schroeter. He was educated at Gonville and Caius College, Cambridge University, and would build a career as a British diplomat and Orientalist, serving

Sir Eric Tiechman, who was murdered by Private George Edward Smith on 3 December 1944.

as adviser to the British Embassy at Chungking. That day Sir Eric sat contentedly in front of a cosy fire in the drawing room of his home, Honingham Hall, enjoying the peace and quiet with his wife, Lady Ellen. Then, from outside, came the sound of shots. Sir Eric got out of his chair and growled, 'I'm going out to stop this damned poaching.' He then left the house, unarmed, and never returned. Two US soldiers, Private George Edward Smith and Private Leonard S. Wojtacha, who were serving as part of the ground echelon with 784th Bombardment Squadron, 466th Bombardment Group (H), had entered the woods on the Teichman estate. Both men were armed with service carbines and, after passing near the house, on an old, abandoned road, they began shooting at a squirrel. They continued to fire as the animal leapt from tree to tree, until they reached a point near the top of a hill, which was about a mile from the airfield and some 300yd from Sir Eric's home. It was in a wooded area, overgrown with bracken about 3ft high. Suddenly, Smith said, 'Watch out that there's an old man approaching behind you.' Sir Eric, who walked with a severe stoop and a cane, asked Wojtacha, 'What are your names?' Wojtacha heard Smith say, 'Get back, pop' and then he heard the sound of a gun. Smith had fired his carbine from his hip. Sir Eric slumped to the ground face down, fatally shot. They quickly left the area and on the return trip to the airdrome, Wojtacha said he felt frightened, but Smith was happy, calm and normal. After returning to their barracks, they hid the rifles under a table in another soldier's room and parted company. Wojtacha said that Smith lay on his bunk, relaxed and smiling. After failing to return for tea, a search for Sir Eric began, his body being found at about midnight. An autopsy revealed a bullet had entered his right cheek, shattered the jaw completely and was then deflected downward by two vertebrae in the neck, broke two ribs and passed out of his body under the left shoulder blade. On the morning of 4 December 1944, all the men in Smith's section were ordered to turn in their firearms. Smith handed in his carbine. The following day, Smith came up to Wojtacha's table at the mess hall and told him, 'Don't say anything. Let them find out for themselves.' The Provost Marshal learned that Smith and Wojtacha had gone hunting during the afternoon in question and, on 6 December, confronted Wojtacha with this evidence and with casts of footsteps made at the scene of the crime. Wojtacha, scared, made a full statement. The next morning Smith was told he would be charged with murder.

Private George Edward Smith appeared before a GCM in the chapel at RAF Attlebridge, Norfolk, on 8 January 1945. Born on 14 April 1917, in Pittsburgh, Pennsylvania, he was the son of a steelworker. He had been inducted into the US Army on 13 August 1942 when he was on parole, serving a long sentence for auto theft and had a string of other offences behind him. Worse was to come. He had been classed as constitutional psychopathic, two words you may have read previously in this publication. He was described as being tidy in his room, took pride in his appearance and was always shining his buttons and polishing his shoes. He occasionally stood and stared into space, and once became angry at a smoking stove and took it out of the room. He rarely went out with his comrades and never played cards or went out with girls. He was considered a normal, happy soldier and was well liked, but inclined to be excitable and raise his voice. The GCM took five days to complete, as Smith was repeatedly hospitalised as he felt ill. Eventually, the court determined his guilt, and he was sentenced to death by hanging. After the case was reviewed and given the usual considerations, there were several requests for clemency, including one from Lady Teichman. However, General Dwight D. Eisenhower signed the order confirming the death sentence on 3 April 1945. VE Day, 8 May 1945, was a solemn occasion at the 2912th DTC in Shepton Mallet Prison, Somerset. As the Allies celebrated the end of Nazi tyranny in Europe, a young American, who should have been looking forward to going home, was about to lose his life to a British executioner. Major Philip J. Flynn, the DTC commander, oversaw the proceedings that night. Following a silent signal from Flynn, at 2.03 a.m., Smith fell through the trapdoor at the hands of Thomas Pierrepoint and Herbert Morris.

Smith's body was initially buried in Brookwood American Military Cemetery, Surrey. In 1948 it was transferred to the American Military Cemetery in Cambridge and, a year later, it was removed from the ground for a second time and secretly transported to the Oise-Aisne American Cemetery where his remains were reburied in Plot 'E', Row 3, Grave 52. Eric Teichman is buried in the churchyard of St Andrew's Church, Honingham, Norfolk. Remember him.

Friday, 15 December 1944, Italy
Victim   T/5 George W. Brown (black)
                Age: 24
                Service No.: 13017299
                Murdered
Assailant   Corporal Shelton McGhee (black)
                Age: 28
                Service No.: 34529025
                Unit: 3823rd Quartermaster Truck Company

At about 11.30 p.m. on 15 December 1944, in the town of Livorno, on the west coast of Italy, a group of African American soldiers serving with the 3823rd Quartermaster Truck Company was playing dice by the gate, near the guard shack. Amongst the men was Corporal Shelton McGhee and T/5 George W. Brown. The guard broke up the game, but the men then went behind the shack and continued gambling. Private John F. Jones, who lost $10, stopped playing and three more men also dropped out of the game, leaving just Brown and McGhee. They played for another 15 minutes until Brown won all of McGhee's money. Brown started to walk away when McGhee said, 'Nobody takes nothing from me', and Brown replied, 'I took this.' When Brown was about 25 or 30ft away, McGhee reached inside his coveralls and drew out a P-38 pistol, pointed it at Brown and fired one shot. He fell to the ground, and McGhee walked towards him firing another four or five more shots at him as he lay on the floor. When he reached Brown's body, he kicked it twice on the right side of the head, then said he was going to kill everyone, so the group scattered and ran.

First Lieutenant James A. Green, McGhee's company commander, saw him with the P-38 pistol in his hand and witnessed him put a cartridge in the chamber. Green walked towards him and asked, 'What are you doing with the gun?' McGhee, who appeared to be very excited, replied, 'Nobody's going to take this gun from me. I killed one man, and I'll kill you.' When Green ordered McGhee to give him the gun, he said, 'I'll kill you.' He then raised and cocked the pistol, stepped backward and pointed the weapon at Green, who turned and ran toward the gate. As he ran, he looked back and saw McGhee pointing the pistol at him and pulling the trigger. Green escaped with his life. Brown, who was conscious and bleeding from the abdomen, was taken to the 64th General Hospital in a truck by Jones and some other soldiers. He was given plasma treatment but stopped breathing about 5 minutes after his arrival, dying at 12.05 a.m. on 15 December 1944. There was one bullet wound in his side and eight in the front of his body.

Justice was swift and McGhee appeared before a GCM at Livorno on 3 February 1945, where he pleaded not guilty. He took to the witness stand, claiming that he believed Brown had a gun as he had been showing it to other members of the company recently. The witnesses did not support this claim. McGhee was found guilty of the crime in a very short hearing and sentenced to death by hanging. On 4 May 1945, Major W.G. Neiswender, Commanding Officer of the PBS Garrison Stockade No. 1 at Aversa, Italy, presided over the execution of Corporal Shelton McGhee. At 8.12 a.m. the trapdoor opened, sending the soldier to his death. His body was then transported to the US Military Cemetery at Naples for burial. In 1949, his remains were removed from this location and secretly re-buried in the Oise-Aisne American Cemetery in Plot 'E', Row 1, Grave 6.

Under the Return of the Dead Program, the remains of T/5 George W. Brown were shipped back to the United States and buried in Forest Hill Burial Park, Lynchburg, Virginia. Remember him.

Sunday, 17 December 1944, France
Victim   Private Billy Basil Betts (white)
                Age: 27
                Service No.: 39573932
                Unit: 568th Railhead Company
                Murdered
Assailant   Private Robert Wray (black)
                Age: 24
                Service No.: 34461589
                Unit: 3299th Quartermaster Service Company

On the evening of 17 December 1944, Private Robert Wray, a black soldier serving with the 3299th Quartermaster Service Company, stationed in Golbey, France, a suburb of Épinal, asked another soldier if he would lend him a pistol. A short time later, at about 8.00 p.m., Wray walked into the Café Moderne and was seen with a weapon in his hands, which looked like a German P-38. He approached a table at which were seated Private Billy Basil Betts, a 27-year-old from San Gabriel, California, and PFC Victor Piechnik, both of the 568th Quartermaster Railhead Company, and two Puerto Rican soldiers, all of whom had been drinking at the cafe since 6.00 p.m.

They had had a few beers and some wine, but not enough to become drunk. As Piechnik stood by the table, picking up some francs to pay for drinks he had ordered, Wray asked him for 100 francs. Piechnik said, 'I'm sorry, I don't know you well enough to give you a hundred francs.' Wray pulled up the pistol and pointed it at him. Piechnik said, 'If you want it, you can take it all', and started backing away, until he was out of the cafe, where he heard a shot. Meanwhile, there was a struggle inside the cafe to try and disarm Wray, but he went to the door, keeping everyone in the place covered with his weapon. Betts then approached Wray at was described as 'the normal rate', in other words, a normal walk, not in an aggressive manner. Wray pushed him back with his left hand and, with the pistol in his right hand, fired. Betts held himself up on a table, then fell on his back. He was taken to the 2nd Convalescent Hospital dispensary at 8.30 p.m. that night, but was found to be dead on arrival, the bullet having entered his neck and exited through his left shoulder. Wray made his escape, returned to camp and handed back the pistol he had borrowed. He was later picked out of an identification parade by Sergeant Ismael Torres of the 65th Infantry Regiment, who was in the cafe at the time. He recognised Wray by the scars on his face. Private Robert Wray, born on 27 March 1921 in Shelby, North Carolina, was then arrested. He had been inducted to the US Army on 7 November 1942 at Fort Bragg, North Carolina. His section sergeant stated that he was an efficient soldier, who was not a troublemaker, but his Company Commander, Captain John J. Harkins, felt that his character and efficiency were poor. Wray had stood before no less than four courts martial, mainly for misdemeanours, and a subsequent psychiatric examination found that he was uneducated, possibly illiterate, but did not have any pre-existing mental illness.

Wray appeared before a GCM on 23 March 1945 in Luneville, France, where he pleaded not guilty to the charge of murder. He took to the witness stand, where he claimed he had walked into the cafe and a Puerto Rican soldier had pulled a .45 pistol on him. There was struggle and he took the pistol from the soldier, who then ran out of the door. The remaining soldiers had 'jumped' him, so he pulled out the P-38 and shot a soldier advancing towards him, who he thought was the Puerto Rican. This contrasted with the statement he had given to investigators, in which he claimed that a white soldier had called him 'nigger', so he slapped him. There was then a fight and as a soldier approached him, who he believed was the one who slapped him, he pulled out the P-38 and shot him. The jury was unconvinced and found Wray guilty of the charge, sentencing him unanimously to death by hanging. Following a review of the case, the death sentence was confirmed by General Omar N. Bradley on 26 June 1945. On the morning of 20 August 1945, a cool breeze blew over the city of Le Mans, and Private Robert Wray stood before the temporary gallows at the Loire DTC. A crowd of officials, witnesses and spectators watched as Lieutenant Colonel Henry L. Peck led him to the steps of the scaffold. After guards escorted him up the flight of thirteen steps, Master Sergeant John Clarence Woods placed a hood over his head and secured a rope around his neck. Lieutenant Colonel Peck then gave a silent signal and the trapdoor sprang open, sending the soldier to his death. His body was then transported to the US Military Cemetery at Marigny for burial. In 1949, his remains were removed from this location and secretly re-buried at the Oise-Aisne American Cemetery in Plot 'E', Row 4, Grave 75.

Private Billy Basil Betts was buried with the honoured dead in the Épinal American Cemetery, Dinozé, France in Plot B, Row 17, Grave 72. Research for this story revealed that just a few weeks after his death, on 31 January 1945, his brother, Staff Sergeant Frederick R. Betts, was killed serving with the 185th Infantry 40th Division in the Pacific Theatre. He is buried at Fort William Mckinley, Manila, Philippines. Some months later, on 6 May 1945, just two days before the surrender of Nazi Germany, PFC Victor Piechnik, who had been drinking with Billy Betts that fateful night, was killed. Under the Return of the Dead Program, his body was returned to the United States and is buried in the Quincy National Cemetery, Quincy, Adams County, Illinois. Remember them.

Friday, 22 December 1944, Italy
Victim   Alfredo Bechelli, Italian civilian (white)
                Murdered
Assailant   Private Charles H. Jefferies (black)
                Age: 21
                Service No.: 33181343
                Unit: Company 'F', 366th Infantry Regiment, 92nd Infantry Division

The Italian town of Barga is situated in the Media Valle (mid-valley) of the Serchio River and formed part of the Gothic Line in the Second World War. The area was the scene of fierce fighting between the Allies and Germans between October 1944 and April 1945, particularly during the Battle of Garfagnana at the end of December 1944. The centuries-old town was the home of the Bechelli family and, on 22 December 1944, Vittoria Bechelli was at home with her 16-year-old daughter, Silvana, and her young son, Alfredo. Also in the house that afternoon was Giaconda Bonini, her infant daughter, Alda, and Angelo Bertoncini. The house was being used as a billet for a squad of African American troops from Company 'F', 366th Infantry Regiment, part of the all-black US 92nd Division nicknamed the 'Buffalo Soldiers'. One member of the squad was 21-year-old Private Charles H. Jefferies, born on 15 July 1923, in Coatesville, Chester County, Pennsylvania.

At about 4.30 p.m. on 22 December 1944, Staff Sergeant Joe W. Wynn suddenly heard shots being fired. He discovered that it was Private Charles H. Jefferies, who said he was testing his rifle. Later, after a short reprimand, Wynn took the rifle away from the soldier because he was behaving oddly. After a discussion with his Platoon Leader, Staff Sergeant John A. Williams, it was decided to send Jefferies to the Command Post as he was being disruptive in the house. Williams came to fetch the soldier, who was getting his kit ready to move. Wynn gave back his rifle but, as he did so, Jefferies began to argue with another soldier, PFC James Livingston, telling him, 'One day I'll get you.' Wynn, sensing danger, then slapped Jefferies, took his rifle and removed the ammunition. Wynn then handed the rifle back to Jefferies and sent him to the Command Post with Staff Sergeant Williams. With Jefferies out of the way, the squad sat down to eat their evening meal and, although they were not eating with them, the Italian family was also in the room. Just as they finished supper, Wynn saw the door of the room ease open and before he could say anything Jefferies appeared and began firing his rifle. All hell broke loose. PFC John B. Walker took a bullet in the shoulder, PFC Livingston was shot in the arm and leg and PFC Manse Bonnett wounded in the leg. Silvana Bechelli suffered wounds in both knees and the stomach, Giaconda Bonini was hit in the right hip and her baby, Alda, suffered a slight flesh wound. Far worse, Alfredo Bechelli, just a small child, was struck by a bullet which pierced his heart, and he died a few moments later in his mother's arms. Staff Sergeant Williams had managed to fire one shot in defence. Angelo Bertoncini had jumped out of the window, but came back to the room, which was filled with screams for help, and found Vittoria Bechelli holding her dead child.

Private Jeffries had run off but was soon found. Lieutenant French, his platoon leader, marched him to the scene of the crime with his hands tied behind his back, where the soldier claimed that French had fired a round and then told him to run for his life. Jeffries later claimed that First Sergeant Parkman had knocked him down and kicked him before taking him to Captain Harold J. Barnett, the Company Commander. This was never confirmed but is not surprising in the circumstances. Private Charles H. Jefferies appeared before a GCM on 28 February 1945, where he pleaded not guilty to the crimes of murder and wounding with intent. He opted not to take to the witness stand and was quickly found guilty of his crimes, and unanimously sentenced to death by hanging. Lieutenant Alonzo G. Ferguson, a black officer, approved the sentence and General Joseph T. McNarney signed the order of execution on 21 April 1945, just a week before German forces unconditionally surrendered in Italy. On 5 July, Captain Glenn A. Waser, Commanding Officer of the PBS Garrison Stockade No. 1 at Aversa, Italy, presided over the execution of Jeffries. At 8.10 a.m., with just eight officials and witnesses present, the trapdoor opened, sending the soldier to his death. His body was then transported to the US Military Cemetery at Naples for burial. In 1949, his remains were removed from this location and secretly re-buried in Oise-Aisne American Cemetery in Plot 'E', Row 4, Grave 78.

There is little doubt that the soldiers who were wounded that day were absent when the German forces made a surprise attack on Barga a few days later on 26 December 1944. The town was overrun but decisive action by the British Indian Division, led by Major General Dudley Russell, stabilised the situation. Barga was recaptured a week later and by the New Year, the front in the western Gothic Line was stabilised and remained so until late March 1945. By the time Jefferies was executed, there was peace in the town. The Italian population made every effort to continue with their lives, with the exception of Alfredo Bechelli. His mother never forgot those few terrible moments when her son died in her arms. Remember him.

Sunday, 31 December 1944, Italy

Victims	Ettore Lombardi, Italian civilian (white)
	Murdered
	Palmira Lombardi, Italian civilian (white)
	Murdered
	Carmela Lombardi, Italian civilian (white)
	Murdered
Assailant	Private John H. Mack (black)
	Age: 34
	Service No.: 34042053
	Unit: Battery 'C', 599th Field Artillery Battalion

This wasn't a case of rape or robbery and there was no grudge or ill feeling. So, what led to the cold-blooded murder of three Italian civilians at a time of the year when they were celebrating peace and good will to all men?

The medieval town of Pietrasanta lays on northern coast of Italy. In winter 1944, it was home to Ettore Lombardi, his wife, Palmira, their daughter, Carmela, and four other members of the Lombardi family, Concetta, Cecelia, Angelo and Prego. On the upper floor of the house lived Lutaldo Lombardi and his niece, Diletta Lombardi, along with her mother and grandmother. At about 2.00 a.m. on 31 December 1944, the family were in bed when there was a knock on Diletta's bedroom door. When she asked who was there, a voice said, '*Paisano*' (a friend). Diletta called out to see if anyone had been let into the house, but all the responses were negative, and it appeared someone had broken into the home. Family members began to wake up and Ettore and Palmira made their way to the kitchen, where she lit a fire. There was no electricity in the property, so a number of candles began to be lit. Diletta made her way to the kitchen, where she found Ettore and Palmira, along with a black US soldier, who had laid his carbine on the table. After asking if there were any other soldiers with him, the family checked the house to find he was the only one present. The soldier seemed quite calm and was talking about having his laundry washed, but suddenly there was complete panic. A shot rang out and Ettore fell to the floor. Diletta ran out of the room, screaming that they were all being murdered by the invader. The soldier was, by now, dragging Carmella out of the kitchen with her aunt, Concetta, hanging on to her screaming, '*Piasano, piasano*, be good', but the soldier pushed Concetta to the floor and dragged Carmella outside. Then, as quickly as it began, it ended. The soldier was gone. After about 30 minutes, Diletta descended into the kitchen. Her eyes fell upon a devastating scene. She found Ettore, who had been killed instantly, bullets entering his left jaw and the base of his neck. Palmira was close to him and had been shot through the head.

Then, Carmella, who had said good morning to the soldier when she first saw him, was found dead in a ditch 500yd from the house, with nine bullet wounds in her young body. The police and military authorities were called, with Dr Giovanni Bambini and Major Harry S. Beckwith, Regimental Surgeon, examining the bodies and Sergeant Peter Yaskell, 3131st Signal Service Company, taking photographs of the scene. Perhaps the killer would have got away with murder had he not been seen before. Lutaldo Lombardi had seen the soldier the night before, when he took a small box to a friend of his at the nearby camp of 599th Field Artillery Battalion. First Lieutenant John W. Logan interviewed the soldier, 24-year-old Private John H. Mack of Battery 'C'. When he was asked why he had killed the civilians, he said he was 'just forced to do it'. Mack claimed that two civilians had asked him if he wanted a drink of wine and they brought him to the house where this took place. After he entered the house the two civilians looked like they were mad, and the woman picked up a bottle, so he shot her. The man jumped on him, so he shot him. When Mack was asked why he killed the girl, he said she ran out of the house hollering, so he chased her for about 200yd then he killed her because he was afraid.

Mack appeared before a GCM on 18 January 1945, charged with three counts of murder. He pleaded not guilty and changed his story. He claimed that Palmira and Carmella had been to the camp a few days before and accused him of stealing cigarettes and $2, so he killed them in revenge. There had, in fact, been a complaint about theft, but this was concerning two other soldiers, not Mack, and it is uncertain who made the complaint. The court wasted no time and found him guilty of all three killings, unanimously sentencing him to death by hanging. General Joseph T. McNarney signed the order of execution on 19 February 1945. On 20 March 1945, Captain Glenn A. Waser, Commanding Officer of the PBS Garrison Stockade No. 1 at Aversa, Italy, presided over the execution of Private John H. Mack. At 9.48 a.m., with just eight officials and witnesses present, the trapdoor opened, sending the soldier to his death. His body was then transported to the US Military Cemetery at Naples for burial. In 1949, his remains were removed from this location and secretly re-buried in Oise-Aisne American Cemetery in Plot 'E', Row 1, Grave 4.

The lives of the remaining Lombardi family would never be the same again. Remember them.

Chapter 8

1945: The Spoils of War

Tuesday, 2 January 1945, Italy
Victim   Corporal Milton M. Winstead (black)
               Age: 19
               Service No.: 33446508
Assailant   Private Kinney Bruce Jones (black)
               Age: 31
               Service No.: 34120505
               Unit: 3rd Platoon, Canon Company, 371st Infantry
                    Regiment, 92nd Division

On many occasions violent and impetuous conduct has been the result of an older man resenting orders given by someone younger, particularly if they felt they were being treated differently to their comrades. Was it this that caused a man to suddenly and dramatically take the life of a young NCO?

Corporal Milton M. Winstead was born on 1 August 1925 in North Carolina. A married man, he enlisted in the US Army in Fort Myer, Virginia, on 10 October 1942 and was assigned to the 3rd Platoon, Canon Company, 371st Infantry Regiment under the command of the US 92nd Division. On 2 January 1945, the platoon was in what was described as a 'Howitzer position' in the village of Rousina, north of Pietrasanta, Italy. Here Private Ellis Beard, of the Medical Detachment, was standing in the door of his sleeping quarters and saw 19-year-old Corporal Winstead meet with another soldier, Private Kinney Bruce Jones, a 31-year-old man, who was born on 15 March 1914 in Greenville, South Carolina. Winstead said, 'When you finish putting your equipment in your pup tent, go relieve the man on the bridge.' Jones immediately began firing his M-1 rifle at Winstead from a distance of about 3ft, firing a total of thirteen rounds towards the young NCO's chest and abdomen. Winstead was taken to the 1st Battalion aid station, where he was examined by Captain Bruce P. McDonald, the surgeon. He was dead, and there were eight to ten gunshot wounds in his body.

Private Kinney Bruce Jones appeared before a GCM on 17 January 1945, charged with murder. He pleaded not guilty, did not admit to committing the crime and did not take to the witness stand. Witnesses, T/5 Benjamin H. Belcher and Private Robert Campbell, described how the two men seemed to get along together, that there had been no aggression between them before the shooting and that Winstead was unarmed. The only issue appeared to be that all the men of the platoon were sleeping in a building, where there was a fire, and Jones was being made to sleep in a pup tent. Lieutenant Leonard S. Morgan had instructed this to happen, as Jones had been drunk the day before, so had ordered him out of the building. There was no evidence that Winstead was involved in this decision, but Jones claimed the corporal said, 'You son-of-a-bitch, come on. I'm going to work the hell out of you today.' There was no confirmation of this, and the court wasted no time in finding Jones guilty of murder and unanimously sentencing him to death by hanging. Major General Edward Almond, commanding the 92nd Division, approved the sentence on 21 January 1945 and General Joseph T. McNarney signed the order of execution on 19 February 1945, the second one he authorised that day. On 20 March 1945, Major W.G. Neiswender, Commanding Officer of the PBS Garrison Stockade No. 1 at Aversa, Italy, presided over the execution of Private Kinney Bruce Jones. At 9.00 a.m., with just eight officials and witnesses present, the trapdoor opened, sending the soldier to his death. His body was then transported to the US Military Cemetery at Naples for burial. In 1949, his remains were removed from this location and secretly re-buried in the Oise-Aisne American Cemetery in Plot 'E', Row 2, Grave 42.

There was some confusion in the court records regarding the location of the crime, and it was stated it had happened approximately 5km north of Pietrasanta at Rousina. This location cannot be confirmed. Records show that Winstead was disinterred from a grave at Castelfiorentino and shipped to the United States under the Return of the Dead Program. On 15 December 1948, he was finally buried in the Arlington National Cemetery, Virginia, Plot 12, Grave 5733. The grave next to him, 5732, was reserved for his wife. Remember him.

Saturday, 6 January 1945, France

Victim   Captain William E. McDonald (white)
                  Age: 26
                  Murdered
                  Service No.: O-408591
Assailant   Sergeant Clete Oscar Norris (black)
                  Age: 27
                  Service No.: 37082314
                  Unit: 3384th Quartermaster Truck Company

The night of 6 January 1945 was dark and snowy in the little Belgian town of Boëlhe, about 20 miles from the city of Liège. A shot rang out in the darkness, an officer fell dead and a soldier was destined for the gallows.

That night Sergeant Clete Oscar Norris, who was born on 1 March 1918 in Palestine, Texas, was drinking, as soldiers do, in a local cafe with other members of his unit, the 3384th Quartermaster Truck Company. They were being loud and soon attracted the attention of the Sergeant of the Guard at their billets, which were located about 150yd away in a large chateau. He found them, intoxicated, playing with their weapons, but seemingly having a good time. The sergeant attempted to get them to leave the cafe and return to their billets, but Sergeant Norris picked up his carbine and menacingly pointed it at the NCO. Most of the men left at the sergeant's request and, after another drink or two, Norris finally departed carrying his carbine and a German P-38 pistol that he had taken from another soldier, T/5 Jesse Stevenson. Shortly after, several pistol shots were heard and Captain William E. McDonald, who was on his way to the cafe, saw Norris and Stevenson and took away their carbines.

Captain William E. McDonald, who was murdered by Sergeant Clete Oscar Norris on 6 January 1945.

McDonald then carried on to the cafe where he ordered the remaining men to leave. It appears Norris had, for some reason, decided to make his way back to the cafe and claimed he found a pistol by the side of the road, which he picked up. Suddenly, a flashlight appeared and a voice said, 'Halt.' Norris raised the pistol and fired, the flashlight fell to the ground and the sound of a steel helmet hitting the street was heard. Norris ran back to catch up with Stevenson, where he said, 'Here is your pistol, come on, I am going to bed.' Captain William E. McDonald, born in Ohio on 21 February 1918, was found outside the cafe, along with two carbines and a damaged steel helmet with two bars painted on it. He was carried, unconscious, into the cafe and laid on a sofa, and was quickly removed to hospital where he was found to have a penetrating wound on the right side of the head. Despite all the medical services did for him, he died from his injuries at 5.45 a.m. on 9 January 1945.

Norris was arrested by MPs the morning after the shooting and appeared before a GCM on 9 February 1945 in St Trond, Belgium, where he pleaded not guilty to the charge of murder. He had joined the US Army at Jefferson Barracks, Missouri, on 25 September 1941 and was regarded as a good soldier. After a 6-hour hearing, the jury found him guilty of the charge, sentencing him, unanimously, to death by hanging. Following a review of the case, the order of execution was signed by General Dwight D. Eisenhower on 3 April 1945.

On the morning of 31 May 1945, a clear, bright day in the city of Le Mans, France, Sergeant Clete Oscar Norris stood before the temporary gallows at the Loire DTC. A small group of officials, witnesses and spectators watched as Lieutenant Colonel Henry L. Peck led him to the steps of the scaffold. After guards escorted him up the flight of steps, Master Sergeant John Clarence Woods placed a hood over his head and secured a rope around his neck. Lieutenant Colonel Peck then gave a silent signal and the trapdoor sprang open, sending the soldier to his death. His body was then transported to the US Military Cemetery at Marigny for burial. In 1949, his remains were removed from this location and secretly re-buried in Oise-Aisne American Cemetery in Plot 'E', Row 4, Grave 79.

The body of Captain William E. McDonald was laid to rest amongst the honoured dead at the Henri-Chapelle American Cemetery, Belgium in Plot C, Row 7, Grave 21. Remember him.

Friday, 8 January 1945, Italy

Victim   Carlo Franceschi, Italian civilian
                   Murdered
Assailant   PFC General Lee Grant (black)
                   Age: 23
                   Service No.: 34557976
                   Unit: Company 'D', 366th Infantry Regiment, 92nd Infantry Division

The small town of Viareggio sits on the Italian coast, about 16 miles from the city of Lucca, which in early 1945 formed part of the formidable Gothic Line. Here lived Carlo Franceschi, his wife, Annunziato, his daughter, Tereza, and two small children. Life was not easy, there was great uncertainty and soldiers, from all armies, could appear at any time demanding supplies. At about 6.00 p.m. on 8 January 1945, PFC General Lee Grant, born on 23 May 1921 in Union Point, Georgia, left his unit, in the full knowledge he was going AWOL. He had joined the US Army on 27 November 1942 and had been assigned to 92nd Infantry Division, the famous 'Buffalo Soldiers'. As Grant passed the Franceschi house he saw a man outside, Guiseppe, Carlo's brother. Grant said, 'Come Stata, how do you do?' Guiseppe replied, 'Alright.' Grant asked to go into the house, then requested wine and again Guiseppe replied, 'Alright.' They went into an adjoining room where the Franceschi family were located, along with two white soldiers, Private John C. Strong and Private Sam T. Mcfalls, both members of the 248th Field Artillery Battalion. Here, Grant began talking to Tereza. He then asked Carlo for some wine and, according to Private Strong, Carlo acted like he did not want him to have it, so Grant asked the old man again. Carlo said, 'Yes, I will give you a glass of wine', to which Grant replied, 'No, I want a bottle.' Allegedly, Grant then said, 'You are just going to give me a glass?' As Carlo walked past Grant, the soldier seized him with his left hand, pulled out a .45 calibre pistol from the rear pocket of his trousers and fired it. Guiseppe jumped on Grant's back and there was a struggle in which two more shots were fired, one of which struck Guiseppe's young nephew in the shoulder. Carlo now came towards Grant, who then fired a shot that hit the Italian directly in the heart and Carlo fell to the floor, killed outright. Grant was immediately arrested. First Lieutenant John W. Logan interviewed him on 9 January and he admitted being at the house, but claimed he acted in self-defence. He claimed Annunziato and one of the white soldiers attacked him, pushing and shoving him out of the house. Frightened by their actions, he pulled out the .45 pistol and started firing it in the air, something that Private Mcfalls would confirm. During this struggle, Grant fired the pistol at Carlo as he came towards him, believing he was going to be attacked.

Grant appeared before a GCM at 7.10 p.m. on 8 February 1945. He pleaded not guilty to the crimes of being AWOL and murder. It seems that he elected not to say anything, which may have been the advice of his defence counsel. The two white soldiers appeared as prosecution witnesses. In his testimony, Private Strong claimed he left the room after the second shot, perhaps an odd reaction for a combat soldier witnessing two Italian civilians struggling with an armed soldier, and that he only heard the last shot. For his part, Mcfalls stated that Carlo had pushed the pistol up in the air and that Grant fired it twice, perhaps confirming Grant's claim that he was trying to scare the civilians off. Private Mcfalls claimed Grant had fired a third time, as he was backing out of the door, and Carlo then fell on his face. After Grant left the room Mcfalls heard a fourth shot in an adjoining room and 'the boy' came in holding his stomach. Guiseppe Franceschi testified that with the aid of his nephew and his wife he got Grant to the front door where he managed to take the gun off him. Grant then ran outside the house and Guiseppe returned. He found Carlo dead and gave the pistol to Mcfalls, who in turn gave it to the MP. The defence counsellor, Captain Francis L. Robison, chose not to raise any objections to the prosecutions case, nor introduce any evidence in the accused's defence. The court wasted no time, finding Jones not guilty of being AWOL, but guilty of murder, and unanimously sentenced him to death by hanging. General Joseph T. McNarney signed the order of execution on 28 February 1945.

On 27 March 1945, Major W.G. Neiswender, Commanding Officer of the PBS Garrison Stockade No. 1 at Aversa, Italy, presided over the execution of PFC General Lee Grant. At 2.09 p.m., with just eight officials and witnesses present, the trapdoor opened, sending the soldier to his death. His body was then transported to the US Military Cemetery at Naples for burial. In 1949, his remains were removed from this location and secretly re-buried in Oise-Aisne American Cemetery in Plot 'E', Row 3, Grave 11. However, in 1952, the ABMC moved the remains for a third time, and they now rest in Row 3, Grave 59.

There is no doubt there was a struggle that day, and no doubt that PFC General Lee Grant shot and killed Carlo Franceschi, but was it murder, what actually took place. We shall never really know. Grant is buried in France and Carlo in his hometown on the Italian coast. Remember them.

1945: THE SPOILS OF WAR

Tuesday, 23 January 1945, Italy
Victim   PFC Earl Johnson (black)
                Age: 44
                Service No.: 34555582
                Murdered
Assailant   Private John W. Taylor (black)
                Service No.: 37485128
                Unit: 371st Infantry Regiment, 92nd Infantry Division

There are some cases where the motive is quite apparent, the crime straightforward with numerous witnesses. In cases such as these, justice would be swift and records of investigation limited, especially for a combat unit on the move.

On 23 January 1945, the guard for the regimental Command Post, 371st Infantry Regiment, was quartered on the second floor of a building in Pietrasanta, a town on the northern coast of Italy. In winter 1945, it was close to the formidable Gothic Line and was one of the combat units making up the 92nd Infantry Division, an all-black formation nicknamed the 'Buffalo Soldiers'. One of the guard members was Private John W. Taylor. At about 6.00 p.m. that evening, Taylor entered the guard quarters holding an M-1 rifle. PFC Earl Johnson was sitting on a bed writing a letter, and a man was lying behind him on the same bed. Taylor did not speak, but simply fired a shot at Johnson from about 8ft. Johnson 'keeled over' without uttering a word. Taylor then said, 'Get up, get up', and the man who was lying on the bed behind Johnson rolled off his bed. Taylor then walked to within one pace from the bed, raised his rifle to his shoulder, aimed and fired two more shots. He then turned and left the room. The headquarters company commander, Captain Robert. E. Moock, was a short distance away, and on hearing the shots went towards the quarters. There he met Taylor who said, 'I shot him three times, and I'm all right, now.' Captain Albert M. Davis, Medical Corps, examined Johnson, who was dead. He had been shot in the head, abdomen and left hand.

Taylor made a pretrial statement to Captain Fred A. Brewer, investigating officer, who stressed the fact that any such statement might be used against him in court. The soldier had first had problems with Johnson the week before, when he oversaw the CP guard and Johnson couldn't be woken to take his turn on guard duty. The two men had a verbal altercation and, eventually, Johnson took his place on guard. Then, two days before the shooting, Taylor was passing out the cigarette ration in the guard quarters. Johnson asked him for a packet of Camels but was told these had already been promised to other men, but Taylor would try to get him some the following day. Johnson then reached over and took a packet out of the box on the table and knocked all the cigarettes, chewing gum and chocolate over the floor. The two soldiers grappled with each other, both pulling out knives, although they were not used, and the altercation quickly broke up. On the evening of 23 January, Taylor was discussing with some of the other men about giving a young Italian who was there some food. Taylor asked one of the other men for a cigarette, remarking that he had traded his cigarettes that day for wine. Johnson then said, 'You're a liar, you gave it to them whores.' This resulted in a further altercation during which Johnson grabbed his rifle, pointed it at Taylor and threw the safety off. Some of the other men then spoke to Johnson and took his rifle away from him. Taylor was convinced that, at some point, Johnson was going to kill him. He said, 'I thought about the way Johnson had been acting and I decided that I might as well get rid of him for if I didn't, he would probably kill me.' He went downstairs, loaded his rifle and then went back and shot him. He shouted a warning as he was only trying to hit Johnson, and not any of the other men.

Taylor appeared before a GCM at the 92nd Infantry Division Headquarters at Massa Maciniai on 30 January 1945. He pleaded not guilty to the crime of murder. The evidence was overwhelming and his statement, although true, was not favourable to his case. The court found Jones guilty of murder, unanimously sentencing him to death by hanging. The case was reviewed by Brigadier General Adam Richmond, the Theatre Judge Advocate for the MTO, and he recommended that the sentence be commuted to life imprisonment in the circumstances. General Joseph T. McNarney, however, disagreed with the recommendation and signed the order of execution on 26 February 1945. Private John W. Taylor was destined to die. On 20 March 1945, Major W.G. Neiswender, Commanding Officer of the PBS Garrison Stockade No. 1 at Aversa, Italy, presided over the execution, the third to take place in the stockade that day. At 8.00 a.m., with just eight officials and witnesses present, the trapdoor opened, sending the soldier to his death. His body was then transported to the US Military Cemetery at Naples for burial. In 1949, his remains were removed from this location and secretly re-buried in the Oise-Aisne American Cemetery in Plot 'E', Row 1, Grave 24.

PFC Earl Johnson, who was born in Jefferson County, Alabama, in 1901, and joined the US Army in Fort Benning, Georgia, on 15 November 1942 at the age of 42, is buried with the honoured dead at the Florence American Cemetery, Italy, in Plot C, Row 2, Grave 12. Remember him.

Sunday, 28 January 1945, France

Victim   Captain Ignacio Bonit (Puerto Rican)
                   Age: 32
                   Service No.: O-401967
                   Murdered
Assailant   Private Victor Ortiz-Reyes (Puerto Rican)
                   Age: 31
                   Service No.: 30405077
                   Unit: 3269th Quartermaster Service Company,
                        245th Quartermaster Battalion

Ignacio Bonit was born on 17 April 1912, although some records show his birth date as either 17 March or 30 April. He was the son of Rafael Bonit Y Fuente and Josefa Betancourt De Bonit, and enlisted in the US Army on 1 August 1941. A good soldier, he soon achieved officer rank and by winter 1945, found himself in command of the 3269th Quartermaster Service Company, part of the 245th Quartermaster Battalion, a supply unit entirely manned by Puerto Rican troops. By 28 January 1945, the unit was stationed outside Marquette, France, just north of the city of Lille. On this day, Private Victor Ortiz-Reyes, described as being illiterate and from a very poor background, had been performing guard duty on a 4 hours on, 8 hours off basis for some 24 hours at the unit's fuel point. At 1.00 a.m. on 28 January, the sergeant of the guard, Sergeant Ramon Ortiz, awakened Ortiz-Reyes and ordered him to get up as it was time for him to go on guard again. The soldier stated that he wasn't going to do guard duty as he had not been asleep, and asked to see the captain of the guard. Wearing nothing more than his underwear and pants, without a shirt, Ortiz-Reyes stood before Captain Ignacio Bonit and repeated his remonstrations. The captain, who had been asleep himself, stood up, pointed his finger at the soldier, and said, 'You got to do the guard, because you are in the Army now.' Undeterred, Ortiz-Reyes said he would not perform the duty and asked the captain to prefer charges against him. Captain Bonit made it clear to the soldier he was going to perform the duty, saying, 'You are going on guard and if you don't go on guard, I will personally take you there, even if I have to drag you with a truck.' Ortiz-Reyes left the room without saying a word or saluting the captain, returned to his cot, prepared himself for guard duty, picked up his .30 rifle and returned to the orderly room, where the captain had gone back to sleep. The guard on duty, roughly 12ft from the orderly room, heard two shots at about 1.20 a.m. hours. The lights went on and he heard a second series of shots. Captain Ignacio Bonit was dead, shot twice through the chest. Private Victor Ortiz-Reyes was placed under arrest by members of the MP, who found him sitting on his cot with his rifle at port arms. He was heard by the First Sergeant of the Company to say, 'The thing I have done is done.'

Ortiz-Reyes appeared before a GCM on 1 March 1945 at Lille, France, where he pleaded not guilty to the charge of murder. In a hearing that lasted three days, the Puerto Rican soldier claimed that he had asked for his place to be taken by another soldier and would have performed guard duty later in the morning. After the refusal by Captain Bonit, he had made himself ready for duty, then went to the orderly room, where he asked the captain if a replacement had been found. He claimed the captain was 'in a bad mood' and after an exchange of words he reached for a pistol that was on his desk. Believing the captain was going to shoot him, Ortiz-Reyes fired his carbine at the officer. However, both the guard outside the orderly room and Second Lieutenant Israel I. Sylvan, who was also asleep in the room, testified that there were two shots in the dark, then the lights came on and there were two more shots. It was only at this point that he saw Captain Bonit's body on the ground. Sylvan also confirmed that the officer's pistol was still in the drawer of his desk, where he had left it the night before. This was sufficient for the court, which found him guilty of the charge, sentencing him, unanimously, to death by hanging. Following a review of the case, the order of execution was signed by General Dwight D. Eisenhower on 6 May 1945. Ortiz-Reyes was held in a prison at Roubaix, near Lille, until he was transferred to the Loire DTC for execution. On the morning of 21 June 1945, a cool and overcast day in the city of Le Mans, France, Private Victor Ortiz-Reyes stood before the temporary gallows, where a small group of officials, witnesses and spectators watched as Lieutenant Colonel Henry L. Peck led him to the steps of the scaffold. After guards escorted him up the flight of steps, Master Sergeant John Clarence Woods placed a hood over his head and secured a rope around his neck. Lieutenant Colonel Peck then gave a silent signal and, at 11.03 a.m., the trapdoor sprung open, sending the soldier to his death. His body was then transported to the US Military Cemetery at Marigny for burial. In 1949, his remains were removed from this location and secretly re-buried in Oise-Aisne American Cemetery in Plot 'E', Row 4, Grave 87.

For Captain Ignacio Bonit a long journey lay ahead, and it would be many years before he was finally put to rest. Originally, he was buried in a temporary US military cemetery in France. In spring 1948, under the Return of the Dead Program, his body was removed by members of the Grave Registration Service and transported to Fort Brooke Military

Cemetery, San Juan, Puerto Rico, where it was buried in Section C, Grave 50. Finally, on 17 February 1960, it was again disinterred and reburied in the Puerto Rico National Cemetery, Bayamon, Puerto Rico, where it rests in Plot C, Grave 571. Remember him.

Monday, 29 January 1945, Italy
Victim   Ireni Rossi Martini, Italian civilian
                  Raped
Assailants   Private Henry W. Nelson (black)
                  Age: 21
                  Service No.: 35726029
                  Unit: Company 'A', 371st Infantry Regiment, 92nd
                     Infantry Division
                  Private John T. Jones (black)
                  Age: 32
                  Service No.: 38315973
                  Unit: Battery 'B', 599th Field Artillery Battalion, 92nd
                     Infantry Division

Massa Maciniai is a small commune about 4 miles south-east of the city of Lucca, Italy, which, in 1945, was close to the Gothic Line. Here lived Angelo Martini, his wife Ireni, their 13-year-old daughter, two sons and a young boy named Silvio Georgia.

On 29 January 1945, the Martini family was sitting downstairs by the fire when two black soldiers knocked on the door and, when Angelo asked who was there, one of them replied, 'The Police, American Police.' It was the same old story, Angelo opened the door and the two soldiers entered, one armed with a carbine. The assailants were Private John T. Jones, an artilleryman, and Private Henry W. Nelson, an infantryman, both serving with the 92nd Infantry Division. They wanted to go upstairs, so Silvio took a candle and showed them the way. One of the rooms had a ladder that led to an attic room which was closed and locked. Attilio Rovai, the next-door neighbour of the Martinis, had some of his belongings stored in there. The soldiers shouted for it to be opened, but Silvio was unable to open it quickly enough for them and they fired a shot into the ceiling. They then pointed their weapons at Angelo and Silvio and pushed them outside the house, where they got them to line up. At that moment Attilio Rovai, who had been summoned by Angelo, came to the house and tried to enter. He was shoved outside and the soldier with the carbine fired three shots at him, the second shot hitting Attilio in the eye. Meanwhile, Ireni had remained inside the house with her daughter, Anna, and son, Alberti. After the shots were fired Ireni moved away from the door toward the fireplace and as she did so, Jones gave her two slaps in the face because she was screaming for help. He knocked her to the ground and held her there, with one hand over mouth, and something cold pressed against her throat, which she believed was a knife. The two soldiers then took it in turns to rape the terrified mother, in front of her family and their neighbour. Jones and Nelson then travelled about a mile down the road to the home of Luigi Decanini and his wife, Ida. Here, the drunken soldiers repeated the excuse they used earlier for entering the little house. They roamed about the property and stole two rings and a watch, although they did not rape Ida. After shooting the radio, for no apparent reason, they then stole two bicycles, which they loaded into the truck Jones was driving and made their escape.

Jones was apprehended at Pietrasanta the following day by First Sergeant Nicholas F. Piazza and PFC Dominic J. Maglione of Company 'C', 101st Military Police Battalion along with a Sergeant Stack. He was questioned by the MPs and spilled the beans, telling them how he had picked up Nelson when he was driving his truck near the town of Viareggio. They had stopped after a while at a little wine shop and had a drink or two. It wasn't long before they were drunk and decided to find some more drink. Following the statement made by Jones, the three MPs went to a house in Pietrasanta, whey they found a carbine hanging on the wall. After removing the ammunition, they approached the bed where they found Nelson asleep. They pulled the sheet off, arrested him and then drove him to the MP Headquarters in Lucca. Here, Nelson told a remarkably similar story to that of Jones but admitted shooting Attilio Rovai and raping Ireni Martini. Jones never admitted to the sexual assault on Ireni and claimed that Nelson was the one with the carbine, him being unarmed.

Jones and Nelson appeared before a GCM at Massa Maciniai on 17 March 1945 at the 92nd Division Headquarters. They pleaded not guilty to the crimes of rape and robbery, and they both made unsworn statements to the court. Their defence counsel refuted their original statements on the grounds that neither of the soldiers had been advised of their rights by the MPs, something that was accepted. Jones, who was born in Silver Creek, Lawrence County, Mississippi, on 11 August 1912, had enlisted in the US Army on 3 November 1942. Nelson, who was missing seven teeth and was riddled with syphilis and gonorrhoea, was younger having been born on 28 May 1924 in East Saint Louis, St Clair County, Illinois, and had enlisted in the US Army on 5 March 1943 at

Fort Benjamin Harrison, Indiana. Both men had previous convictions before a court martial. Neither Ireni, her husband or Attilio Rovai were able to identify Jones or Nelson as their attackers. Anna, however, unequivocally identified Jones and it was abundantly clear from the statements they made that Jones and Nelson were the perpetrators of the crime. The court found them both guilty, unanimously sentencing them to death by hanging.

Lieutenant Colonel William T. Thurman, the Judge Advocate for the 92nd Division, reviewed the case and approved the sentences. Brigadier General Adam Richmond, the Theatre Judge Advocate for the MTO, recommended the sentences be commuted to life imprisonment. General Joseph T. McNarney, however, disagreed with the recommendation and signed the order of execution on 21 April 1945. On 5 July 1945, Captain Glenn A. Waser, Commanding Officer of the PBS Garrison Stockade No. 1 at Aversa, Italy, presided over the execution of the two soldiers. At 8.44 a.m., with just eight officials and witnesses present, the trapdoor opened, sending Private Henry W. Nelson to his death. Private John T. Jones passed through the trapdoor at 9.20 a.m. Their bodies were then transported to the US Military Cemetery at Naples for burial. In 1949, their remains were removed from this location and secretly re-buried in Oise-Aisne American Cemetery in Plot 'E'. Nelson is buried in Row 1, Grave 1 and Jones is buried in Row 2, Grave 48.

Attilio Rovai was treated at the 170th Evacuation Hospital by Major Vernon D. Stephens on 30 January 1945 but had lost his left eye forever. Anna Martini, who had lit a match that night so that she could help Attilio with his wound, never forgot his face or that of her mother's rapist as it was revealed in the darkness. Remember them.

Thursday, 1 February 1945, France
Victim   Private Charles P. Williams (black)
                  Service No.: 36796816
                  Murdered
Assailant   Private William A. McCarter (black)
                  Age: 38
                  Service No.: 34675988
                  Unit: 465th Quartermaster Laundry Company

On Christmas Eve 1945 the body of General George S. Patton was laid to rest at the Luxembourg American Cemetery in the Hamm district of Luxembourg City, buried amongst the men of the US Third Army. Close by is the grave of Private Charles P. Williams, a black soldier born in

The grave of Private Charles P. Williams in Luxembourg American Cemetery, Luxembourg City. Williams was murdered by Private William A. McCarter on 1 February 1945.

Mississippi, who had only recently joined the the 465th Quartermaster Laundry Company, and who was referred to as 'C.P.'. Unlike Patton, little has been written about him, even in official court-martial records. The work of the laundry company was hard and tiresome, but Williams was a good soldier, who worked hard and gave no trouble. Any time off was an opportunity to relax, maybe have a drink and even play a little game of dice. On 31 January 1945, the unit was stationed at Thionville, France, some 43 miles south of Luxembourg city. On the third floor of a barrack building, a noisy dice game was in progress. C.P. Williams was there along with other members of the unit, including Private William A. McCarter, a hard-working 38-year-old former laundry employee who was born in Charlotte, North Carolina, on 22 October 1906, and had joined the US Army on 22 June 1943. Although the game was boisterous, it was friendly, but by 2.00 a.m. on 1 February, there were only three players left, Privates James F. Hunt, C.P. Williams and McCarter. Just before the game broke up, McCarter claimed that someone had taken his pocketbook, containing about $20. He went into the room of Corporal Thomas Williams, on the third floor of the barracks, and repeated this claim. According to the corporal, McCarter seemed to direct his accusations towards C.P. Williams. A short time later, Private Hunt and C.P. Williams came into the room and offered to be searched to satisfy McCarter that they were innocent of his accusations. They removed some of their clothing, but he declined to examine it or to search them.

McCarter then went to the guardhouse and asked Private Kadell Mitchell whether anyone had been out that night. Mitchell believed that the only person who had been outside the barracks was C.P. Williams, who had gone over to the hospital mess hall. McCarter then said, 'I'll get him; he's got my money.' About 15 minutes later, Mitchell heard a voice in the darkness say, 'Is that you Williams?', the reply was, 'Yes, it's C.P.' The sound of a carbine filled the air and McCarter appeared, and said, 'I got him.' At the same time, Mitchell saw C.P. Williams lying on the ground about 6yd away, close to the steps of the barracks, struggling for breath. McCarter ran off saying, 'I hope the MPs hurry up and come and get him.' Sergeant Reginald Dyson, awakened by the sound of shooting, saw McCarter come into the barracks and say, 'Somebody better go out there, he's laying out there.' McCarter then reported his own crime to the Barrack Corporal, also making his comrades aware of his actions. Sergeants McDonald and Dyson and Corporal Williams found Williams outside the barracks lying face downwards in a pool of blood. He was taken to hospital, arriving there about 3:30 am on 1 February 1945 and was immediately pronounced dead. His death was due to haemorrhage and shock from the gunshot wounds he had sustained. An autopsy established that he had been shot in the back five or six times. Wounds were apparent in the back of the neck, beneath the ribs, behind the right shoulder, in the head and in the back of the right leg.

McCarter appeared before a GCM on 16 February 1945 at Thionville, France. It was a straightforward case. He believed Williams had stolen his money, so he shot him in the back five times and killed him, but he still pleaded not guilty. The court took just 2¼ hours to find McCarter guilty of the charge, sentencing him, unanimously, to death by hanging. Following a review of the case, the order of execution was signed by General Dwight D. Eisenhower on 29 March 1945. On the morning of 28 May 1945, an overcast day in the city of Le Mans, France, Private William A. McCarter stood before the temporary gallows at the Loire DTC. A group of forty-eight officials, witnesses and spectators watched as Lieutenant Colonel Henry L. Peck led him to the steps of the scaffold. After guards escorted him up the flight of thirteen steps, Master Sergeant John Clarence Woods placed a hood over his head and secured a rope around his neck, whilst the guards strapped his ankles together. Lieutenant Colonel Peck then gave a silent signal and at 11.03 a.m. the trapdoor sprung open, sending the soldier to his death. His body was then transported to the US Military Cemetery at Marigny for burial. In 1949, his remains were removed from this location and secretly re-buried in the Oise-Aisne American Cemetery in Plot 'E', Row 4, Grave 91.

The body of Private Charles P. 'C.P.' Williams, one of Patton's Third Army, was laid to rest amongst the honoured dead at Luxembourg American Cemetery, Luxembourg City, in Plot G, Row 8, Grave 3. He is entitled to the following awards: World War II Victory Medal, American Campaign Medal, Army Presidential Unit Citation, Army Good Conduct Medal and European-African-Middle Eastern Campaign. Remember him.

Sunday, 4 February 1945, Italy

Victim	PFC George W. Jones (black)
	Service No.: 36796415
	Murdered
Assailant	Private Abraham Smalls (black)
	Age: 34
	Service No.: 34512812
	Unit: Company 'L', 370th Infantry Regiment, 92nd Infantry Division

For a variety of reasons, some records are decidedly lacking in content. Such is the case of a black soldier, PFC George W. Jones, who was a member of Company 'L', 370th Infantry Regiment, part of the 92nd US Infantry Division. On 4 February 1945, his unit was bivouacked in a rest area, about 2 miles from the town of Viareggio, Italy. At 8.00 a.m., Abraham Smalls, who had been assigned to Company 'L', was in front of his tent washing his face. Just a short distance away, Sergeant Willie B. Adams was doing the same thing. Jones was also planning to have a wash but had no soap. He asked Smalls for the soap but got no response, so he asked Sergeant Adams, who said the soap belonged to Smalls. Jones again asked Smalls for the soap, and Smalls said he was going to give it to Adams. Jones, who was unarmed, threatened, 'I will strike your tent.' Smalls replied, 'I will shoot you.' Jones reached down and pulled out the front pegs of the tent, and as he straightened up, Smalls suddenly shot him with his M-1 carbine. Jones fell to the ground and rolled onto his face. Despite the efforts of Sergeant Adams to stop Smalls, he pumped another six rounds into Jones' body. Captain Eugene L. Young Jr, surgeon for the 370th Infantry Medical Detachment, determined Jones had died from two gunshot wounds, one in the right chest and the other in the left chest.

An investigation began, during which Private Cicero Clark reported that in December 1944 Jones had called Smalls out of his tent, pointed his rifle at him and said he was going to kill him, then struck him several times. However, he did not fire. Clark also said that at some point before the shooting Jones had stolen money from Smalls, soon after he had been paid. On the night before the shooting, Smalls said the money belonged to him and asked for $10, but Jones refused to give it to him. Another soldier, PFC Walter Hills, said that Jones had repeatedly bullied Smalls over money.

Private Abraham Smalls appeared before a GCM on 17 February 1945. The 32-year-old had been inducted into the army in Fort Jackson, Columbia, South Carolina, on 7 November 1942, pleaded not guilty to the crime of murder. Smalls made a lengthy voluntary statement in which he admitted shooting Jones after warning him repeatedly not to keep pestering him for $100. On the morning of the killing, Jones said to Smalls, 'Either you give me that money today or I will spray your tent with gas', having previously threatened to burn the tent with Smalls inside. He said that after they argued about the soap Jones started to strike his tent, and he shot him. The evidence was overwhelming and his statement, which appears to be true, was not favourable to his case. The court found Jones guilty of murder, unanimously sentencing him to death by hanging. Major General Edward Almond, commanding the 92nd Division, approved the sentence on 6 February 1945. The case was then reviewed by Brigadier General Adam Richmond, the Theatre Judge Advocate for the MTO, who approved the sentence on 28 February 1945, and General Joseph T. McNarney signed the order of execution on 12 March 1945. On 27 March 1945, Major W.G. Neiswender, Commanding Officer of the PBS Garrison Stockade No. 1 at Aversa, Italy, presided over the execution of Private Abraham Smalls. At 1.35 p.m., with just eight officials and witnesses present, the trapdoor opened, sending the soldier to his death. He was pronounced dead 12 minutes later. His body was then transported to the US Military Cemetery at Naples for burial. In 1949, his remains were removed from this location and secretly re-buried in the Oise-Aisne American Cemetery in Plot 'E', Row 1, Grave 23.

PFC George W. Jones is buried with the honoured dead at the Florence American Cemetery, Italy, in Plot G, Row 8, Grave 15. Remember him.

Friday, 23 February 1945, France

Victims   PFC John H.W. Hoogewind (white)
Age: 32
Service No.: 36157563
Unit: Civil Affairs Division
Murdered

Sergeant Royce Arthur Judd Jr (white)
Age: 22
Service No.: 15100920
Unit: Battery 'B', 376th Parachute Field Artillery
       Battalion, 82nd Airborne Division
Murdered

Assailant   PFC Alvin R. Rollins (black)
Age: 20
Service No.: 34716953
Unit: 306th Quartermaster Railhead Company

Just over 100 miles south-east of Paris, France, lays the town of Troyes. An important railhead, and a crossing point for the River Seine, it was captured by the 35th US Infantry Division on 25 August 1944. In February 1945, the 306th Quartermaster Railhead Company, an African American unit, was stationed in the town. The men worked hard to keep the supplies moving, items so desperately needed by the Allied forces as they progressed across the European battlefields. Amongst them was PFC Alvin Rollins, born on 5 December 1924 in Chattanooga, Tennessee. He had joined the army at Camp Forrest, Tennessee, on 15 June 1943, and his company had been posted to Boughton, Northamptonshire, and then on to Troyes, France.

On 23 February 1945, Rollins and the men in his barracks were told that they had failed an inspection and were

PFC John H.W. Hoogewind, who was murdered by PFC Alvin R. Rollins on 23 February 1945. He is buried in the American Cemetery in Épinal, France.

restricted to camp. Rollins was recognised as a hard worker, so it was understandably disappointing for him, but he decided to slip out of camp anyway. Borrowing a field jacket from a buddy, he left the camp and made his way into the town, where he had a few drinks in a cafe. He then moved on to the Cafe Number 27, which was out of bounds to all troops. He went in anyway and met up with another man from his company, Private E.C. Williams. Whilst they were there, a jeep pulled up outside and the cafe owner shouted 'MPs!' Rollins and Williams tried to dive out the back door, but a voice said, 'Just a minute. I got to take you down. Don't you know it is off limits?' This was Sergeant Royce Arthur Judd Jr, an MP from Ohio, who was serving with the 82nd Airborne Division and been assigned to the Guard Platoon that day. Judd entered the cafe with another MP, Corporal Victor H. Paul. Rollins pleaded for a break, and then asked if this was about his colour. Judd said, 'No, I would take anybody in that I found in this place.' Judd and Paul escorted the two soldiers outside and placed them in the back of the jeep, with Rollins seated behind the driver, and the two MPs sat together in the front. Their driver that day was PFC John H.W. Hoogewind, who had joined the US Army on 14 June 1941 in Kalamazoo, Michigan. He was serving with the Civil Affairs Division and had also been assigned to the Guard Platoon that day. The two MPs now made a stupid, but catastrophic mistake. Rollins was carrying a fully loaded German Luger pistol, hidden in his field jacket, and the MPs had not searched either of the two soldiers. Hoogewind pulled away in the jeep and as he did so a shot was fired from behind the front seat at very close range. Corporal Paul immediately threw himself out of the moving vehicle, but his foot got caught under the dashboard, and he was dragged along the street for about 30ft, during which time more shots were fired at him. The jeep stopped when it struck a wall, Williams and Rollins jumped out and ran down the street in the opposite direction from that which the jeep faced. Williams ran back to camp, but Rollins broke off, returning to camp later that night. In the meantime, Corporal Paul had stopped a passing jeep, which took him with the two victims to a hospital. Judd was dead on arrival, having been shot in the neck. Hoogewind was fatally wounded, one bullet having passed through his helmet liner and his head and another through his left jaw. He later succumbed to his injuries.

An identification parade was held at the 306th Quartermaster Railhead Company, and Corporal Paul picked out Rollins as the killer. He appeared before a GCM on 13 March 1945 in Reims, France, where he pleaded not guilty to the charge of murder. He made a sworn statement claiming he suffered from blackouts and that he had left camp that night to sell the gun to another soldier. In a previous statement he claimed that Williams was carrying a revolver and that it was him who had fired the shots. At the GCM Williams testified against Rollins. The jury were unconvinced and found Rollins guilty of the charge, sentencing him unanimously to death by hanging. The sentence was confirmed by General Dwight D. Eisenhower on 29 April 1945.

On the morning of 31 May 1945, a clear, bright, sunny day in the city of Le Mans, PFC Alvin R. Rollins stood before the temporary gallows at the Loire DTC. A crowd of thirty officials, witnesses and spectators watched as Lieutenant Colonel Henry L. Peck led him to the steps of the scaffold. After guards escorted him up the flight of steps, Master Sergeant John Clarence Woods placed a hood over his head and secured a rope around his neck. Lieutenant Colonel Peck then gave a silent signal and the trapdoor sprang open, sending the soldier to his death. His body was then transported to the US Military Cemetery at Marigny for burial. In 1949, his remains were removed from this location and secretly re-buried in the Oise-Aisne American Cemetery in Plot 'E', Row 3, Grave 51. The *Chattanooga Daily Times*, dated 17 June 1945, reported that PFC Alvin R. Rollins had died from 'wounds received in Europe'.

PFC John H.W. Hoogewind is buried with honour in the American Cemetery in Épinal, France.

The day of his murder should have his last day of service in France before being shipped back to the United States, and perhaps he had thoughts of home on his mind as he pulled away from the cafe. Under the Return of the Dead Program, the body of Sergeant Royce Arthur Judd Jr was shipped back to the United States and is buried at Greenlawn Cemetery, Tiffin, Seneca County, Ohio. On 6 October 1948, the *Toledo Blade* reported that Judd had died from 'accidental gunshot wounds'. Remember them.

Friday, 30 March 1945, Germany

Victim	Second Lieutenant John Bernard Platt (white)
	Age: 28
	Service No.: O-509505
	Murdered
Assailant	Private Henry Clay Philpot (Native Indian)
	Age: 28
	Service No.: 39080069
	Unit: 234th Replacement Company, 90th Infantry Battalion

The grave of Second Lieutenant John Bernard Platt in the Ardennes American Cemetery, Neupré, Belgium. He was murdered by Private Henry Clay Philpot on 30 March 1945 in Bad Neuenahr, Germany.

John Bernard Platt was born on 30 May 1916 in Milwaukee, Wisconsin, the son of John and Bertha Platt, one of three brothers. He attended the Shorewood High School, Wisconsin, and was later employed as a salesman. On 18 February 1939, he married 25-year-old Helen Pinkley at the Scared Heart Cathedral, Davenport, Iowa, as war clouds were looming over Europe. On 16 October 1940, the 24-year-old registered for the draft. His education would lead him to the officer corps and, as a young second lieutenant, he would see service in the ETO, from where he would never return.

By 30 March 1945, John Platt was commanding the 234th Replacement Company, stationed at Bad Neuenahr, Germany, south of the city of Bonn, and looking forward to the war ending, so that he could get back home to his wife. At 5.40 p.m. that afternoon, Platt was made aware there was a problem in the mess hall. Private Henry Clay Philpot, a 27-year-old Native American, was drunk and causing a disturbance. Platt took a four-man detail to arrest the unruly soldier and place him in the stockade. He was arrested and then escorted from the mess hall, with his M-1 rifle slung over his shoulder. When they reached the corner of the hall, a sergeant intercepted them and handed Platt the confinement papers. Philpot said he did not want to be confined but wanted to eat, and Platt said it was all right for him to 'go ahead and eat'. Philpot then dropped his mess kit and took his rifle off his shoulder. He pulled off the safety catch, worked the bolt back, looked into the chamber, let the bolt go forward, put his finger on the trigger and waved the rifle around at all members of the detail. He then pointed it directly at Platt for about 5 minutes, ordering him to back up or he would shoot. Platt stepped back three paces, but Philpot shot him, and the lieutenant fell over on his back. The sergeant who had brought the confinement

papers, grabbed the barrel of the carbine and struck Philpot over the head, at the same time a corporal struck Philpot with a .45 calibre pistol. He dropped the rifle as he fell to the ground and tried to grab it, but the sergeant threw him into a wall. The body of Second Lieutenant Platt lay on the street, motionless, with blood all around him. He was taken to a hospital where an examination revealed that the officer had died almost instantaneously from a bullet wound that had severed his spinal cord. Philpot claimed that he still had a clip in his rifle after shooting on the range that morning, that he had been drinking wine incessantly since mid-morning and when Lieutenant Platt told him he would be confined he 'just flared up'. He remembered the shooting but did not remember pulling the trigger.

Philpot, who was born on 20 June 1917 in Redding, Shasta County, California, and was inducted into the army in Sacramento, California, on 7 May 1941, appeared before a GCM on 23 April 1945 at Marburg, Germany, where he pleaded not guilty to the charge of murder. There were no witnesses for the defence and he was quickly found guilty and unanimously sentenced to death by hanging. Following his trial, Brigadier General Edwin C. McNeil, the chief of the branch office of the JAG, proposed that Philpot undergo a psychological assessment. This was carried out at the 235th General Hospital, and it was found that although Philpot's early life was troubled, he was able to tell the difference between right and wrong and was judged to be sane. Brigadier General Ewart G. Plank approved the sentence and, following a review of the case, the death sentence was confirmed by General Dwight D. Eisenhower on 7 June 1945.

On the morning of 10 September 1945, a clear, bright, sunny day in the city of Le Mans, Private Henry Clay Philpot stood before the temporary gallows at the Loire DTC. A group of officials, witnesses and spectators watched as Lieutenant Colonel Henry L. Peck led him to the steps of the scaffold. After guards escorted him up the flight of steps, Master Sergeant John Clarence Woods placed a hood over his head and secured a rope around his neck. Lieutenant Colonel Peck then gave a silent signal and the trapdoor sprang open, sending the soldier to his death. His body was then transported to the US Military Cemetery at Marigny for burial. In 1949, his remains were removed from this location and secretly re-buried in the Oise-Aisne American Cemetery in Plot 'E', Row 4, Grave 89.

Following his murder, Second Lieutenant John Bernard Platt was laid to rest in a temporary grave at the newly opened Neuville-en-Condroz Cemetery, some 12 miles south-west of Liège in Belgium. In 1960, this was dedicated as the Ardennes American Cemetery, Neupré, Belgium. He rests in Plot D, Row 32, Grave 12. Remember him.

Sunday, 1 April 1945, France
Victim   Yvonne Louise Le Ny, French civilian (white)
                  Age: 35
                  Murdered
Assailant   Private Charles M. Robinson (black)
                  Age: 22
                  Service No.: 38164425
                  Unit: 667th Quartermaster Truck Company,
                     66th Infantry Division

Yvonne Louise Le Ny was born on 2 October 1909 in Sainte-Maure, Aube, France, the daughter of Prosper Le Ny and Louise Briendo. It seems she was unmarried and sadly may have fallen into a life of prostitution, as she was well known to soldiers who visited the Café de Sport in the small town of Messac, about 15 miles south-west of the city of Rennes.

At the end of March 1945, the 667th Quartermaster Truck Company was camped outside of Messac, and Yvonne was acquainted with one of the soldiers serving with the unit, Private Charles M. Robinson, and even carried his photograph in her handbag. But it seems that Yvonne was also acquainted with other members of the unit, and on the night of 31 March 1945, she slept with another black soldier named 'Jimmy' in the same tent where Robinson slept with five other soldiers whilst he was there. The following afternoon, at about 2.30 p.m., Yvonne was returning to camp with another woman, and met Robinson and another soldier on the road. She seemed quite happy, but he was clearly

Yvonne Le Ny, who was murdered by Private Charles M. Robinson for sleeping with another soldier. (*JAG File*)

upset with what she had done. They talked for about half an hour, and then Robinson told her to 'go and get Jimmy'. She walked away and when she was about 5ft from him he pulled out a pistol from his trouser pocket and shot Yvonne through the head. She died instantly. Three witnesses saw him shoot Yvonne, and one saw him standing over the body with the smoking gun in his hand. Robinson ran back to the camp where he was found a short time later, in a tent sitting behind an officer who was playing a piano. A mud-covered pistol, which had been recently fired, was found in a ditch close to where Robinson had last been seen. He was arrested 15 minutes after the shooting.

Charles M. Robinson, born on 4 April 1924 in Houston, Texas, had been inducted into the US Army in Fort Sam Houston, Texas, on 2 July 1942. He was brought before a GCM on 19 April 1945 in Ploërmel, France, where he pleaded not guilty to the charge of murder and claimed that he had been the victim of several beatings from MPs to make him confess. There were no witnesses for the defence, but several witnesses had seen him shoot Yvonne and dispose of the weapon. He was quickly found guilty of the charge, and unanimously sentenced to death by hanging. Following his trial, Major General Herman F. Kramer, commanding the 66th Infantry Division, to whom Robinson's unit was attached, approved the sentence and, following a review of the case, the death sentence was confirmed by General Dwight D. Eisenhower on 6 May 1945. On the morning of 28 September 1945, a clear, bright, sunny day in the city of Le Mans, Private Charles M. Robinson stood before the temporary gallows at the Loire DTC. A group of officials, witnesses and spectators watched as Lieutenant Colonel Henry L. Peck led him to the steps of the scaffold. After guards escorted him up the flight of steps, Master Sergeant John Clarence Woods placed a hood over his head and secured a rope around his neck. Lieutenant Colonel Peck

Private Charles M. Robinson. (*JAG File*)

then gave a silent signal and the trapdoor sprang open at 11.02 a.m., sending the soldier to his death. His body was then transported to the US Military Cemetery at Marigny for burial. In 1949, his remains were removed from this location and secretly re-buried in the Oise-Aisne American Cemetery in Plot 'E', Row 3, Grave 70.

Yvonne Louise Le Ny is believed to be buried in Messac, France. Remember her.

Sunday, 15 April 1945, Germany
Victims   Ulita Obichwist, Polish refugee
               Raped and murdered
               Peter Lobacz, Polish refugee
               Murdered
Assailants   Private Woodrow Parker (black)
               Age: 27
               Service No.: 34561139
               Private Sidney Bennerman Jr (black)
               Age: 27
               Service No.: 34174757
               Unit: 163rd Chemical Smoke Generator Company

At times, it can be difficult to summarise a particular case, especially if it is exceptionally harrowing. On this occasion, the Board of Review provided wording that prepares the reader for what is about to follow, 'No more revolting case has come before the Board of Review. The utter obliviousness of the accused to the accepted principles of civilized conduct caused by their bestial, lust-crazed selfishness and resulting in the murders and rapes merit the extreme punishment to which they have been sentenced.'

At about 9.00 p.m. on Sunday, 15 April 1945, five US soldiers were sitting at a table drinking wine with two Polish refugees in the Displaced Persons Camp at Heilbronn, Germany, a former Wehrmacht army barracks. Three of the soldiers were white, the other two black. The latter were Private Woodrow Parker and Private Sidney Bennerman Jr, who were serving with 163rd Chemical Smoke Generator Company which was encamped nearby. Bennerman, a married man with two children, was born in Wilmington, New Hanover County, North Carolina, on 31 January 1918. A seasoned veteran, he had entered the US Army in Fort Bragg, North Carolina, on 22 November 1941. He had a poor disciplinary record, had been demoted from staff sergeant and had spent six months in military prison following a previous court martial.

A building in the Displaced Persons Camp in Heilbronn, Germany, where Polish refugees Ulita Obichwist and Peter Lobacz were murdered by Private Woodrow Parker and Private Sidney Bennerman Jr. Ulita was also subjected to an horrific sexual assault.

Parker, born in Coosa County, Alabama, on 17 August 1918, had been inducted into the US Army on 12 December 1942, and does not appear to have had any prior service.

Whilst they were drinking, Bennerman asked one of the white soldiers about a .22 calibre German rifle he had and was given it as a souvenir. Sitting at a nearby table was Peter Lobacz, a Polish refugee who was in the camp with his family. Another refugee, Ulita Obichwist, had shared a room in the barracks with a man she knew, but he had now left the camp and she was afraid to sleep alone. So, she asked Peter Lobacz if he would stay with her for the night. He agreed and then accompanied his two daughters, Eweline and Anna, his brother, John, and his brother's wife, Malvina, along with Luba Kot and Konstantine Salofwaue, to the cellar where they usually slept. He obtained a bed cover from the shelter and then returned to the barracks, an act of kindness that would cost him his life. An hour or so later, Parker and Bennerman entered the cellar, struck matches and started asking about 'mademoiselles'. One of the soldiers attempted to drag John Lobacz out of the cellar, whilst the other made advances towards his wife, but then they both left the cellar without further incident. An hour later they returned, and this time one of the soldiers threw Malvina on the bed and it was obvious what they were trying to do. Terrified, the Lobacz daughters and Luba Kot hid under the bed. John Lobacz shouted at the two soldiers, telling them he was going to call the MPs. Parker and Bennerman then left the cellar and did not return.

The following morning, the bodies of Peter Lobacz, and Ulita Obichwist were discovered. Peter, who had agreed to sleep in Ulita's room so she wouldn't be frightened, was still in his bed. His skull had been smashed in with a large blunt instrument. Ulita was found outside with devastating injuries to her head and face, her legs splayed apart and her clothes had been pushed up over her breasts. On her back were superficial lacerations that had been caused by her body being dragged over a rough surface, and cinders were embedded in her shoulders and buttocks. A trail of bloodstains led from the sleeping quarters to where her body lay, and she had been sexually assaulted. Around her body investigators found three pieces of a broken German rifle, exactly like the one the white soldier gave to Bennerman. A guard at their camp had seen Bennerman with a similar rifle that night, but when he returned to camp, he did not have it with him. It didn't take investigators too long to realise what had happened and the two individuals were apprehended.

Bennerman, who was interviewed on 17 and 18 April, gave a sworn statement detailing how the pair, who were drunk, had entered the room occupied by Peter Lobacz, and Ulita Obichwist. On seeing them, Ulita, terrified, jumped out of her own bed and into Peter's. The two soldiers argued with Peter and expressed a desire to 'get some of this pussy'. Parker said, 'I'm going to kill those son-of-a bitches', and struck Peter's head with his carbine, holding it in both hands by the barrel. He heard no outcry from the man. Parker then hit the girl on the head with the carbine, and again struck the man, breaking the stock. Parker grabbed the German rifle from Bennerman, announcing he was 'going to finish killing these son-of-a-bitches', then hit the girl on the head two or three more times. He then took her by the legs and started to drag her out of bed. When she began to scream, he silenced her by striking her on the head again. Parker dragged her by the legs out onto the road and alongside a building, a short distance away. He then pulled the girl's clothes up leaving her naked from the waist down, spread her legs apart and had sex with her. Parker returned to the barrack where he found the barrel of the rifle, which he threw alongside the road saying, 'I believe I killed those sons-of-a-bitches.' They stopped a short time later, slept and returned to their company at about daybreak. For his part, Parker gave pretty much the same statement, except he felt that neither of them was drunk and, therefore, were fully aware of what they were doing. During the attacks, Bennerman ensured they could see what they were doing by continually lighting matches.

The two soldiers were brought before a GCM at Bad Canstatt, near Stuttgart, Germany, on 28 April 1945. They pleaded not guilty to the crimes but opted not to take to the witness stand. The court found them both guilty of their crimes and sentenced them to death by musketry. There is no evidence to explain why this method of execution had been chosen. The sentences were confirmed by Major General Withers A. Burress, commander of the 100th Infantry Division, to whom their company was attached. General Dwight D. Eisenhower signed the orders of execution on 4 August 1945. Both men were transferred to Camp Miami, near Reims, France, after which they were moved to the Delta DTC, at Camp des Milles, France. Here in the early hours of 15 October 1945, they were shot by firing squad. Their bodies were then transported to the US Military Cemetery at Marigny for burial. Like most other soldiers featured in this book, in 1949 their remains were removed and secretly re-buried in the Oise-Aisne American Cemetery in Plot 'E'. Bennerman is in Row 3, Grave 57 and Parker is in Row 3, Grave 56.

There is no record of where the remains of Ulita Obichwist and Peter Lobacz were buried. One can only hope they knew little of their ordeal and now rest in peace. Remember them.

Monday, 16 April 1945, Germany
Victims   Märta Jenny Sofia Gary, Swedish civilian (white)
             Age: 41
             Murdered
             Babette Kuhndorfer, German civilian (white)
             Age: 21
             Raped
             Elfriede Weissbarth, German civilian (white)
             Age: 54
             Attempted Rape

Assailant   PFC Blake Waskee Mariano (Native Indian)
Age: 29
Service No.: 38011593
Unit: Company 'C', 191st Tank Battalion, 45th Infantry Division

On 15 April 1945, the German fortress town of Lauf an der Pegnitz was captured by US forces, including the battle-hardened 191st Tank Battalion, part of the US 45th Division, which had slogged its way across Europe from Southern France and was now poised to assault one of the most renowned cities in the Nazi empire, Nuremberg. Amongst the soldiers serving with the unit was 29-year-old PFC Blake Waskee Mariano, a Navajo Indian, whose home was in McKinley County, New Mexico. He had enlisted in Santa Fe, New Mexico, on 8 March 1941 and had seen combat in North Africa, Italy, including Anzio, and across Europe for almost three years.

A tank trundles through the ruins of Lauf an der Pegnitz where Märta Jenny Sofia Gary, a Swedish woman, was murdered by PFC Blake Waskee Mariano on 16 April 1945.

Civilians were hiding in the cellars and air-raid shelters of the rubble-strewn town, including a woman who records commonly refer to as Martha Gary. She was, in fact, Märta Jenny Sofia Holmgren, a Swedish woman, who was born on 17 December 1903 in Nacka, Stockholm, Sweden, the daughter of Karl John Emil Holmgren and Jenny Mellner. Not much is known about her life, but on 29 August 1935, she married Ernst Gary in the town of Bälinge, Uppsala, Sweden, just over 50 miles outside Stockholm. Her sister, Ingeborg Rohlin, was an opera singer whose husband, Bror Rohlin, imported German dentistry equipment into Sweden. Quite why Märta was a thousand miles from her home in April 1945 is uncertain, but she was never to return there.

On 16 April, Märta was amongst a group of fourteen civilians who were assembled in a large cellar underneath Lauf castle, which was used as an air-raid shelter and had just a single light. At about 4.00 a.m., Blake W. Mariano entered the cellar, along with a Pole and another US soldier. Mariano pointed his rifle at 54-year-old Elfriede Weissbarth and motioned her to leave the shelter. He followed her, with a rifle at her back, until they were outside. Mariano attempted to tear off Elfriede's clothes, but to spare her clothing she opened her coat. Mariano then forced her into a corner, pulled down her underwear, forced her to lie down and then raped her. Elfriede did not resist Mariano because the soldier constantly pointed his rifle at her, and whilst he raped her he kept his hand over her mouth so she could not scream. Within 10 or 20 minutes, Mariano returned to the cellar where he questioned 41-year-old Märta Gary. She showed him her Swedish passport, gave him her pocketbook and ring, but these were returned. Mariano put his hands to his chest and then threw them to his sides, and the others told Gary, 'He wants you to undress.' She began to do so, but slowly, and all the while Mariano held his rifle in the ready position. Märta had undressed until the top of her sanitary pad became visible and Mariano pointed his finger and asked, 'What is that?', she replied, 'I am ill.' Mariano suddenly shot her and she fell backwards, fatally injured. Mariano now turned his attention to 21-year-old Babette Kuhndorfer. He pointed his rifle at her and motioned for her to exit the cellar. Mariano followed with his rifle on his arm. They went up to the ground floor, undressed and then Mariano laid down his rifle and raped Kuhndorfer. By now it was about 6.30 a.m. and Märta had lain on the floor, wounded, for over an hour. She said, 'I have to die' and asked for coffee. By 09.00 a.m., she had died from her injuries. A later examination would find that she had a small bullet hole in her right side, which exited the right side of her back, tearing a large hole in it.

Mariano was not arrested until 8 May 1945, VE Day, and was brought before a GCM on 25 May, at Munich, Germany, where he pleaded not guilty to murder and rape. He took to the witness stand where he claimed he was so drunk that he could not remember what he had done. He had been drinking cognac and schnapps and could only recall waking up in the turret of his tank the next morning. Mariano, born on the 4 April 1916, had had a difficult early life. He had been married, but later divorced, and was the father of three children. His army classification test score and a medical board deemed him to be classed as a 'high grade moron'. Despite this, Mariano had been serving overseas since 6 August 1942 mainly as a gunner on Sherman tanks. His commanding officer and crew described him as a soldier who was calm and composed in battle, and always obeyed orders. Alcohol was his downfall, and he would go wild when drunk. He had fought valiantly at Anzio, Italy, and had been wounded by shrapnel at Épinal, France, a soldier who had seen a lot of combat and, in his own words, 'had killed a lot of Germans'. One witness at the trial, a German doctor, stated that Elfriede Weissbarth had not been raped, and the charge was amended to assault with intent to rape. Mariano was found guilty of the crimes and sentenced to death. The commander of the 45th Division, Major General Robert T. Frederick, approved the sentence and General Dwight D. Eisenhower signed the order of execution on 4 August 1945.

On the morning of 10 October 1945, a clear, bright, sunny day in the city of Le Mans, PFC Blake Waskee Mariano stood before the temporary gallows at the Loire DTC. A group of officials, witnesses and spectators watched as Lieutenant Colonel Henry L. Peck led him to the steps of the scaffold. After guards escorted him up the flight of steps, Master Sergeant John Clarence Woods placed a hood over his head and secured a rope around his neck. Lieutenant Colonel Peck then gave a silent signal and the trapdoor sprang open at 11.02 a.m., sending the soldier to his death. His body was then transported to the US Military Cemetery at Marigny for burial. In 1949, his remains were removed from this location and secretly re-buried in the Oise-Aisne American Cemetery in Plot 'E', Row 1, Grave 12.

Märta Jenny Sofia Gary was never to return home to Sweden and is buried in the town of Lauf an der Pegnitz, Germany, where records regard her as Czechoslovakian. Remember her.

Thursday, 24 May 1945, France

Victim	Second Lieutenant Eddie Lee May (black)
	Age: 26
	Service No.: O-1110096
	Murdered
Assailant	Private Ellsworth Williams (black)
	Age: 23
	Service No.: 34200976
	Unit: Company 'E', 1349th Engineer General Service Regiment

The Second World War in Europe drew to a close on 8 May 1945, and for servicemen such as Second Lieutenant Eddie Lee May the future had already begun to look a little brighter with a sense of optimism in the air. The war was over, and the Allies were victorious. Eddie, born on 17 July 1918 in Macon, Mississippi, was the second son of Ellis John May Sr and Mary Jane Strode, one of five children. By 1940, his family were living in Beloit, Wisconsin, where his father worked for Fairbanks Morse and Eddie attended Beloit College, a private liberal arts institution, and it was from here that he joined the US Army, becoming a rare black member of the officer corps. With an engineering background, he served with 383rd Engineer Battalion, stationed in Fleet, Hampshire, from early 1943, preparing engineering works for the Normandy invasion. The unit constructed camps, facilities, roads, vehicle hardstanding and the Weymouth LST ramps to enable the housing, transportation and shipping of the Allied troops for D-Day. Following the invasion of France, the 383rd was engaged in reconstructing battle-damaged facilities and constructing new ones to support the front-line troops. In August 1944, after much lobbying by their officers, the battalion was re-constituted 1349th Engineer General Service Regiment.

In May 1945, Private Ellsworth Williams was assigned to Company 'E' of the 1349th, stationed in Le Havre, France, at the time. On 24 May, Williams was on guard duty at the firing range near Le Havre Airport, when Sergeant Minor R. Davis arrived at the location. Lieutenant May told Davis what he wanted done during the day. Williams, who had been on duty since 2.00 a.m., was heard to tell Lieutenant May, 'It doesn't matter to me from out here at all, if you don't send me from out here at all.' Lieutenant May replied, 'If it takes that you'll remain.' Shortly after this confrontation, a weapons carrier arrived at the site and Williams asked the driver where he was going. He then told the guard sergeant, 'Sir, this is my relief', and turned and walked toward

May. Suddenly, Sergeant Davis heard a loud voice say, 'Don't come up to me, don't come up to me, Lieutenant.' He saw Williams with a rifle pointed at the lieutenant, holding the gun between his waist and shoulder. Before Davis could intervene, Williams fired and Lieutenant May collapsed to the ground, suffering perforating gunshot wounds to the chest and abdomen. The soldier then simply turned his back on May and walked away. Davis ran to injured officer, who was hollering, 'Get a doctor, I have been shot.' After placing the wounded officer in the weapons carrier, so he could be taken to hospital, Davis went to Williams and said, 'Soldier, give me that rifle.' He replied, 'Sergeant, you take the rifle, take the ammunition, take everything.' Williams was then arrested. On arrival at hospital, Captain Edward John Dill, Medical Corps, examined Lieutenant May and found the bullet had entered his left side, between the ninth and tenth ribs. The exit wound was in his back 3in to the right of the spine, at the level of the eleventh and twelfth vertebrae. Second Lieutenant Eddie Lee May died from his injuries two days later on 26 May 1945 and would never see home again.

Ellsworth Williams appeared before a GCM on 19 June 1945 at Le Havre, France. He pleaded not guilty and claimed he was unloading his rifle when it went off accidentally. He denied arguing with Lieutenant May and said he had not pointed his rifle at him. Private Daniel Boone, who was supervising a prisoner of war detail at the scene of the incident, heard Williams scream, 'I been out here a long time. I been out here too long', reminiscent of the scene involving Private David Cobb, who was executed for murdering his officer in similar circumstances. Williams, who had joined the US Army in Camp Blanding, Florida, on 24 January 1942, was convicted of the murder and sentenced to death. The details of executions which occurred in the period after the ending of hostilities do not appear to have survived. What is known is that Private Ellsworth Williams was transported to Mannheim Military Prison, Germany, where he was hanged on 5 January 1946, and was buried near the place of his execution. His remains were exhumed by the Graves Registration Service in 1949 and secretly moved to the Oise-Aisne American Cemetery in Plot 'E', Row 2, Grave 32. Williams is believed to have been the last US serviceman to be hanged by Master Sergeant John Clarence Woods.

Second Lieutenant Eddie Lee May is buried amongst the honoured dead at the Normandy American Cemetery, Colleville-sur-Mer, France in Plot B, Row 9, Grave 23. Remember him.

Chapter 9

The Execution of Private Edward Donald Slovik

Friday, 25 August 1944, France
Private Edward Donald Slovik (white)
Service No.: 36896415
Unit: Company 'G', 109th Infantry Regiment

The case of Private Edward Donald 'Eddie' Slovik, the only US soldier to be executed for desertion since the American Civil War, is one that has been studied in detail and become the subject of books, movies and ongoing controversy. His GCM stands out as an example of the precise application of the letter of the law. But it leaves disturbing questions about whether, given the circumstances, it was a fair trial.

Born in Detroit, Michigan, on 18 February 1920, to a Polish immigrant father and a US mother, Eddie and his siblings grew up in a poor home environment and by the age of 15 he had dropped out of school. Described

Private Edward Donald Slovik, the only US soldier to be executed for desertion during the Second World War. His remains were repatriated to Woodmere Cemetery, Detroit, Michigan, to rest by the side of his beloved wife.

220

as a follower, not a leader, he was repeatedly in trouble with the law. Between 1932 and 1938 he was convicted on six occasions and in each case was placed on parole. In 1937, he was sentenced to six months to ten years for embezzlement, and in 1939 was again confined for unlawfully driving away an automobile. He was still imprisoned when the United States entered the Second World War and, when he was released in April 1942, he was given the classification '4F' as an ex-convict. This meant he had initially escaped the draft, as the army had sufficient manpower and did not need to recruit convicted felons. It was at this point in his life that he married Antoinette Wisniewski, in a ceremony that took place at a Polish National Catholic Church in Detroit, Michigan, on 7 November 1942. In late 1943, however, facing an increased need for able-bodied young men, the War Department reclassified Slovik, defining him as available and fit for general military service, and he was quickly inducted into the army.

After completing his basic training at Camp Wolters, Texas, Eddie Slovik was posted to Europe in August 1944, where he was assigned to the 109th Infantry Regiment, a part of the 28th Infantry Division, nicknamed the 'Bloody Bucket Division'. He was amongst fifteen replacements who were sent to the village of Elbeuf, France, to join their unit when he and a companion, Private John F. Tankey, became separated from the rest of the men. They stumbled upon a Canadian Provost unit that took them in. Here, it seems, they performed a variety of roles, remaining with the Canadians for the next forty-five days. On 4 October 1944, the Canadians turned the two men over to the US Military Police, who reunited them with their parent unit, which by now was in Elsenborn, Belgium. No charges were brought, as replacements getting lost early in their tours of duty was not unusual, so when Slovik reported back to Company 'G', 109th Infantry Regiment, three days later, he was in the clear. However, it appears that he was questioned by his Company Commander, Captain Ralph O. Grotte, about this absence, and Slovik stated that he was 'too scared, too nervous' to serve with a rifle company and would desert again if ordered to fight. Slovik was then ordered to remain in the company area. Shortly thereafter, he returned to Captain Grotte and asked: 'If I leave now, will it be desertion?' When Grotte confirmed it would, Slovik left without taking his weapon. The next day, he surrendered to a nearby field kitchen unit and handed over a signed, hand-printed note to a cook that said:

> I, Private Eddie D. Slovik, 36896415, confess to the desertion of the United States Army. At the time of my desertion, we were in Albuff

[*sic* Elbeuf] in France. I come to Albuff as a replacement. They were shelling the town and we were told to dig in for the night. The following morning, they were shelling us again. I was so scared, nerves and trembling that at the time the other replacements moved out I couldn't move. I stayed there in my fox hole till it was quiet and I was able to move. I then walked in town. Not seeing any of our troops so I stayed over night at a French hospital. The next morning, I turned myself over to the Canadian Provost Corp. After being with them six weeks I was turned over to American M.P. They turned me loose. I told my commanding officer my story. I said that if I had to go out their again, I'd run away. He said there was nothing he could do for me, so I ran away again, and I'll run away again if I have to go out their [*sic*].

After being returned to his unit on 9 October, Slovik's commander told him that the note was damaging to his case and that he should take it back and destroy it. He refused to do so and was confined to the division stockade. On 26 October, Lieutenant Colonel Henry P. Sommer, the Division Judge Advocate, offered Slovik a deal. If he would go into the line, that is accept a combat assignment, he could escape court martial. Slovik refused this offer and on 29 October his case was referred to trial by general court martial.

At 10.00 a.m. on 11 November 1944, described by one of the attending officers, Benedict B. Kimmelman, a dentist, as a cold, grey day with snow falling off and on, Slovik was tried for desertion inside a scarred two-storey building in the village of Roetgen, Germany. In the grimmest of surroundings, and during the worst time the division had endured, he was charged with two specifications of desertion, in violation of the 58th Article of War. He pleaded not guilty and elected to remain silent. He was represented by Major Edward Woods, a young staff captain who was not an attorney but had served on previous courts martial. Five witnesses were heard. The cross examinations were perfunctory. The defence made no closing argument. The court then recessed for 10 minutes, resumed and retired almost immediately afterward. Three ballots were taken in closed court, the verdicts unanimously guilty on all counts. In open court once more, the president announced the verdict and the sentence. Private Slovik was to be dishonourably discharged, forfeit all pay and allowances due, and to be shot to death with musketry. The proceedings closed at 11.40 a.m. and Slovik was confined to the Seine Disciplinary Centre in Paris.

General Dwight D. Eisenhower upheld the sentence and Slovik was shot by a twelve-man firing squad led by Sergeant Albert H. Bruns, in the walled-in garden of an estate in the small town of Sainte-Marie-aux-Mines, Alsace, France, on 31 January 1945. The execution report makes grim reading, detailing how Slovik needed no assistance and replied quietly to those trussing him up and placing the hood over his head. His body stiffened at the impact of the bullets and pieces of his flesh splattered from his back onto the board panel behind the post. Slovik slumped forward, restrained only by the support straps, his body then made several movements that were reported as 'involuntary muscle reflexes', but not everyone present was convinced of this. Slovik's heart was still beating when the Chief Medical Officer examined him and it was thought that a second volley may be required, but Slovik was pronounced dead a few moments later. His body was laid to rest in the American Military Cemetery at Épinal, France. In 1949, it was removed from this location and reinterred at the Oise-Aisne American Cemetery in Plot 'E', Row 3, Grave 65.

Slovik's case records contain a piece of vital evidence that did not appear until 18 November 1976, when the officer in charge of his training at Camp Wolters, Texas, First Lieutenant Arnold C. Shaw, wrote:

> We recognised this man's total inability as a combat soldier, through no fault of his own. He was popular with the troops, non-comms and officers, but badly cast as an infantryman. We tried every means to get his discharge, failing this, we tried to get him transferred to a non-combat unit. Here again, we failed. As a last resort, we tried to remove his fear of weapons and simulated combat conditions. Tragically, we failed again.

Perhaps it was this tragic failure that caught the attention, in 1981, of Bernard B. Calka, an Assistant Fire Chief for the City of Sterling Heights, Michigan, who read about the case of Eddie Slovik. In 1987, Calka began a campaign that culminated in President Ronald Regan authorising Slovik's body being removed from Plot 'E' and returned home, where it was laid to rest at the Woodmere Cemetery, Detroit, Michigan, next that of his beloved wife, Antoinette. Bernard Calka passed away himself on 10 October 2010, but always believed one of his greatest achievements was seeing Slovik's body returned home. He felt the soldier was guilty of desertion, as many others were, but it was clear he was made the sole example and Calka believed his execution was an historic injustice. Remember him.

Chapter 10

A Case of Double Murder

Tuesday, 16 January 1945, Italy
Victims   Arnolfo Carresi, Italian civilian (white)
                  Murdered
                  Maria Carresi, Italian civilian (white)
                  Raped
Tuesday, 31 July 1945, Italy
Victim   Pietro Testini, Italian civilian (white)
                  Murdered
Assailants   Private Charlie Ervin (black)
                  Age: 26
                  Service No.: 34042926
                  Private Mansfield Spinks (black) (16 January only)
                  Age: 20
                  Service No.: 36793241
                  Private Elmer Sussex (black) (31 July only)
                  Age: 22
                  Service No.: 38354458
                  Unit: 'I' Company, 366th Infantry Regiment,
                      92nd Infantry Division

The last two US soldiers to be executed by firing squad as a result of crimes committed in the Second World War were Private Charlie Ervin and Private Mansfield Spinks. The cases were complicated, and their stories read more like a movie script.

By January 1945, the Allied campaign in Italy had become a long, arduous and frustrating slog. The men of the all-black US 92nd Infantry Division, nicknamed the 'Buffalo Soldiers', had found themselves thrown back from the Gothic Line, a series of fortified passes and mountain tops that stretched from the Adriatic coast through to the Ligurian Sea, in December 1945. They were now engaged in a cat-and-mouse game of opposing patrols with a combined German and Italian force. On 16 January 1945, Arnolfo Carresi, his wife, Maria, and a number of children and family members were living in the coastal town of Forte Dei Marmi, about 3 miles from Pietrasanta. That evening, two black US soldiers entered their home. These were Private Charlie Ervin and Private Mansfield Spinks, who were then serving with Company 'I', 366th Infantry Regiment. Both men had been drinking heavily, and when they arrived at the house Arnolfo welcomed Ervin in through the kitchen door, as though he had been there before. Spinks, who had never been in the home previously, then entered the kitchen, even though Arnolfo had tried to stop him. The two soldiers were provided with chairs and blankets and warmed their feet on the fire, whilst Arnolfo and Maria went to bed. It appears that Ervin then hatched a plan to provoke Arnolfo into attempting to shoot them both in order that he could kill him. Evidence suggests that Maria had been providing Ervin with sexual favours and wanted rid of her husband, and it seems Ervin was happy to oblige. Arnolfo had placed a large chest against the bedroom door in order to keep the two soldiers away from his wife. Spinks started to bang on the door, shout and make a commotion in order to get the Italian to come out. Eventually, Arnolfo appeared and in an effort to keep the soldier quiet, went with him to the kitchen. Here, Spinks picked up his rifle and fired a shot into the fireplace, then placed his rifle on the kitchen table, knowing that the firing mechanism was faulty. Arnolfo picked up the M-1 and, as he did so, Erving shot him through the head. On hearing the shots, Maria put a coat on over her nightdress and ran out of the house to fetch help from a neighbour. Ervin and Spinks grabbed her and marched down the street. When they reached an empty house, they dragged her inside and then took turns in raping her.

A few days later, on 19 January, Maria Carresi picked Spinks out of an identification parade as one of her rapists. He, in turn, indicated that Ervin was the killer. Both men were arrested and faced a GCM. On 7 February 1945 Spinks was brought before a military court, but Ervin was absent as he had been admitted to the US 170th Evacuation Hospital. Sergeant Weston Hoffman, of the Criminal Investigation Division, was quizzed over his investigation of the case in which he claimed that Spinks had 'broke down and confessed' to the crimes, even though it seems he had indicated he did not want to make a statement. The convening authority withdrew the charges and specification and a new trial was ordered for 28 April 1945, and Spinks was to be tried for a second time. Then, a few days later, on 17 February 1945, Ervin escaped from hospital and went on the run. A defendant was on the loose and Spinks now had to face a GCM alone, as the military justice machine continued to grind on without one of the culprits. The trial went ahead and Private Mansfield Spinks, born on 7 November 1924 in Chicago, Illinois, pleaded not guilty to both charges. Maria Carresi testified that she had never seen Spinks before the night of the murder and claimed the two soldiers had left her alone in the dark after they had raped her. She did, however, confirm what Spinks had said in his statement, that he had sex with her twice and Ervin four times. She had not resisted their attentions as she was fearful of what they may do to her or her family. Spinks, in his defence, claimed that the woman had not resisted at all and was a willing participant, as she had made a pact with Ervin. Despite the suggestion that the killing was a question of murder for hire, the fact that Spinks had not pulled the trigger on Arnolfo Carresi and the second defendant was still missing, he was found guilty of both crimes and sentenced to death by musketry. The case passed through the varying stages of review and confirmation and the order of execution was signed by General Joseph T. McNarney on 20 June 1945. Spinks was to be executed on 10 August 1945 but was also required to appear at the GCM of Private Charlie Ervin, who had now been recaptured following a second murder case.

There is every possibility that Ervin may have got away with his first crime, had he not done two things. Firstly, he spent six months hanging around the coastal town of Pietrasanta instead of heading for a big city, where he could lay low. Secondly, he continued his killing spree, this time with a new companion, Private Elmer Sussex. On the evening of 30 July 1945, a group of eight Italian civilians were making their way to the city of Genoa with a truck load of lemons. They were some 70 miles from their destination, near the town of Pietrasanta, when the vehicle broke down. The owner of the cargo decided to make his way to Genoa for assistance, whilst the remaining occupants passed the night away at the scene. One of the passengers, Giorgio Gamberini, opted to sleep on the cases of lemons along with his brother-in-law, Pietro Testini. At about 4.00 a.m. the following morning, one of the civilians woke up to find two black soldiers bothering the driver. One of the soldiers asked to see a permit and upon being shown a civilian identity card said that it was 'no good'. The second soldier climbed partly up the side of the truck, and Giorgio pointed at the soldier's arm and said, 'You are not from the military police.' Thereupon, the soldier asked Giorgio for his permit and simultaneously drew a knife, with which he jabbed at Giorgio as he drew his pocketbook from his trousers. Pietro Testini, seeing that there was trouble coming, picked up a box of lemons and threw it at Elmer Sussex. As he did so, two shots rang out. One struck Giorgio Gamberini in the leg, the other entered the right side of Pietro Testini, causing a devastating and fatal injury. The two soldiers made good their escape, and the civilians managed to find help for their injured fellow travellers. The two men were taken to Pietrasanta Hospital, where Pietro died from his injuries at 6.30 a.m. that morning.

On 2 August 1945, MPs found Private Charlie Ervin and Private Elmer Sussex asleep in a school building in Pietrasanta. They were arrested and their weapons sent for examination by a ballistics expert. The two soldiers were brought before a GCM on 22 August 1945, the last to be held in Europe for crimes committed before VE Day in which a sentence of death was to be pronounced. Both men pleaded not guilty to the charges against them, but Ervin already had a death sentence hanging over his head and his chances of evading it were practically zero. Born on 18 February 1918 in Lexington, Tennessee, he had been inducted in the US Army on 23 April 1941 in Fort Oglethorpe, Georgia. Even though he had been awarded a Purple Heart for a wound he received on 31 December 1944, and a combat infantryman's badge, his overall army record was a poor one. He had stood before a Summary Court Martial on four separate occasions and had been admitted to hospital numerous times with both syphilis and gonorrhoea infections. The ballistics expert confirmed that two cartridges found at the scene of the shooting had come from the weapon issued to Sussex, which was being carried by Ervin. This was confirmed by Ervin himself, who had left his own rifle behind when they went in search of civilians to rob as they had no money. The court was quick to make its decision and Private Elmer Sussex was sentenced to life imprisonment for his part in the attempted robbery. Ervin was to join Private Mansfield Spinks in front of a firing squad.

At 8.00 a.m. on 19 October 1945, in a specially prepared execution pit at the PBS Garrison Stockade No. 1, in Aversa, Italy, Private Mansfield Spinks was tied to a stake before a group of officials and witnesses. Following the word, 'Fire!', he slumped forward and was pronounced dead a short time after. Just 9 minutes later, Private Charlie Ervin suffered the same fate. Both men were then buried at the US Military Cemetery in Naples. In 1949, they, along with several others, were secretly removed from their resting place and transported to the Oise-Aisne American Cemetery, where they rest in Plot 'E'. Spinks is in Row 3, Grave 49 and Ervin is in Row 3, Grave 54.

It is thought Arnolfo Carresi and Pietro Testini rest in the locations where they fell. Remember them.

As for Maria, I leave the reader to make their own decision as to her part in the murder of her husband.

Chapter 11

A Grave Mystery

This chapter looks specifically at Grave 83 in Plot 'E' of the Oise-Aisne American Cemetery. A variety of records state that both Private Willie Lane and Private Archie Hall are buried in the same location. Trial records demonstrate that each of these soldiers, separately, murdered a comrade in arms. They appeared before a GCM and were found guilty of their crimes and sentenced to death. No execution records exist for them, so it is not possible to say, with any certainty, if the executions were actually carried out. The ABMC have confirmed that neither man is buried in Plot 'E'. So, who rests in Grave 83?

The ABMC have confirmed that the soldier buried in this grave is actually Private Willie Hall, whose name, oddly, is a combination of both the others. This soldier was found guilty of manslaughter, following the death of comrade, but appears to have lost his life whilst in custody, either by his own hand or that of another. The stories of each man and their victims are outlined below.

16 January 1944
Victim   T/5 George L. Robinson (black)
                 Age: 23
                 Service No.:13050668
                 Accidentally killed
Assailant   Sergeant Willie Hall (black)
                 Age: 36
                 Service No.:33268841
                 Unit: Company 'B', 402nd Engineer Battalion

Willie Hall, a black soldier, was born on 24 November 1907 in Winston-Salem, North Carolina. He was to serve eighteen months in the

Allegheny County Workhouse from March 1939 to September 1940 for larceny. He enlisted in the US Army on 3 June 1942 in Pittsburgh, Pennsylvania, and married Catherine Jackson on 16 September 1942. He was shipped overseas in January 1943. Hall and T/5 Ealie Lewis were both serving with the 357th Engineer General Service Regiment when they were convicted of killing T/5 George Robinson, Company 'B', 402nd Engineer Battalion, at Koudiat, near Bizerte, Tunisia, on 16 January 1944, in a quarrel over the ownership of a pistol. During a physical struggle for the weapon, it went off and Robinson was struck in the forehead. He died within minutes of being shot. Both men appeared at a GCM held in Bizerte, Tunisia, on 31 January 1944 and, on the basis that the death of Robinson was deemed to be accidental, were both found guilty of manslaughter and sentenced to life imprisonment. A hospital record shows that Hall died from a bullet wound on 30 March 1944. The ABMC state that he died in prison, and it is he who is buried in Plot 'E', Row 4, Grave 83.

T/5 George L Robinson who was born in Abbeville, South Carolina, on 4 December 1919, was brought home to the United States under the Return of the Dead Program and is buried in the Bethel Baptist Church Cemetery, Unionville, Orange County, Virginia. Remember him.

Monday, 14 May 1945

Victim	PFC Willie Leroy Dumas (black)
	Age: 19
	Service No. 34793729
	Murdered
Assailant	Private Willie Lane (black)
	Age: 23
	Service No.: 34750115
	Unit: 791st Engineer Dump Truck Company, 1321st Engineer General Service Regiment

A petty argument over a light socket escalated out of control to the point where a teenager lost his life and his killer spat out words that would ensure his own demise.

Willie Leroy Dumas was born in Jacksonville, Duval County, Florida, on 25 July 1925, the son of Hattie Dumas, a widow. He worked for the Seaboard Air Line Railroad until he was inducted into the US Army on 2 October 1943 in Camp Blanding, Florida, and was attached to the 791st Engineer Dump Truck Company, part of the 1321st Engineer General Service Regiment. The unit arrived in Liverpool,

The grave of PFC Willie Leroy Dumas in the Épinal American Cemetery, Dinozé, France. He was murdered by Private Willie Lane on 14 May 1945 in an argument over a light socket.

England, on 15 October 1944 and moved to Le Havre, France, on 6 December 1944. The regiment then went to work repairing roads and bridges, establishing depots and constructing facilities in the north-eastern Vosges area of France to support the Seventh Army's advance towards Germany. The 1321st crossed the Rhine on 24 April 1945 and rebuilt damaged roads and bridges along the autobahn, and by 14 May 1945 was stationed at Leonberg, Germany.

At about 12.30 a.m. on 14 May 1945, PFC Willie Dumas and Private Willie Lane were engaged in a fist fight in the presence of seventeen other members of the company over a light socket which Lane had demanded from Dumas. Sergeant Weathers separated them, and Dumas sat on his bunk and then reached for a carbine, but did not manage to get it. Lane reached into his coveralls and pulled out a Luger pistol, which he pointed at Dumas, but Sergeant Weathers took it away from him. The sergeant then took Lane out of the room and talked to him. He agreed to forget about the matter and returned to the room. However, he went straight to his footlocker and drew a .32 calibre pistol, turned around and shot Dumas four times with it. Dumas grabbed his stomach, fell on the bed and began to scream. Captain William Pahl arrived and Lane said to him, 'I just shot a man and I meant to kill him.' Dumas had been shot once in his leg and three bullets had entered his face and neck. His condition was critical, and on 17 May 1945, he was loaded onto a medical air evacuation flight for emergency treatment but died as a result of his wounds en route to hospital.

There appears to have been little need for any further investigation and Private Willie Lane was brought before a GCM at Mannheim, Germany, on 5 June 1945 and was charged with murder. Lane, who had been inducted into the US Army on 6 May 1943 in Fort Benning,

Georgia, pleaded not guilty and claimed self-defence as Dumas was reaching for a carbine, and he believed his life was in danger. The court felt that his claim to Captain Pahl that he intended to kill Dumas was sufficient for them to find him guilty of the charge and it sentenced him to death. The sentence was approved by the Commanding General, Continental Advance Section, and the Commanding General, European Theatre, confirmed the order of execution. There are no execution records to evidence that fact that Private Willie Lane was hanged. It is believed that he died at Mannheim Military Prison, Germany, either by his own hand or that of another. The ABMC have confirmed he is not buried in the Oise-Aisne American Cemetery, France in Plot 'E'.

PFC Willie Leroy Dumas is buried amongst the honoured dead at the Épinal American Cemetery, Dinozé, France in Plot B, Row 22, Grave 64. Remember him.

Wednesday, 30 May 1945
Victim   Private Sidney Benard Fountain (black)
                Age: 21
                Service No.: 34873094
                Murdered
Assailant   Private Archie Hall Jr (black)
                Age: 20
                Service No.: 34900858
                Unit: 3135th Quartermaster Service Company

Private Sidney Benard Fountain arrived at Camp Shelby, Mississippi, on 17 September 1943 to begin his service with the US Army, one that would ultimately lead to his death, not through combat but as a result of nothing more than an idle threat. Born on 26 March 1923 in Fayette, Jefferson, Mississippi, the son of William and Susan Fountain, and one of at least six children. After leaving school, he worked at the Case Lumber Company and upon entering the army was assigned to the 3135th Quartermaster Service Company. In May 1945, the unit was stationed in Senouches, France, about 80 miles south-west of Paris. Here they had the job of guarding German prisoners of war, an arduous and monotonous task.

At about 7.30 a.m. on 30 May 1945, Private Archie Hall and other members of his company, including Sidney Fountain, were sitting in their barracks prior to going on guard duty. It seems that Fountain was trying to take a nap when Hall told him to wake up and teased him about 'prisoner chasing'. Fountain, who it was alleged had a short temper, became angry and made a derogatory remark about the mother of 'whoever rubbed him over the head'. He then got up, walked over to his bed, picked up his rifle and loaded it. He then sat back down beside Hall with the rifle on his knee, pointing toward the ceiling. Things started to turn ugly, and Hall asked Fountain several times who he had got the rifle for. Fountian responded by saying, 'If you don't stop your foolishness, I am going to shoot you.' It seems that Hall was afraid that Fountain might actually shoot him, so when Fountain stepped out to the latrine, Hall loaded his rifle and waited for the soldier to return. As he did so, Hall asked him if he meant to do what he said and when Fountain answered 'Yes', Hall immediately shot him with his rifle. Private Fountain was taken to hospital, where he died on 3 June 1945 from the effects of his injury.

Archie Hall, born on the 21 April 1925, in Nashville, Tennessee, the son of Archie and Hattie Hall and one of ten children, appeared before a GCM at Le Mans, France, on 14 June 1945, where he pleaded not guilty to the charge of murder. Before joining the US Army, he worked as a driver for the Atlantic Ice & Coal Company in Nashville and was inducted into the army in Camp Forrest, Tennessee, on 19 October 1943. He elected to testify, claiming that another soldier had touched the head of Private Fountain and that he was fearful of his life. Major Joseph Shimpa, a psychiatrist, testified that he had examined Hall and believed his 'reasoning was faulty' and that he 'perhaps thought' he was fully justified in shooting Fountain. However, he could distinguish right from wrong, both on 30 May and on the day of the trial, and was deemed to be sane. His mental condition was described as 'about that of an adult' and 'at least of the average of his race'. The court felt that Hall's testimony tended to raise an issue as to whether he acted in the heat of sudden or uncontrollable passion aroused by adequate provocation under circumstances which might reduce the offence to manslaughter. It appears that they chose to ignore all circumstances, found Hall guilty and sentenced him to death. There are no further records relating to the sentence or any execution, but the ABMC have confirmed he is not buried in the Oise-Aisne American Cemetery, France, in Plot 'E'.

Private Sidney Benard Fountain is buried amongst the honoured dead in the Normandy American Cemetery, Colleville-sur-Mer, France, in Plot A, Row 3, Grave 31. Remember him.

Chapter 12

In Circumstances Unknown

There are two US soldiers buried in Plot 'E' in the Oise-Aisne American Cemetery whose crimes are not known, nor the outcome of any GCM they may have faced. Details are scant, and the destruction of records in the 1973 archives fire means that we may never know much more about these two soldiers other than what is set out below.

Private William N. Lucas
Service No.: 36639075

William N. Lucas was a white soldier from Illionis. He appears to have died as a result of hepatitis in April 1945 whilst in custody. He is listed as a GP (General Prisoner) and, according to official records, he was originally buried in Plot 4, Grave 24, but this is believed to be an administrative error as Grave 24 is actually in Row 1 and contains the body of Private John W. Taylor. The ABMC was unable to provide a date or cause of death but have confirmed that he is now buried in Plot 'E', Row 4, Grave 96.

Private Joseph J. Mahoney
Age: 33
Service No.: 12008332

Joseph J. Mahoney was a white soldier born in New Jersey in 1911. He enlisted in the US Army on 2 August 1940 in Newark, New Jersey, and is listed as a GP (General Prisoner) and was in military custody at the time of his death. A hospital record states he died from a haemorrhage in February 1944. The ABMC state that he died in prison and have confirmed he is currently buried in Plot 'E', Row 1, Grave 11.

Sources and Bibliography

Official Publications and Documents

File Unit: 314.6 T/O (European) Weekly Burial Reports 100: 1944, 1939–1954
File Unit: 314.6 T/O (European) Weekly Burial Reports 86–95: 1944
'Final Disposition of WW2 Dead 1945–51', Steere & Boardman, *QMC Historical Studies,* Series II No. 4, Office of the QMG, Washington, 1957
'History of 2913th Disciplinary Training Centre, March–June 1944', *NARA*, 1 July 1944
'History of 2913th Disciplinary Training Centre, 15 September–15 December 1943', *NARA*
'Statistical Returns of General Prisoners – Office of the Theatre Provost Marshal', European Theatre of Operations, September 1945
US Army (1945), *Board of Reviews of the Branch Office of the Judge Advocate General with the North African and Mediterranean Theatre of Operations*, Volumes 1–7.
US Army (1945), *Board of Reviews of the Branch Office of the Judge Advocate General with the European Theatre of Operations*, Volumes 1–34

Books and Articles

Buckton, Henry, *Friendly Invasion – Memories of Operation Bolero – The American Occupation of Britain 1942–1945*, Phillimore & Co., 2006
Clark, Mark, *Calculated Risk*, Harper & Brothers, 1950
Clarke, John, *London's Necropolis: Guide to Brookwood Cemetery*, Stenlake Publishing, 2018
Diamond, William J., 'Water is Life: Story of Water Supply in World War II', *The Military Engineer*, 1947
Dickson, Chris, *The Foreign Burial of American War Dead: A History*, McFarland & Co., 2011
Eddleston, John J., *The Encyclopaedia of Executions*, John Blake Publishing, 2004
Fielding, Steve, *Pierrepoint: A Family of Executioners*, John Blake Publishing, 2006

Fielding, Steve, *The Executioner's Bible*, John Blake Publishing, 2008
Hargrove, Hondon, *Buffalo Soldiers in Italy: Black Americans in World War II*, McFarland & Co., 1985
Johnson, Paul, *The Brookwood Killers*, Frontline Books, 2022
Klein, Leonora, *A Very English Hangman: The Life and Times of Albert Pierrepoint*, Corvo, 2006
McCormick, Dr Leanne, *Dirty Girls and Bad Houses*, Manchester University Press, 2009
MacLean, Col. French L., *The Fifth Field*, Schiffer, 2013
MacLean, Col. French L., *American Hangman*, Schiffer, 2019
Opinions, European Theatre of Operations (ETO), Washington, Office of the JAG, 1945
Opinions, Mediterranean Theatre of Operations (MTO), Washington, Office of the JAG, 1945
Patton, John R., '6677th Disciplinary Training Centre', *Trading Post Magazine*, April–June 2011
Pierrepoint, Albert, *Executioner: Pierrepoint*, Harrap, 1974
Reynolds, David, *Rich Relations: The American Occupation of Britain, 1942–1945*, Phoenix Press, 2000
Reynolds, David, *America, Empire of Liberty*, Allen Lane, 2009
Roland, Paul, *The Nuremberg Trials*, Arcturus Publishing, 2012
Russell, Harrold E., Jr., *Company I 366th Infantry*, RoseDog Books, 2008
Smith, Graham, *When Jim Crow Met John Bull: Black American Soldiers in World War II*, Taurus, 1987
Stone, Allen, *Shepton Mallet: A Visible History*, Shepton Mallet Local History Society, 2005
Wakefield, Ken, *Operation Bolero – The Americans in Bristol and the West Country 1942–45*, Crecy Books, 1994
Webb, Simon, *Execution: A History of Capital Punishment in Britain*, The History Press, 2012
Webb, Simon, *British Concentration Camps*, Pen & Sword, 2016
Webb, Simon, *Fighting for the United States, Executed in Britain*, Pen & Sword, 2021
Wilson, R. Michael, *Legal Executions by the United States Military: A Complete Record, 1942–1961*

Websites

www.ancestry.com
www.dpcamps.org
www.findmypast.com
www.fold3.com
www.thefifthfield.com
www.loc.gov

Index

Victims

Adams, PFC William D. 141–3
Alexander, PFC James Edward 76–8

Barry, Lucienne 143–4
Bechelli, Alfredo 182–4
Bechelli, Vittoria 182–3
Bellery, Victor 153–5
Betts, Pvt. Billy Basil 180–2
Bignon, Noémie 116–19
Bignon, Victor 116–19
Bocage, Louise 78–80
Bonit, Capt. Ignacio 195–6
Bouton, Constint 117–18
Bouton, Jeannine 117–18
Bouton, Marie-Louise 117–18
Brockman, Pvt. John Henry 70–2
Broome, Joyce 174
Broussard, Cpl Laurence 168–70
Brown, T/5 George W. 178–80
Brown Jr, Cpl John P. 55–7
Bryant, Pvt. Wilbur Lee 52–5

Carresi, Arnolfo 224–8
Carresi, Maria 224–8
Cobner, Lt Robert James 18–20
Collomp, Cesar 111–14
Collomp, Lucy 111–14
Coogan, Harry 65–8
Cope, Agnes 100–2

Dehu, Germaine 139
Dehu, Raymonde 137–41
Deremince, Henriette Tillieu Ep 163–5
Drouin, Adolphe Paul 126–8
Dumas, PFC Willie Leroy 230–2
Dupont, Marie 87–9

Evison, First Sgt Thomas 62–5

Fawden, Muriel Joyce Rosalie 40–4
Ferretti, Eolo 155–6
Fontaine, Denise 131
Fontaine, Julienne 130–3
Fountain, Pvt. Sidney Benard 232–3
Franceschi, Carlo 191–2

Garrett, Cpl Tommie Lee 170–2
Gary, Märta Jenny Sofia 4, 214–17
Gourdin, Marie Josef 102–5
Gourdin, Pierre 102
Green, Betty Dorian Pearl 121–6

Hailstone, Henry 45–9
Hebert, Just 86
Hèbert, Renée 95
Hèbert, Xavier 95, 98
Herbaut, Julia 98–100
Holmes, Dorothy 58–62
Honore, Aimée Hellondais 105
Hoogewind, PFC John H.W. 204–6

Hudson, Sgt Johnnie E. 137–40
Hualle, Lucie 147–9

Jackson Jr, Pvt. Randolph 166–8
Jenkins, PFC Harry Mosby 20–3
Johnson, PFC Earl 193–4
Jones, PFC George W. 202–3
Judd Jr, Sgt Royce Arthur 204–6

Kuhndorfer, Babette 214, 216

Lagouche, Louise 84, 86
Lay, Cynthia June 40–4
Lebarillier, Auguste Louis Clement 95–8
Lebocey, Albert 146–7
Lebocey, Germaine 146–7
Lefèbvre, Auguste 159–61
Lepoittevin, Marie 84–6
Leveziel, Louis 84–6
Lobacz, Peter 211–4
Lombardi, Carmela 184–6
Lombardi, Ettore 184–6
Lombardi, Palmira 184–6

McDonald, Capt. William E.
Martin, Jeanne 78–9
Martini, Ireni Rossi 197–9
May, Second Lt Eddie Lee 218–19
Morana, Giovianana Incatasciato 37–40

Nunez, Carmen 30–3
Ny, Yvonne Louise Le 209–11

Obichwist, Ulita 211–14
Osouf, Marie 95–8

Pivel, Christiane 143–4
Pivel, Germaine 143–4
Platt, Second Lt John Bernard 206–8
Pouliquen, Germaine Marie Françoise 119–21

Quellier, Madeleine 128–30
Quick, Pvt. David 49–51

Raby, Pvt. Alfred Edwin 23–5
Reynolds, Beatrice Maud 89–92
Robert, Berthe 161–3
Robertson, First Sgt Loyce M. 107–11
Robinson, T/5 George L. 229–30

Sabatini, Carla 172–3
Skrzyniarz, Aniela 72–5
Sondej, Zofia 73
Souillet, Therese 131–2
Staples, Doris May 33–7

Tackett, Cpl William Lynn 28–30
Testini, Pietro 224–8
Tiechman, Sir Eric 176–8
Tournellec, Eugene 114–16

Vaudevire, Yvonne Emilienne Eugenia 25–7
Vingtier, Alexina 134–7
Vingtier, Raoul 134–7

Weber, Mireille 143
Weissbarth, Elfriede 214–17
Williams, Pvt. Charles P. 199–200
Winstead, Cpl Milton M. 187–8
Wylie, Patricia 150–2

Zanchi, Anna 81–4

Assailants

Agee, Pvt. Amos 134–7
Anderson, Pvt. Roy W. 78–80

Bailey, Pvt. Fred Thomas 23–5
Bailey, Pvt. Milbert 159–61
Baldwin, Pvt. Walter James 126–8
Bennerman Jr, Pvt. Sidney 211–14
Brinson, Pvt. Eliga 58–61
Burns, Pvt. Lee A. 172–4

INDEX

Clark, Cpl Ernest Lee 121–5
Clay Jr, Pvt. Matthew 153–5
Cobb, Pvt. David 18–20
Cooper, Pvt. John David 143–5
Crews, Pvt. Otis Bell 52–5

Davis, Pvt. Arthur Eddie 105–7
Davis, Pvt. Lee Andrew 40–4
Davis, Pvt. William E. 119–21
Davison, Pvt. Tommie 128–30
Donnelly, Pvt. Robert L. 55–7
Downes, Pvt. William Clifton 84–7

Ervin, Pvt. Charlie 224–8

Farrell, Cpl Arthur J. 147–9

Gordon, Pvt. Tom E. 168–9
Grant, PFC General Lee 191–2
Green Jr, Pvt. George 170–1
Guerra, Pvt. Augustine Miranda 121–5

Hall Jr, Pvt. Archie 229, 232–3
Hall, Sgt Willie 229
Harris, Pvt. Willey 63–9
Harrison Jr, Pvt. William 150–2
Heard, PFC Haze 162–3
Hendricks, PFC James E. 116–19
Holden, Pvt. Mervin 163–6
Hollingsworth, Pvt. L.B. 111–13
Hopper, Pvt. Benjamin F. 166–7

Jefferies, Pvt. Charles H. 182–4
Johnson, Pvt. Willie 130–3
Jones, Pvt. Cubia 174–6
Jones, Pvt. Edwin P. 3, 23–5
Jones, Pvt. James L. 159–61
Jones, Pvt. John T. 197–9
Jones, Pvt. Kinney Bruce 187–8
Jordan, Pvt. Charles H. 105–7

Kendrick, Pvt. James E. 30–3
Kluxdal, PFC Paul Mauritz 107–11

Lane, Pvt. Willie 230–2
Leatherberry, Pvt. J.C. 45–9
Lucas, Pvt. William N. 234

McCarter, Pvt. William A. 199–201
McCutcheon, Pvt. Riggle 79
McGann, Pvt. Theron Watts 3, 25–7
McGhee, Cpl Shelton 178–9
Mack, Pvt. John H. 184–6
Mack, Pvt. William 114–16
McMurray, Pvt. Fred A. 81–4
Mahoney, Pvt. Joseph J. 234
Mariano, PFC Blake Waskee 4, 215–17
Martinez, Pvt. Aniceto 100–2
Maxey, Pvt. Curtis L. 111–14
Megaw, Eileen 66–8
Miranda, Pvt. Alex Flores 62–5

Nelson, Pvt. Henry W. 197–9
Newman, T/5 Oscar Neil 137–40
Norris, Sgt Clete Oscar 189–90

Ortiz-Reyes, Pvt. Victor 165–6

Parker, Pvt. Woodrow 211–14
Parrott, Pvt. James Robert 85–7
Pearson, Cpl. Robert L. 174–6
Pennyfeather, Pvt. William Drew 98–100
Philpot, Pvt. Henry Clay 206–8
Pittman, Pvt. Willie A. 37–40
Potts, Pvt. J.C. 119–21
Pygate, Pvt. Benjamin 76–7

Robinson, Pvt. Charles M. 209–10
Rollins, PFC Alvin R. 204–6

Sanders, T/5 James Buck 78–80
Schmiedel, Pvt. Werner E. 155–8
Scott, T/5 Richard Bunney 87–9
Slovik, Pvt. Edward Donald 2, 10, 156, 220–3
Smalls, Pvt. Abraham 202–3
Smith, Pvt. Charles H. 28–30

Smith, Pvt. George Edward 176–8
Smith, Pvt. Grant U. 85–7
Smith, Pvt. Harold
  Adolphus 20–2
Smith, Pvt. John Cleveland 134–7
Smith, Pvt. Willie 58–61
Spears Pvt. Charles E. 49–51
Spencer, Pvt. Elwood J. 163–6
Spinks, Pvt. Mansfield 224–8
Stroud, Pvt. Harvey 37–40
Sussex, Pvt. Elmer 224–7

Taylor, Pvt. John 193–4
Teton, Cpl. Wilford 147–9
Thomas, Pvt. Madison 89–92
Till, Pvt. Louis 81–4
Twiggs, Pvt. James W. 141–2

Valentine Sr, T/5 Leo 137–40

Waters, Pvt. John H. 33–7
Watson, Pvt. Frank 134–7
Watson, Pvt. Joseph 102–5
Watson, Pvt. Ray 70–2
White, Pvt. Armstead 37–40
White, Pvt. David 37–40
White, Pvt. Theodore 61
Whitfield, Pvt. Clarence 14,
  72–5
Williams, Pvt. Ellsworth 218–19
Williams, Pvt. Olin W. 146–7
Wilson, Pvt. Florine 78–80
Wilson, Pvt. J.P. 143–5
Wimberly, T/5 Willie 102–5
Wray, Pvt. Robert 180–2

Yancy, Pvt. Waiters 95–8

Personalities

Adams, Pvt. James W. 156
Adams, Sgt Willie B. 202
Adrieu, Hillion 148
Almoslino, T/5 Peter 154

Armstrong, Head Constable James
  (RUC) 67
Austin, Pvt. Odell 146

Bambini, Dr Giovanni 185
Barnes, Lt Col. Gilbert C. 115
Barnett, Capt. Harold J. 183
Barresi, Sgt Frank J. 56–7
Beard, Pvt. Ellis 187
Beckwith, Maj. Harry S. 185
Belcher, T/5 Benjamin H. 188
Benschoten, Col. Charles Matthew
  Van 61
Berthelot, Marcel 106
Bertoncini, Angelo 182–3
Best, Cpl Willie J. 169
Betts, Brig. Gen. Edward C. 107, 167
Blaskett, Peggy 122
Blight, Jean Elizabeth 90–1
Bocchini, Camillo 156
Bodiles, Jean 131
Boet, Leon 134, 136
Bonini, Giaconda 182–3
Bonnett, PFC Manse 183
Bonza, Pietro 156
Booker, Cpl Richard 120
Boston, Pvt. George 113
Bowles, PFC Leroy, 120
Bradley, Lt Gen. Omar Nelson 13,
  38, 40, 75, 110, 181
Brannon, Col. Ernest M. 74
Brown, PFC John D. 169
Bryant, PFC Miller J. 52, 55

Calka, Bernard B. 223
Campbell, Maj. Harry M. 149
Campbell, Pvt. Robert 188
Cangelosi, Maj. Theo F. 69
Carter, James E. 83
Cederberg, Capt. Walter G. 145
Champion, Harry 122
Christian, Maj. Mortimer H. 27, 89,
  100, 104, 111, 119
Churchill, Robert 43

INDEX

Clark, Pvt. Cicero 203
Cloud, Sgt Henry E. 35–6
Coet, Pvt. Chester 146
Coleman, Pvt. Richard W. 54
Collins, Brig. Gen. Leroy P. 69
Connor, Agent James E. 175
Cooley, T/5 Harold A. 127
Cravens, Staff Sgt Edward J. 86
Crilly, Dr James 67
Cullens, Maj. James C. 36–7, 44, 49, 61, 69

Davis, Capt. Albert M. 193
Davis, Sgt Minor R. 218
Descormiers, Andre 148
Descormiers, Denise 148
Devers, General Jacob L. 13, 22, 44, 51, 57, 71, 113
Dill, Capt. Edward John 219
Dillon, Brig. Gen. Joseph V. DePaul 39–40
Dobrin, Agent Victor 53
Dorman, Michael 151
Dorman, Peter, 151
Doughty, Sgt Arthur 175
Draper, Detective Inspector William 48
Duqueroux, Henri 128–30
Durbin, Police Sgt William 63

Eisenhower, General Dwight D. 3, 13, 14, 27, 30, 33, 36, 39, 49, 61, 75, 80, 87, 89, 92, 97, 99, 102, 104, 107, 116, 118, 121, 124, 129, 132, 136, 140, 142, 145, 147, 149, 152, 154, 163, 165, 167, 169, 171, 175, 178, 190, 196, 201, 206, 208, 210, 214, 217, 223
Elliott, P.C. James Herbert 91
Evrard, Basile 126

Ferguson, Lt Alonzo G. 183
Flanders, First Lt Russell Frank 127
Flynn, Maj. (Capt.) Philip J. 77, 102, 152, 178

Ford, Special Agent Harold F. 101
Foster, Maj. Ferris U. 44
Fowler, Pvt. George 47–9
Francesco, Mattero 51
Frederick, Major General Robert T. 217
Fredericks, Pvt. Stephen 71
French, Capt. Willard G. 173
Fuller, Agent Robert E. 154

Galieti, Libero, 156
Gamberini, Giorgio 226–7
Garner, Capt. Earl R. 68
Gestin, Michel 120
Gibson, Lt Col. White E. 64
Glanville, Dr Albert 175
Goldsmith, Agent Jack 88
Graham, Sgt Stephen J. 48
Graham, Agent William P. 145
Grant, T/5 Lawrence L. 141
Green, Pvt. Carl F. 155
Green, First Lt James A. 179
Griffith, Cpl Ray 71
Grotte, Capt. Ralph O. 221
Guilloche, Jules 162

Hagan, Bernard 151
Hale, P.C. William G., 59
Hall, Capt. Horace L. 110
Hall, Sgt James O. 59–60
Harkins, Capt. John J. 181
Harman, Capt. D.J. 60
Heffernan, PFC Edward J. 58–60
Herron, Sgt William (RUC) 67
Heyue, First Lt Edward C. 106
Hocking, Dr Frederick D.M. 91
Hodges, Lt Gen. Courtney H. 167
Hoffman, Sgt Weston 225
Hope, Leading Aircraftsman Ivan (RAF) 71
Hornstein, First Lt N.M. 140
Hunt, Pvt. James F. 200
Huntress, Capt. William W. 57

Isabelle, Pvt. Ira 120

Jenkins, T/5 Lawrence R. 171
Jones, Sgt James E. 110

Kapp, First Lt Jerome Frank 60
Kayes, Second Lt Alfred E. 115
Keely, Pvt. Patrick R. 79
Keruzec, Ernest 120
Kilgore, Agent Obed T. 165
Kleinbeck, T/5 Herbert A. 87
Kot, Luba 213
Kramer, Major General Herman F. 210

Land, Agent Eugene F. 157
Lane Jr, CWO Earl E. 129
Laslett, Maj. Herbert R. 92, 124, 175–6
Lazar, Capt. Isidor 136
Lewis, Cpl Dewey 172
Lipinski, Agent Bernard 53
Livingston, PFC James 183
Lobbrecht, Emile 98
Lock, Priscilla 61
Logan, First Lt John W. 185, 191
London, Sgt John W. 67
LoPinto, T/Sgt John 156–9
Lord, Brig. Gen. R.B. 129
Lorieux, Edouard 135–6
Lupernant, Gisele 135–6

Mabardy, Maj. Mitchell Abraham 38
McCowen, Congressman Edward 152
Mace, Auguste 96–7
McFarlane, Pvt. Delmar Joseph 155, 158
McNarney, Lt Gen. Joseph Taggart 13, 14, 55, 84, 158, 173, 183, 186, 188, 192, 194, 199, 230, 226
McNeil, Brig. Gen. Edwin Colyer 61, 208
McQueen, Sgt Otto 168
Maglione, PFC Dominic J. 198

Marsh, Capt. George W. 110
Martin, Capt. Donald H. 140
Martinez Jr, Louis 2, 65
Masi, John 82–3
Mendenhall, Sgt Earl F. 119
Merklein, Staff Sgt James A. 63–4
Mitchell, Pvt. Kadell 201
Montague, Daniel 151
Moock, Capt. Robert E. 193
Morehen, Mabel 60
Morris, Capt. Cecil B. 172–3
Morris, Pvt. David 54
Morris, Insp. Henry 35
Morris, Herbert 152, 176, 178
Morton, Cpl William H. 127
Mosley, Sgt Richard A. 119

Neal, Pvt. John H. 142
Nehme, Michel 112–13
Neiswender, Maj. W.G. 174, 179, 188, 192, 194, 203
Nesfield, Staff Sgt John V. 97
Newall, Dr Frederick J. 122
Nichols, Pvt. James 70–1
Nixon, Colonel Thomas A. 104

O'Connor, Sgt James 68
Orio, Rafael Di 51
Oxx, Brig. Gen. Francis H. 52–5, 83, 156, 158

Parks, Dr Edward Burdon 60
Patch, Lt Gen. Alexander M. 113, 169
Patton, Gen. George S. 103, 105–6, 110, 145, 199, 202
Paul, Cpl Victor H. 205
Pauly, Second Lt Paul E. 131–2
Peck, Lt Col. Henry L. 98, 116, 121, 128, 130, 133, 136–7, 140, 142, 145, 149, 154, 155, 161, 163, 165, 167, 169, 171, 181, 190, 196, 201–2, 206, 208, 210, 217
Penchansky, Capt. Samuel 55
Pepper, Senator Claude 61

INDEX

Perimony, Dr George 126
Piazza, First Sgt Nicholas F. 198
Piechnik, PFC Victor 180–2
Pierrepoint, Albert 15–17, 20, 22, 92, 102, 124
Pierrepoint, Thomas 14–17, 20, 22, 36, 44, 49, 61, 69, 75, 92, 102, 124, 152, 176, 178
Pionnier, Madeleine 138
Piva, Fausta 157
Pope, Pvt. William L. 79
Prete, Raffaella del 53
Provendier, Dr Henri 139
Pyland, Capt. Vadie P. 86

Railland, T/5 Robert J. 80
Reber, Staff Sgt Leroy 110
Reed, Capt. Harrison P. 35–6
Reed, PFC Leon P. 131
Reeves, First Lt Maurice C. 148–9
Reynolds, Chief Writer Thomas Henry (RN) 90
Richmond, Brig. Gen. Adam 173, 194, 199, 203
Riggs, First Lt Albert C. 175
Riley, Alexander 15, 36, 44, 69
Rinaldo, Lorenzo 172
Robert, Roger 117
Robinson, T/3 Thomas F. 87
Robinson, First Lt Vinson K. 142
Rollman, Capt. Henry 97
Romano, Pasquale 156–8
Rovai, Attilio 197–9
Roye, Capt. J.G. 60

Salofwaue, Konstantine 213
Schwartz, Capt. George 77
Searcy, Col. Cyrus H. 118
Sharshel, Cpl Donald L. 99
Shaw, First Lt Arnold C. 223
Shimpa, Maj. Joseph 233
Shultz, Agent Robert A. 154
Siciah, Second Lt Walter S. 74
Slade, Det. Con. Ernest Wilfrid 59

Smeed, Superintendent Francis Herbert 122
Smith, PFC Earl M. 71
Snowling, Constable Edgar 47
Sommer, Lt Col. Henry P. 222
Sorbello, First Lt Michael 86
Stevenson, T/5 Jesse 189–90
Stewart, Pvt. James 70
Stoops, Maj. Charles D. 111
Sullivan, Capt. Edward M. 111
Swetnam, Sgt Eric 158
Swiren, Capt. Abraham J. 136

Taburel, Joseph 106
Talley, Col. Benjamin B. 99
Tauscher, Captain Roland L. 73
Tavolieri, Pvt. Anthony 155
Thomas, Pvt. Arthur J. 99
Thomas, Pvt. James 82
Thrasher, Brig. Gen. Charles O. 77, 92
Thurman, Lt Col. William T. 199
Tobeas, PFC Philip 70
Torres, Sgt Ismael 181
Totterdell, Superintendent George H.R. 47
Tournay, Arthur 122
Tucker, Lt Donald F. 118

Vandervoort, Lt Col. Benjamin Hayes 78
Vaughan Jr, Brig. Gen. Harry B. 102
Venanzoni, Alfredo, 156
Villemez, First Lt Clarence L. 43

Walkeley, Police Inspector Charles E. 60
Walker, PFC John B. 183
Wall, Dr Henry J. 123
Waser, Capt. Glenn A. 183, 186, 199
Watts, Chaplain William T. 55
Webber, Captain John J. (Canadian) 46–9
Webster, First Lt James P. 73–4

Wehking, Cpl Joel R. 63
Wesley, T/5 James W. 63
Whalen, Maj. Joseph D. 97
Wheeler, Pvt. J.C. 43
Williams, Pvt. Thomas 200
Wojtacha, Pvt. Leonard S. 177
Wood, Capt. William G. 57
Woodland, Dr Frederick Albert John 91
Woods, Master Sgt John Clarence 14–17, 80, 87, 98, 104, 109, 111, 116, 121, 128, 133, 136, 140, 142, 145, 147, 149, 155, 161, 163, 165, 168–9, 171, 181, 190, 201, 206, 208, 210, 217, 219
Worthey, Pvt. Aldene 172
Wynn, Staff Sgt Joe W. 182–3

Yaskell, Sgt Peter 185

Ziegler, Pvt. Milton K. 53–4

Locations

Antrain, France 86
Anzio, Italy 215–17
Ardboe, Northern Ireland 150
Au Fayel, France 148
Aversa, Italy 55, 72, 84, 113, 158, 174, 179, 183, 186, 188, 192, 194, 199, 203, 227

Bad Canstatt, Germany 214
Barga, Italy 182–4
Barrafranca, Sicily 38
Beaunay, France 139–40
Bellefontaine, France 141
Bishops Cleeve, England 58–9
Bizerte, Tunisia 230
Boëlhe, Belgium 189
Boughton, England 204
Bricquebec, France 95–7
Brest, France 102, 114

Caltanissetta, Sicily 38
Cambridge, England 20, 176
Campofelice di Rocella, Sicily 39
Castelfiorentino, Italy 188
Châlons-en-Champagne, France 139
Champigneulles, France 170
Chard, England 174–5
Cheltenham, England 59, 60
Cherbourg, France 25, 86–7, 89, 97–9, 154
Cisterna, Italy 81
Colchester, England 45–9

Devonport, England 89, 91

Elsenborn, Belgium 221
Etienville, France 85–7
Exeter, England 64

Ferme de Marville, France 143
Fontenay-sur-Mer, France 153–5
Fromentières, France 138

Genoa, Italy 226
Golbey, France 180
Granville, France 129, 132, 163
Guiclan, France 120
Gunnislake, England 90–1

Hameau au Pigeon, Quettetot, France 98
Heilbronn, Germany 211–12
Henley-on-Thames, England 34, 37
Herbesthal, Welkenraedt, Belgium 166
Hindley Green, England 62
Honiton, England 62–3
Horham, England 61

Koudiat, Tunisia 230

La Pernelle, France 159–61
La Rouennerie en Montour, France 159–61

INDEX

Le Chêne Daniel, France 146–7
Le Havre, France 218, 231
Le Mans, France 126–7, 167, 181, 190, 196, 201, 206, 208, 210, 217, 233
Le Pas en Ferre, France 103
Leonberg, Germany 231
Lérouville, France 144–5
Lewisburg, Pennsylvania, United States 113, 140
Lichfield, England 102
Liège, Belgium 166, 189, 208
Liverpool, England 44, 63, 230
Livorno, Italy 83, 178–9
Locmenven, France 119
Lucca, Italy 190, 197–8

Maggiano, Italy 172
Mannheim, Germany 219, 231–2
Marlborough, England 40, 43–4
Marquette, France 195
Marseille, France 168
Massa Maciniai, Italy 194, 197–8
Mesnil-Clinchamps, France 162
Messac, France 209, 211
Montmort-Lucy, France 139
Montour, Ille-et-Vilaine, France 105–7
Morlaix, France 116–21
Moussy-le-Vieux, France 110
Munich, Germany 217

Namur, Belgium 164–5
Nancy, France 145, 170–1, 174
Naples, Italy 50–1, 54–7, 71, 156–7
Neuville-au-Plain, France 78
Nuremberg, Germany 215

Oran, Algeria 25, 29, 30, 33, 50
Orto D'Atella, Italy 53

Paris, France 25, 80, 104, 111, 136, 204, 222, 232

Pentreff, Le Drennec, France 114, 119
Pietrasanta, Italy 184, 187–8, 193, 198, 225–7
Plabennec, France 116
Plumaudan, France 117
Poyntzpass, Co. Down, N. Ireland 66
Prise Guinment, France 128–9

Rambouillet, France 136
Reims, France 140, 205, 214
Rennes, France 131, 149, 209
Renouf, France 86
Rigauderie, France 126–7
Roetgen, Germany 222
Rousina, Italy 187–8

Saint-Lô, France 25, 27, 75
Sainte-Marie-aux-Mines, France 223
Sainte-Mère-Église, France 78, 80, 85, 95
St Sabine, France 104
St Sauveur, France 97
Saint-Sulpice-des-Landes, France 149
Saint-Tropez, France 112–13
Salisbury, England 41
Savernake, England 40–3
Secondigliano, Italy 70
Sézanne, France 138
Shepton Mallet, England 14, 16, 20, 49, 61, 65, 77, 92, 102, 124–5, 152, 176, 178
Soumagne, Belgium 167

Thorpe Abbotts, England 61
Troyes, France 204

Venafro, Italy 55
Viareggio, Italy 191, 198, 202
Vierville-sur-Mer, France 73

Watford, England 36

US Military Cemeteries

Ardennes, Neupré, Belgium 207, 209

Brookwood, England 20, 23, 37, 44, 49, 61, 65, 69, 77, 92, 102, 125, 152, 176, 178

Cambridge, England 10, 37, 44, 49, 61, 65, 69, 77–8, 92, 102, 125, 152, 176, 178

Épinal, France 40, 182, 204, 206, 223, 231–2

Florence, Italy 194, 203

Henri-Chapelle, Belgium 190

Limay, Meurthe-et-Moselle 145

Marigny, France 27, 75, 87, 89, 98, 100, 107, 116, 119, 121, 128, 130, 133, 137, 142, 147, 149, 155, 161, 163, 168–9, 171, 181, 190, 196, 202, 206, 208, 211, 214, 217

Monte Soprano, Italy 40

Naples, Italy 40, 50–1, 55–7, 72, 84, 113, 158, 174, 180, 184, 186, 188, 192, 194, 199, 203, 227

Nettuno, Italy 40

Neuville-en-Condroz, Belgium 208

Normandy, Colleville-sur-Mer, France 143, 219, 233

Sicily-Rome, Italy 56–7

Solers, France 80, 105, 111, 140

US Army Units

1st Tank Destroyer Group 20

No. 2 Combat Crew Replacement Centre 150

2nd US Convalescent Hospital 181

2nd US Evacuation Hospital 152

4th Infantry Division 62

4th Special Service Company 97

5th Engineer Special Brigade 15

14th Armoured Field Artillery Battalion 30–1

17th Cavalry Reconnaissance Squadron, 147

17th Criminal Investigation Section 154

18th Replacement Battalion 23, 155

18th US General Hospital 47

27th Armoured Field Artillery Battalion 23

28th Infantry Division 221

28th US Field Hospital 140

29th Signal Construction Battalion 78

32nd Military Police Criminal Investigation Section 175

32nd Signal Construction Battalion 29

35th US Infantry Division 204

36th Field Artillery Battalion 55

37th Engineer Combat Battalion 15

42nd Field Artillery Battalion 62

45th Infantry Division 215, 217

56th Military Police Company 71

57th Military Police Company 55–6

64th US General Hospital 179

65th Infantry Regiment 181

66th Infantry Division 209, 210

73rd Field Artillery Brigade 109

79th US General Hospital 152

82nd Airborne Division 78

90th Infantry Battalion 206

91st US Infantry Division 55

92nd US Infantry Division 172, 182, 191, 193–4, 197, 202, 224

93rd Bomb Group (H) 152

95th Bombardment Group (H) 61

100th Bombardment Group (H) 61

100th US Infantry Division 214

INDEX

101st Military Police Battalion 198
101st US Evacuation Hospital 97, 127
109th Infantry Regiment 220–1
112th Military Police POW Detachment 70
116th Infantry Regiment 21
163rd Chemical Smoke Generator Company 211
170th US Evacuation Hospital 173, 199, 225
177th Port Company 81–2, 84
191st Tank Battalion 215
200th Field Artillery Battalion 107, 109
218th Military Police Company 28–9
229th Quartermaster Salvage Collecting Company 87
234th Replacement Company 206–7
235th US General Hospital 208
240th Port Company 72, 74
245th Quartermaster Battalion 195
248th Field Artillery Battalion 191
248th Quartermaster Battalion 40, 43
249th Quartermaster Battalion 37
255th Military Police Company 59
257th Signal Construction Company 102–3
306th Fighter Control Squadron 121, 123–4
306th Quartermaster Railhead Company 204–5
354th Engineer Regiment 43
356th Engineer (General Service) Regiment 45
363rd Infantry Regiment 55
366th Infantry Regiment 182, 191, 224–5
370th Infantry Regiment 202–1
371st Infantry Regiment, 187, 193, 197
376th Parachute Field Artillery Battalion 204
383rd Engineer Battalion 218
386th Engineer Battalion 70
387th Engineer Battalion 49
396th Quartermaster Truck Company 137–8, 140
402nd Engineer Battalion 229–30
403rd Replacement Company 155
427th Quartermaster Troop Transport Company 128
434th Port Company 159, 161
465th Quartermaster Laundry Company 199, 200
466th Bombardment Group (H) 176–7
494th Port Battalion 72
501st Port Battalion 159
503rd Military Police Battalion 106
504th Military Police Battalion 112
505th Parachute Infantry Regiment 78
511th Military Police Battalion 120
563rd Quartermaster Battalion 119
568th Railhead Company 180
574th Ordnance Ammunition Company 126
578th Field Artillery Regiment 114–15
597th Ordnance Ammunition Company 85–6
599th Field Artillery Battalion 184–5, 197
626th Ordnance Ammunition Company 65–6, 68
644th Quartermaster Troop Transport Company 124
646th Quartermaster Truck Company 163
667th Quartermaster Truck Company 209
712th Railway Operating Battalion 137–8
784th Bombardment Squadron 176–7
791st Engineer Dump Truck Company 230

792nd Ordnance (Light Maintenance) Company 172
795th Anti-aircraft Artillery Automatic Weapons Battalion 86
827th Engineer Battalion (Aviation) 18
960th Quartermaster Service Company 76
964th Quartermaster Service Company 89, 91
998th Quartermaster Salvage Collecting Company 170
1285th Military Police Company (Aviation) 61
1293rd Military Police Company 86
1323rd Engineer General Service Regiment 141
1349th Engineer General Service Regiment 218
1391st Engineer Forestry Battalion 148
1511th Engineer Water Supply Company 95, 97
1698th Engineer Combat Battalion 174–5
2651st Military Police Company 53
2912th Disciplinary Training Centre 16, 36, 44, 49, 61, 69, 124, 175, 178
3105th Quartermaster Service Company 162–3
3121st Quartermaster Service Company 119
3131st Signal Service Company 185
3135th Quartermaster Service Company 232
3170th Quartermaster Service Company 166
3236th Quartermaster Service Company 153
3251st Quartermaster Service Company 168
3269th Quartermaster Service Company 195
3277th Quartermaster Service Company 111
3299th Quartermaster Service Company 180
3326th Quartermaster Truck Company 105, 116, 118
3327th Quartermaster Truck Company 105
3384th Quartermaster Truck Company 189
3423rd Quartermaster Truck Company 52, 54
3704th Quartermaster Truck Company 73
3823rd Quartermaster Truck Company 178
3868th Quartermaster Truck Company 98
3966th Quartermaster Truck Company 143
3984th Quartermaster Truck Company 130
4090th Quartermaster Service Company 58–9
4133rd Quartermaster Company 113
4194th Quartermaster Service Company 146